Making Theatre in Northern Ireland

Exeter Performance Studies

Series editors:
Peter Thomson, Professor of Drama at the University of Exeter;
Graham Ley, Reader in Drama and Theory at the University of Exeter;
Steve Nicholson, Reader in Twentieth-Century Drama at the
University of Sheffield.

From Mimesis to Interculturalism: *Readings of Theatrical Theory Before and
After 'Modernism'*
Graham Ley (1999)

British Theatre and the Red Peril: *The Portrayal of Communism 1917–1945*
Steve Nicholson (1999)

On Actors and Acting
Peter Thomson (2000)

Grand-Guignol: *The French Theatre of Horror*
Richard J. Hand and Michael Wilson (2002)

The Censorship of British Drama 1900–1968: *Volume One 1900–1932*
Steve Nicholson (2003)

The Censorship of British Drama 1900–1968: *Volume Two 1933–1952*
Steve Nicholson (2005)

Freedom's Pioneer: *John McGrath's Work in Theatre, Film and Television*
edited by David Bradby and Susanna Capon (2005)

John McGrath: Plays for England
selected and introduced by Nadine Holdsworth (2005)

*Theatre Workshop: Joan Littlewood and the Making
of Modern British Theatre*
Robert Leach (2006)

'In Comes I': *Performance, Memory and Landscape*
Mike Pearson (2006)

Also published by University of Exeter Press

Extraordinary Actors: *Essays on Popular Performers*
Studies in honour of Peter Thomson
edited by Jane Milling and Martin Banham (2004)

Making Theatre in Northern Ireland

Through and Beyond the Troubles

TOM MAGUIRE

UNIVERSITY
of
EXETER
PRESS

First published in 2006 by
University of Exeter Press
Reed Hall, Streatham Drive
Exeter EX4 4QR
UK
www.exeterpress.co.uk

British Library Cataloguing in Publication Data
A catalogue record for this book is available
from the British Library.

Paperback ISBN 10: 0 85989 739 7
ISBN 13: 978 0 85989 739 6
Hardback ISBN 10: 0 85989 738 9
ISBN 13: 978 0 85989 738 9

Typeset in 10/12½pt Plantin Light
by XL Publishing Services, Tiverton

Printed in Great Britain by Antony Rowe Ltd, Chippenham

Contents

List of illustrations		vi
Acknowledgements		vii
List of abbreviations		viii
Chronology of key events		ix
1	Introduction: Staging Northern Ireland	1
	Terms and Definitions	4
	The Critical Context	12
	Theatre, Ideology and Propaganda	16
	The Shape and Approach of the Book	18
2	Direct Engagement	21
3	Authentic History	44
4	Failed Origins	60
5	Utopian Myths	77
6	Gendered Troubles	97
7	Let the People Speak: Community and Theatre	118
8	Theatre after the Cease-fires	137
9	The Art and Politics of Staging the Troubles	158
Notes		173
Bibliography		184
Playography		206
Index		215

Illustrations

1. *The Flats* by John Boyd, Lyric Theatre, Belfast.
   Photographer: Chris Hill   15
2. *The Interrogation of Ambrose Fogarty* by Martin Lynch,
   Lyric Theatre, Belfast. Photographer: Chris Hill   27
3. *Northern Star* by Stewart Parker, Lyric Theatre, Belfast.
   Photographer: Chris Hill   64
4. *Observe the Sons of Ulster Marching Towards the Somme* by
   Frank McGuinness, Lyric Theatre, Belfast.
   Photographer: Chris Hill   73
5. *The Pursuit of Diarmuid and Gráinne* by Zoe Seaton,
   Big Telly Theatre Company, Riverside Theatre, Coleraine.   87
6. *Carthaginians* by Frank McGuinness, Lyric Theatre, Belfast.
   Photographer: Jill Jennings   108
7. *A Night in November* by Marie Jones, Dubbeljoint Productions,
   Belfast Institute of Further & Higher Education.
   Photographer: Jill Jennings   140
8. *As the Beast Sleeps* by Gary Mitchell, Lyric Theatre, Belfast.
   Photographer: Jill Jennings   147

Acknowledgements

This book is the result of a research project supported by the Arts and Humanities Research Board and the Faculty of Arts at the University of Ulster. My thanks go to Ophelia Byrne, Hugh Odling-Smee and Jane Moore for all their assistance with the theatre archive of the Linenhall Library in Belfast, their insight and encouragement. Thanks too to Clare Coleman for her tireless work on my behalf in the archives of Belfast's Newspaper Library, and to the staff there. I owe a huge debt to the theatre makers who gave of their time to speak to me and point me in the right directions. I am grateful too for the support, comments and advice of John Bennett, Ben Francombe, Helen Gilbert, Nadine Holdsworth, Royona Mitra, Lionel Pilkington, the readers at University of Exeter Press, and my editor, Simon Baker. Of course, any faults or inaccuracies are solely my responsibility.

I have received invaluable support from my colleagues and students in the Faculty of Arts at the University of Ulster, particularly John Hill, Gerry McCarthy, Paul Moore, Carole-Ann Upton and Robert Welch; also from research student Paul Devlin and the students with whom I have shared discussions of many aspects of theatre at Ulster and at Liverpool Hope.

I continue to be blessed with the patient support of my family. I owe so much to my parents, Roisin and Buddy, who tried to keep the Troubles from our door and who have done so much to teach me the meaning of tolerance and the value of loyalty.

Abbreviations

ACNI   Arts Council of Northern Ireland
DUP   Democratic Unionist Party
GAA   Gaelic Athletic Association
INLA   Irish National Liberation Army
IRA   Irish Republican Army
NILP   Northern Ireland Labour Party
PIRA   Provisional Irish Republican Army
PSNI   Police Service of Northern Ireland, which replaced the RUC
RIRA   Real IRA, which continued its military campaign after the PIRA cease-fire.
RTE   The state broadcasting body in the Republic of Ireland
RUC   Royal Ulster Constabulary
SDLP   Social Democratic and Labour Party
UDA   Ulster Defence Association
UDR   Ulster Defence Regiment
UFF   Ulster Freedom Fighters
UUP   Ulster Unionist Party
UVF   Ulster Volunteer Force

Chronology of key events

1920   Government of Ireland Act leads to partitioning of Ireland.

1921   First NI parliament is elected.

1967   Northern Ireland Civil Rights Association formed.

1968   First civil rights march takes place.
NI Prime Minister O'Neill issues in a reform package to address nationalist demands.

1969   RUC is armed and part-time mobilisation of 'B' specials by O'Neill.
O'Neill resigns as NI Prime Minister.
Rioting in Derry and Belfast with troops called in. Peacelines erected in Belfast.

1970   Nationalist Falls Road area of Belfast placed under curfew while army carries out searches for arms.

1971   Internment without trial introduced.

1972   Bloody Sunday in Derry when British soldiers kill fourteen people in total. Widgery Report largely exonerates the army.
Special Category status granted to republican and loyalist prisoners.

1973   UK and Republic of Ireland join European Economic Community.

1974   Ulster Workers' Council strike brings down the power-sharing executive formed under the Sunningdale Agreement.

1978   Start of 'dirty protests' in the Maze Prison, Long Kesh.

1979   Margaret Thatcher leads Conservatives to victory in UK General Election.

1980   First hunger strike by republican prisoners in the Maze Prison, Long Kesh.

1981   Second hunger strike by republican prisoners in the Maze Prison, Long Kesh results in deaths of ten hunger strikers including Bobby Sands, MP for Fermanagh-South Tyrone.

1985   Anglo-Irish Agreement signed.

1987   IRA bombs a Remembrance Day ceremony in Enniskillen killing eleven people.

1988   SDLP leader John Hume and Sinn Féin's Gerry Adams begin talks.
UK Home Secretary announces a broadcasting ban on members of Sinn Féin.

1989   Guilford Four released by the Court of Appeal.
1990   Margaret Thatcher replaced by John Major as British Prime Minister.
1993   Hume–Adams joint statement.
1994   First PIRA cease-fire; followed by loyalist paramilitary cease-fires.
1996   PIRA ends cease-fire with bomb attack on Canary Wharf, London.
1997   Tony Blair is elected as British Prime Minister.
        Second PIRA cease-fire announced.
1998   Tony Blair announces setting up of Saville Inquiry into 'Bloody Sunday'.
        Good Friday Agreement signed and elected Northern Ireland Assembly takes control of devolved government.
        Real IRA car bomb in Omagh kills 29 people.
1999   Patten Report on policing proposes far-reaching changes.
        An executive for the NI Assembly is formed.
        Irish government formally amends Articles 2 and 3 of the Constitution which lay claim to NI.
2005   PIRA declares an end to all military activities and undertakes a final act of decommissioning.

1

Introduction

Staging Northern Ireland

In a televised broadcast on 9 December 1968, the then Prime Minister of
Northern Ireland, Captain Terence O'Neill, announced that 'Ulster is at the
crossroads'. He identified that moment as the last opportunity to avoid a
descent into violent political conflict, in asking directly:

> What kind of Ulster do you want? A happy and respected province, in
> good standing with the rest of the United Kingdom? Or a place continu-
> ally torn apart by riots and demonstrations, and regarded by the rest of
> Britain as a political outcast?. . . Make your voice heard in whatever way
> you think best, so that we may know the views not of the few but of the
> many. For this is truly a time of decision and in your silence all that we
> have built up could be lost.
>
> (1969: 140–6)

Little could he know then that it would not be until the Good Friday
Agreement of 1998 that a negotiated resolution to what would prove to be
thirty years of conflict would become possible: Ulster once again at a political crossroads. Yet still, as I am writing, media images of street riots across
Belfast reinforce around the world the sense of over three decades of undifferentiated violence. 'Northern Ireland' and 'The Troubles' have become
synonymous. The residual image is of cars burning on street corners: bonfires
at the crossroads.

It is ironic, of course, that in writing a book about stage representations of
the Troubles, I may well be contributing to the persistence of this imagery.
This work cannot include the diversity of work which has emerged over the
last thirty years about life in Northern Ireland which has not addressed this
particular political dimension.[1] I am, nonetheless, acutely aware of Connolly's
reminder that 'an implicit assumption that the "real" politics equals institutional politics. . . mars more complex evaluations of the articulation of alternative politics' (1999: 252). Images of bonfires and street riots contribute to

a hegemonic narrative of strife between two equally entrenched tribal communities separated by religious and ethnic identity. This narrative has been
accepted across the world and internalised by many of the people of Northern
Ireland. The theatre has played its part in generating and repeating such
images. Such depictions occlude the variations in involvement which people
have had in the violence and their experience of it. Such variations can be
attributed, for example, to differences in place, social class (Coulter 1999;
Finlayson 1999) and gender (Fairweather et al. 1984; Aretxaga 1997; Sales
1997; Roulston and Davies 2000). Instead, the causes of the conflict are
presented as cultural, such that:

> the roots of the conflict in Northern Ireland lie in a cluster of abnormal
> and problematic values, beliefs and attitudes. These include: an obsession
> with the past conceived in mythical terms, extreme nationalism, religious
> intolerance, an unwillingness to compromise and a willingness to use or
> condone political violence. Each side is said to be in a timewarp, out of
> touch with present-day reality, entrapped in a mythical view of the past
> which leads to an endless repetition of old tribal conflicts.
>
> (Ruane and Todd 1991: 29)

Such cultural views hide the involvement of successive governments in
Northern Ireland, Britain, the Republic of Ireland and the United States
whose policies and practices have implicated them deeply in the causes,
continuation and, latterly, resolution of the conflict (Dixon 2001). Bell notes
that 'Over the last twenty-five years the British state has sought to represent
itself as an honest broker seeking to mediate between two ethnic traditions
locked in an ancient struggle' (1998: 239). Playwrights too have reinforced
this interpretation. In Stewart Parker's *Northern Star* (1984), Henry Joy
McCracken describes the situation as: 'A field, with two men fighting over it.
Cain and Abel. The bitterest fight in the history of man on this earth' (Parker
1989: 57).[2] The image of the burning car and the cultural interpretations
underpinning it upstage too the social, legal and political changes within the
state which have moved Northern Ireland far from its origins in the establishment of what Lord Craigavon had once described as a 'Protestant
Parliament for a Protestant people' (cited Hennessey 1997: 122).

   The focus of this book is not, however, the analysis of the history of the
crisis. Rather, it is to consider the ways in which the circumstances of the
crisis have been mediated in theatrical representation and the ways in which
such representations may have been operative. This is timely given the ways
in which the political dimensions of the conflict have come under negotiation
within the most recent peace processes, which culminated in the signing of
the Good Friday Agreement in 1998 (see Chapter 8) and on 28 July 2005,
the announcement by the Provisional IRA of the end of its armed struggle

with its final act of decommissioning being undertaken two months later. However, the devolved government of the Northern Ireland Assembly and its power-sharing Executive which the Good Friday Agreement ushered in collapsed in November 2002, with a return to direct rule from Westminster. In this context, cultural representation has become an area of contestation (Rolston 1998a). Representation is contested, for example, between those wishing to resolve the conflict by creating new images of unity (Murtagh 1995; Neill 1995; Shirlow and Shuttleworth 1999) and those who believe that only by acknowledging the historical manifestations of the conflict will resolution be achieved. Representation is contested too as communities of identity and interest (see Chapter 7) seek to legitimate their stake in a new political dispensation (often by recourse to narratives of victimhood). Moreover, the resources and prestige unlocked by the Good Friday Agreement's insistence on parity of esteem between different ethno-nationalist identities are the prizes in such conflicts by proxy. Within this context, the public staging of representations of the political situation becomes crucial in determining the sense which people in Northern Ireland have of themselves and in the ways in which they are regarded externally.

Theatres have long been and continue to be used as places where people will gather and recognise themselves as a community or nation through the stage representation (Kruger 1992; Trotter 2001). Such stagings often invoke a metonymic substitution of the part presented for the whole being represented. Thus, part of my enterprise is to explore these metonymic substitutions on the stage and their relationship to the wider whole. This interest in theatrical representation derives from the importance laid by all parties to the conflict on winning what has been termed 'the propaganda war' (Curtis 1984; Miller 1994). The ways in which the conflict has been mediated publicly have contributed and continue to contribute to the determination of how it has developed; how it is experienced; and moreover, how it is perceived both within and beyond the borders of the Northern Irish state. Whilst much of the propaganda on Northern Ireland has been the result of deliberate and sustained policies from all sides, it is important that the fundamental ideological functions of cultural representation are identified if we are to understand in greater depth the relationship between culture and conflict. As McIlroy notes, 'culture and politics are intertwined in Ireland in such a way that no artefact can easily escape into art for art's sake' (1998: 7).

The role of intellectuals likewise (O'Dowd 1991) can be subjected to closer scrutiny, once it is recognised that they function ideologically in their valorisation and criticism of cultural works: that 'political agendas are built into interpretations of culture' (Hohenleitner 2000: 254). While attention has been paid to the perceived politics of Field Day Theatre Company, for example, this dimension of the historiography of the theatre in Northern Ireland has largely gone unremarked. However, especially in the case of Field

Day, there has grown up an orthodoxy around which productions are worthy of attention, an orthodoxy which itself has created a distortion of both theatre history and of the realities which the theatre has sought to represent. Within the mass of critical literature, a small number of works by a smaller number of playwrights have dominated. The discussion here seeks to fill out existing criticism in this respect.

Terms and Definitions

The act of naming is a recurrent focus for drama concerning Northern Ireland. Its consequences as a socio-political act are explored most notably in Brian Friel's *Translations* (1980). The play highlights the centrality of nomen-clature to the current conflict, in 'a culture inundated with labels' (McDonough 2000: 191) where, in the title of Anne Devlin's short story (and later film), 'Naming the Names' (1995) is a political act. To name is to claim authority, to become an agent in the world and to signal membership of partic-ular communities, to be involved in what Silverstein (1992) calls a 'scheme of identification'. It is important therefore to explain which names are to be used in this book and why.

Already I have used a number of terms to cover the political violence in Northern Ireland since the late 1960s: 'the conflict', 'the crisis', 'The Troubles'. The last of these is the most generally used term, but its use carries with it a caveat. The euphemism of 'The Troubles' does not disguise the fact that from the protests of a peaceful civil rights movement against the injus-tices of the unionist state in the 1960s (Purdie 1990; Shirlow and McGovern 1997), a sustained three-way war developed: between republican militants; the security services of initially the Northern Irish government and then the wider British state; and loyalist paramilitaries. The security services of the Republic of Ireland too have been drawn in, albeit more sporadically. The criminalisation of paramilitary combatants was a specific counter-insurgency measure adopted in public by successive British and Irish governments (Pilkington 2001b: 195); while at the same time other more covert initiatives legitimated the status of the conflict as a war (Hennessey 1997: 250ff.; Dixon 2000: 114–17). The analysis of the conflict within this book assumes an acceptance of its fundamentally political basis. That many of the rights to equality within the state have been delivered through the intervention of external political and legal institutions (such as the European Parliament and European Court of Justice) is indisputable; it does not negate the fact that it has been only after sustained campaigns of political violence by republicans that direct negotiation with them has taken place from which in turn further rights have been enshrined within the structures and operation of the state (Patterson 1996). My emphasis rejects narratives of ethnic or religious barbarism which seek both to explain the relentlessness of the violence and to reassure those sections of Irish, British and Northern Irish society who wish to distance themselves from it through processes of what Cornell terms 'psychological withdrawal' (1999a: 71). She identifies this as a particular issue for the British public since:

> Throughout the 1980s representations of Northern Ireland in British television drama impeded efforts to end the violence by encouraging a form of 'psychological withdrawal' from the North on the part of the British public. By depicting Northern Ireland not only as 'alien' but as in fact antithetical to Britain in every way, these representations complemented a political agenda that sought to deny responsibility both for creating the conflict and for failing to bring it to a swift conclusion.
>
> (1999a: 71)

In seeking to meet the challenge of such a position, this work is aligned with the aspiration expressed by the directors of Field Day Theatre Company that the company 'could and should contribute to the solution of the present crisis by producing analyses of the established opinions, myths and stereotypes which had become both a symptom and a cause of the current situation' (Deane et al. 1985: vii). Thus, the conflict is presented not as some inevitable result of ethnic or sectarian hatred but as a failure of the state to accommodate all its citizens due to its 'differential relationship with Irish nationalism on the one hand, and Ulster unionism on the other' (Rolston 1998b: 272). While there is clearly an underlying issue of religious prejudice, this is not just a matter of individual bigotry; 'sectarianism persists not simply because of personal weakness or moral vice but because it is imbricated in real structures of power' (Cleary 1999: 510). Nonetheless, it is important to note that there may be as many positions in relation to the conflict as there are identities within it and experiences of it. Paramilitary organisations have long been linked to general criminal activities (extortion, smuggling and drug dealing, for example) and a large number of incidents of murder and destruction have had a basis only in bigotry, breeding in their turn hatred and an appetite for revenge. The conflict itself has shifted through different phases over the period, further reorientating positions, occasionally so radically as to resemble a political and deadly Mad Hatter's Tea Party.

A further consequence of this insistence on the political basis of the conflict is that I will use predominantly the terms 'unionist' or 'nationalist' to refer to the two major identity blocs within Northern Ireland, rather than 'Protestant' or 'Catholic' respectively. Unionists are those whose political identity is predicated on the continuation of the link with Britain (Aughey 1996), although there is a variety of reasons which underpin this position. Sales notes that unionism may also encompass a number of other dimensions: cultural (linked to notions of 'British identity'); religious (the preservation of the Protestant religion and the Protestant settlement in the Union); supremacist (epitomised in the slogan 'we are the people'); or 'progressive' (emphasising economic ties and links to the British labour and trade union movement).

(1997: 47)

There are divisions within unionism from which a range of competing interests have striven to claim to themselves the position as the authoritative voice of unionism (Finlayson 1999). For example, Todd differentiates Ulster loyalist and Ulster British ideological positions. She notes that 'the essential characteristics of Ulster loyalist ideology are that its primary imagined community is Northern Protestants while its secondary identification with Britain involves only a conditional loyalty' (1987: 3). McIlroy glosses this by suggesting that loyalists 'give *conditional* allegiance to Great Britain as long as their Protestant religion and civil freedoms are supported and protected' (1998: 10–11). Todd describes Ulster British ideology as one whose 'imagined community is Great Britain, although within this there is a secondary regional identification with Northern Ireland. Religious values are not primary in the structure of Ulster British thought although moral principles are important in defining their community. This ideology may be either integrationist or devolutionist at the level of political programmes' (1987: 11).

Just as unionism contains a range of diverse and often competing interests, so too does nationalism (Patterson 1996; Coulter 1999). 'Nationalists' are united, however, in the desire to see a reunification of Ireland and in regarding themselves as primarily Irish. As McIlroy suggests, nationalists believe 'that the geographical limits of the island of Ireland encompass a nation which has been prevented by British imperialism from achieving its natural development and destiny' (1998: 8). Republicans share the nationalist aspiration for the reunification of the island. They are distinguished both by a tradition of armed struggle and, within the context of the current Troubles, a greater commitment to social equity (ibid.: 8) since the republican movement has been strongly rooted within the nationalist working class (Coulter 1999: 90).

'Northern Ireland' is used to refer to the internationally recognised territory upon which the Troubles have been focused, rather than 'Ulster' or the 'North of Ireland'. The latter are more evocative of political aspirations than descriptive of a recognisable political entity. 'Ulster' is motivated by a unionist desire to be seen as separate from the rest of Ireland, politically and culturally (although its use refers to only six of the original nine counties which make up the province). The 'North of Ireland' serves the contrary purpose of asserting that Ireland is one unit, with no more than geographically distinct regions. It is a nationalist denial of the legitimacy (and to some extent reality) of the border. The state of Northern Ireland came into existence with the passing into British law of the Government of Ireland Act of 1920 which partitioned Ireland.[3] The Act called into being what A.T.Q. Stewart has identified as 'the narrow ground' in which members of the two major identity blocs are forced to live together, despite 'their diametrically opposed political wills' (1989: 180).

Northern Ireland has never been hermetically sealed from the rest of the island by the creation of the border, even during the middle decades of the last century when each state sought to insulate itself from the other, in what Hennessey has termed a 'Cold War' lasting from 1928 to 1962 (1997: 56ff.). From partition, through this period and up until the present day, a number of institutions have continued to operate across the whole island including churches, sporting organisations and, notably in this context, both professional theatre and amateur drama organisations. Playwrights, actors, directors and designers have moved between institutions across the border. Both parts of the island have also shared (albeit asymmetrically) influences from the rest of the British Isles and beyond, including, for example, in the development of gender politics, cultural trends and economic changes. Latterly, the development of supranational economic, political and legal organisations have increased the permeability of the border, most notably the European Economic Community and later the European Union. Inward investment by multinational companies has altered economic relations, and increasingly globalised media organisations operate without respect to borders. Each has resulted in a closer homogeneity in much of the patterns and tastes of cultural production and consumption across the island and within the British Isles.

Despite the permeability of the border, however, my insistence remains on 'Northern Ireland'. As Boyce argues, the central problem 'is the very legitimacy of the state—the state that used to be (Northern Ireland) and the state of which that region still forms a part (the United Kingdom)' (1991: 15). A further point is being made concerning the opportunities that might arise by focusing closely on works by Northern Irish theatre makers. There has been a tendency to regard Northern Irish dramatic output as a minor chapter in the canon of Irish dramatic literature. For example, Christopher Murray (1997) devotes one chapter to 'Playing the North', in his *Twentieth Century Irish Drama: Mirror up to Nation*, not unreasonably given that his starting point is 'the assumption that in the Irish historical experience drama. . . and theatre. . . were both instrumental in defining and sustaining national consciousness' (1997: 3). Northern Irish playwrights and dramas may have difficulty in fulfilling that function given the duality of the Northern Irish state, and multiplicity of positions which can be taken in relation to it. In *The Cambridge Companion to Twentieth Century Irish Drama*, edited by Shaun Richards (2004), Northern Irish theatre is largely ignored apart from a single chapter on Brian Friel and a separate one on Field Day.

Another approach has been to avoid separate treatment of 'Northern' plays or playwrights. Margaret Llewellyn-Jones, for example, argues that her deployment of this strategy

> is not to evade the political issue of 'The Troubles' but to facilitate compar-
> ison of ways in which writers and companies have worked in particular
> though different contexts on similar themes. . . Further, the recent
> burgeoning of drama in Ireland has not been a separatist but almost
> entirely, in some way, a 'border-crossing' activity, contributing to a more
> fluid, hybrid approach to cultural identity.
>
> (2002: 10)

However, disaggregating playwrights or plays from Northern Ireland which are concerned with The Troubles from the mainstream of Irish theatre history allows a closer analysis of the ways in which plays in performance are situ-ated as part of the contexts within which they are rendered meaningful. The most important element of this context is that Northern Ireland is *both* Irish *and* British. If this is not acknowledged, much of the cultural specificity of the experience of living and working within or responding to the boundaries of this state is lost. This is of particular significance for a playwright like Gary Mitchell, for example, who refuses to be categorised as an Irish playwright since he is from and seeks to address the experiences of working-class loyal-ists who are resolutely British (Arnold 2000: 64). Likewise, when Seamus Heaney (1985) resists inclusion in an anthology of *British* poetry, one must nonetheless acknowledge that, even for nationalists, living within Northern Ireland has been to a large extent an experience of hybridity, conditioned both by a British state and a sense of Irish identity, however defined.

Issues of context aside, there are also advantages in respect of the investi-gation of dramatic strategies in isolating Northern Irish theatre. As I will argue in detail in succeeding chapters, many of the dimensions of Northern Irish drama in performance will not be appreciated if measured against the values of the dominant Irish theatre tradition. These values derive from two mutu-ally reinforcing categories: the aesthetic and the political. The aesthetic values depend on the identifiable literary merit of the play text, rarely seeking to engage with the performative dimensions of plays in production before spec-ified audiences (Llewellyn-Jones is one of the few writers to attempt this). Trotter (2001), for example, contrasts the emphasis placed on literary merit by the founders of the Irish Literary Theatre with the prominence awarded to performance by the contemporaneous Gaelic League. As Maxwell has commented 'W.B. Yeats asserted "the sovereignty of words" throughout his career as a dramatist. Irish drama generally has acknowledged this sovereignty of words' (1990: 3). This emphasis has obtained in Irish theatre thereafter since, as Lionel Pilkington argues in the institutional theatre, 'the excellence of a given performance depends on its iterability and there is at all times an essential disregard for the contingencies of time and space' (2001: 29). Jocelyn Clarke cites Goldman to argue likewise that theatre reviewers rarely engage with what happens on the stage; instead 'they substitute opinion for analysis and interpretation, and descriptions of the play for descriptions of the production' (2000: 97). In part, as Thomas Crane (2001) identifies, the emphasis on the representational aspects of performance is due to the ongoing prominence of textual analysis within theatre historiography more generally and within Irish theatre historiography in particular. Whilst post-colonial theory has been introduced in some discussions (for example: Silverstein 1992; Worthern 1995; Llewellyn-Jones 2002) and feminist critical approaches are being increasingly developed (for example: Pelan 1999; McDonough 2000; McMullan 2000; Foley 2003), exploration of the ways in which a play in performance might engage its audience has been under-developed.

McAuley, however, dismisses analyses of texts which 'however subtle and intelligent they may be, reveal more about the critic's skill as a reader—or as virtual *metteur en scène*—than they do about theatre practice, and they belong to the literary economy: texts about texts, circulating amongst readers of texts' (1999: 10). A further limitation of this emphasis on the text is that, as Bauman states in relation to verbal art, it places 'severe constraints on the development of a meaningful framework for the understanding of verbal art as a perform-ance, as a species of situated human communication' (Bauman 1975: 291). It is this situatedness that is crucial to analysis in which it is recognised that the performance is not secondary to a pre-existing text as an act of commu-nication, but constitutes such an act in and of itself.

At least in part, the emphasis on the writer and the text of this critical tradi-tion can be attributed to a lack of clarity about the ways in which cultural representations and politics relate. This is, I suspect, a direct consequence of two things. The first is that the reliance of political discourse on metaphor and metonymy, the fundamental elements of the dramatic medium, has produced a highly performative political culture in Northern Ireland which, while appearing theatrical, clouds over the precise ways in which theatre and politics relate. The second is that the implicitly nationalist project of Irish theatre history has assumed a direct correlation between the theatrical act and political action. Moreover, this critical tradition has avoided any close exam-ination of the issue of efficacy for the works under discussion. The analysis of the ideas discernible within plays has substituted for the analysis of how plays construct, successfully or otherwise, an audience's experience of the actual theatrical event and how that experience fits within the wider context of political processes. The critique of Friel's *Making History* (1988) by Hohenleitner (2000) is a case in point. She writes that '*Making History* has been accused of being a bad play, a boring play, an overly intellectual play, a dramatized Field Day pamphlet' (2000: 254), yet nowhere does she connect her own detailed analysis of the text and its origins to the diachronic unfolding of the play for a live audience to explain or refute such criticism. Indeed, she ignores the positive reviews which the play received when it opened in September 1988 in Derry's Guildhall.

In such critical accounts, the priority given to that which is considered as *readable* has downplayed the spectator's presence within the theatrical event and the structures of performance in interaction with which the spectator's integrated psycho-physical experience is organised. Mary Thomas Crane identifies these approaches as one side of a 'constitutive binary. . ., namely the distinction between representation and experience, or discourse and embodiment, which might also be described as a distinction between semiotics and phenomenology' (2001: 170). In semiological criticism, significance is equated to signification in a process through which the interpretation of the performance as text is prioritised over the experience of the spectator present at a performance. The distinction is key: analysis of signification seeks to identify the meanings which are read within a performance; analysis of significance seeks to identify both the ways in which the performance structures the audience's experience and the impact with which that experience is registered. There are, of course, problems in attempting to account for this experience, such as generalising from personal experience and elevating the private anecdote to the status of analytical insight. A brief response to these issues might point out that responses to the literary text are just as likely to be subjective as those based on experience. Bruce McConachie (2001) has proposed a method of explaining the 'normative experiences of most spectators' at a performance event by determining the dominant image schemas of the mainstream culture at that time and examining how these organised the spectator's perception and experience of the production. McConachie's approach is convincing and ties in with concerns of other theoreticians of audience experience who, as De Marinis phrases it, wish to take 'reception from the a-temporal and a-historical island where some want it to be confined, and bringing it back to its only real place: *within culture, hence within society and history*, in order to account for it' (1993: 9; see also Pavis 1983).

Inattention to the reception of performance events has not been operational in isolation within critical discourses. It derives from and is reinforced by a further dominant trend within criticism and art practice. This trend has sought to prioritise the universal over the situated and the objective over the subjective, often disguising the partial and contingent values which are operative therein. These are the values espoused by Yeats and (at least some of) the co-founders of the Irish Literary Theatre. Mengel cites tellingly the letter which they circulated to attract support for their venture emphasising the avoidance of a direct engagement with politics:

We hope to find in Ireland an uncorrupted and imaginative audience trained to listen by its passion for oratory. . . We will show that Ireland is not the home of buffoonery and of easy sentiment, as it has been represented, but the home of an Irish people who are weary of misrepresentation, *in carrying out a work that is outside of all the political questions that divide us.* [Mengel's emphasis]

(1986: 3)

This unwillingness to engage directly with the political world beyond the theatre is an inevitable consequence of the idealist elitism of the ILT. It connects to the 'constructive unionism of its founders' (Pilkington 2001b: 2) since, as Leerssen notes, in the nineteenth century, cultural nationalism was considered 'by the people involved, to be apolitical and. . . the pursuit of Irish culture and antiquity was considered a sanctuary where men of different religious or political persuasion could meet' (1996: 49). Assuming these values today, however, prevents an appreciation of works which engage audiences (not always intentionally) in the consideration of the political situation beyond the theatre; a category into which much Northern Irish drama falls.

The political values of the contemporary mainstream theatre in the Republic may be attributed in part to the ambiguities of living within a state founded through violent conflict but unable to come to terms with such violence in its own development or in the crises within its northern counterpart. In the service of its own internal cohesion which has been threatened by the Troubles 'up North' and in its most recent processes of modernisation, the Republic of Ireland has sought to redefine itself in ways to which militant republicanism and northern nationalism have been, at the very least, an embarrassment. The resolutely nationalist teleology to much Irish theatre historiography (Pilkington 2001a) and other aspects of public cultural activity has ignored the Northern problem. Ian Hill commented: 'In Dublin, there is a comfortable society which, though its Government claims in its constitution to possess the northern six counties, certainly does not want to possess its violent troubles' (1993: 45). This observation was borne out when, even while urging unionist politicians to share power with members of Provisional Sinn Féin, following the General Election of 2002 in the Republic, the returning Taoiseach (Prime Minister), Bertie Aherne, refused any such accommodation within his own coalition government south of the border. This is the result of an acceptance of the crisis as a problem internal to the state of Northern Ireland, a crisis between the two traditions, in which the Republic might engage as a broker, but not as a participant. This acceptance has manifested itself in the reception of plays about the Troubles south of the border. Murray describes the reception of Friel's *The Freedom of the City* in its first production at the Abbey in 1973 within the wider context of Irish theatre:

In effect, the ironic, hard-hitting elements of the play were not appreciated, largely because of the conservatism of Dublin audiences. Although
it was subsequently dismissed in New York as politically biased, *The
Freedom of the City* has since 'gained greatly in stature' as its theatrical skil-
fulness has been better appreciated (Zach 1989, 432). Yet it has never
been revived at the Abbey, and its reception underlines the antipathy in
the South to plays about Northern politics.

(1997: 201–2)

A decade later, Peter Sheridan's *Diary of a Hunger Striker* (1982) was
refused a staging at the Dublin Theatre Festival. According to Sheridan,
'Michael Colgan, who was head of the Dublin Theatre Festival at the time,
said he didn't want a H-Block image in the Dublin Theatre Festival. Imagine,
a play about Ireland—about something as seminal as the hunger strikes—
could not find a home in Dublin' (Sheridan and Mulrooney 2001: 452).
Likewise, in commenting on the poor audiences for the opening of Parker's
Northern Star at the1984 Dublin Theatre Festival, the *Sunday Independent*
reviewer noted 'To my mind, it deserved full houses during the entire festival
first week; that it wasn't so is a reflection on what we down here think of Belfast
and the North generally' (Smith 1985: 17).

Focusing on Northern Ireland as a defining category also allows attention
to be drawn to the inter-relationships between theatrical and other cultural
representations of the conflict. Harrington and Mitchell's edited volume of
essays, *Politics and Performance in Contemporary Northern Ireland* (1999) is a
welcome departure in this respect, in seeking to identify the context in which
performances of plays may be placed alongside a variety of other political
performances. No medium is made or experienced in isolation. Practitioners
and policy makers move between modes of performance and between
theatrical, print and broadcast media. Writers such as Gary Mitchell, Graham
Reid and Christina Reid have adapted work originally presented in one
medium for a different medium. The horizon of expectations and mental
luggage of audiences too are conditioned by exposure to a whole range of
media. Thus it is important to locate theatrical output within a wider understanding of the ways in which culture can intervene in processes of representation and public politics.

The Critical Context

Such a relocation of Northern Irish theatre is part of the goal of this book.
My own interest in interventionist theatre has developed since my exposure
to popular political theatre movements in Scotland in the 1980s and 1990s.
I grew up in the aspirant Catholic working class in North Belfast, living
through the ambiguous cultural context of an Irish nationalism experienced

within the predominantly British state, civic and social structures of Northern Ireland from the mid-1960s. In Scotland I was witness to how theatre could contribute to the development of a civic nationalism and cultural self-confidence which were not reliant on narrow conceptions of ethnic identity. In bringing this experience back to bear on Northern Ireland, I share in a similar nationalist analysis of the political situation that acknowledges two elements. The first of these is that 'the political story of Northern Ireland is a colonial story' (McDonough 2000: 183). In Northern Ireland, this is a particularly complex configuration given the presence of an indigenous population, a long-standing settler colony and the continuing presence of a former colonial power which operates on many levels as a metropolitan centre of influence. Further complexity is added by the involvement of Irish people in the imperial projects of Britain, the current global influence of Irish culture, and the pull of Dublin as a metropolitan centre in its own right. The second presumption is that it has been the failure of the structures of the British state in Northern Ireland to accommodate the needs and aspirations of all the people within it that has fuelled the most recent Troubles (Patterson 1996: 46). These elements need not imply a mechanistic application of concepts generalised from other contexts to Northern Ireland, an approach lambasted by Foster (2001), for example. Each context of colonialism is different in its particularity: post-colonial theory can alert us to ways in which specific power relations, nonetheless, have been configured historically, and continue to be configured across colonised societies. Moreover, institutionalised discrimination, the military saturation of nation-alist areas and social segregation have been experienced as colonial acts by many nationalists without a need to refer to other contexts or abstract theo-ries to explain their lived experience. Thus, without change to the structures of the state, peace is impossible. However, such structures are only part of the process: it is people who make such structures operative. Thus, even if the constitutional position of Northern Ireland were to change, it would still be necessary to find political, economic, social and cultural structures to allow this possibility.

There have been a number of precursors to this work, of course. Philomena Muinzer undertook one of the first surveys of theatrical responses to the Troubles in 1987. In 1990 Maxwell identified key plays in Northern Ireland's legacy of political drama. This was followed by Ian Hill's article 'Staging the Troubles' (1993) and another survey essay by Ashley Taggart in 2000. These have been valuable in giving exposure to the work, with their central focus on providing analysis of the narrative and dramaturgical structures of the plays. As essays they have necessarily been constrained in the level of detail they have provided while attempting to be as inclusive as possible. A similar comment can be applied to surveys of the theatrical institutions themselves, such as Ophelia Byrne's (1997) *The Stage in Ulster from the Eighteenth Century* (see also Byrne 2001a and b; and Grant 2001), which have provided invaluable reference points.

Two more extensive works have also been undertaken. The first, by Nicholas Grene (1999), sets out to identify the relationship between theatre and politics through the recent history of Irish theatre across the island, and it includes discussion of a number of plays concerning the Troubles. More tightly focused on theatre in Northern Ireland is Lionel Pilkington's *Theatre and the State in Twentieth Century Ireland* (2001b). Pilkington sets out to 'counteract the long-standing assumption that Irish theatre stands outside politics and apart altogether from the determining power of the state' (2001b: 1). He examines the origins of the Irish National Theatre in its relationship to the British state and subsequently in its relationship to the Irish state following partition. He also includes two chapters relating to Northern Ireland. Of these, the first on National Theatres in Northern Ireland details the post-partition period in which unionism exercised hegemonic control of the media and cultural institutions of the state. Following the Second World War, the model of direct intervention by the state across the United Kingdom was turned in Northern Ireland to the cause of 'Ulster regionalism' (ibid.: 168): the cultural legitimation of the state. However, attempts to create some kind of 'national' theatre of Northern Ireland foundered on a variety of political and aesthetic disputes. At the same time, private individuals and companies staged a number of plays which directly challenged the sectarian basis of unionist hegemony such as Gerald McLarnon's *The Bonefire* (1951) and Sam Thompson's *Over the Bridge* (1960). With the establishment of the Lyric Players Group in 1951 (later the Lyric Players Theatre Trust), a broadly nationalist perspective was brought to the Northern Irish stage, creating 'a semi-independent public space existing outside of Stormont's political control' (Pilkington 2001b: 188).

The second chapter on 'National Theatre and the Political Crisis in Northern Ireland, 1968–92' provides an outline of the relationship of the state and the theatre in the early years of the Troubles and discusses some of the well-known plays of the early period such as John Boyd's *The Flats* (1971); Friel's *The Freedom of the City* (1973) and *Volunteers* (1975); and Frank McGuinness's much later *Observe the Sons of Ulster Marching Towards the Somme* (1985). His main discussion is reserved, however, for Friel's *Translations*. This discussion has been invaluable in presenting a model through which the aesthetic and the political are related and in part this work attempts to extend its scope across both time and a wider range of material.

Even as the research for this book was underway two books were published in 2003 which intersect directly with the project at hand: Imelda Foley's *The Girls in the Big Picture: Gender in Contemporary Ulster Theatre* and Bernard McKenna's *Rupture, Representation, and the Refashioning of Identity in Drama from the North of Ireland, 1969–1994*. Foley places interviews with contem-

Figure 1. *The Flats* by John Boyd, Lyric Theatre, Belfast.
Photographer: Chris Hill

porary playwrights (Marie Jones, Christina Reid, Anne Devlin and Frank McGuinness) in the contexts of the historical operation of patriarchy within Northern Irish theatre and society as a means of introducing a discussion of the work of each. This discussion is informed by feminist theory and praxis and Foley develops an argument in particular around the French feminist concept of *écriture féminine*. This produces an emphasis on tracing the characteristics of the internal form of the plays and her concentration is on the text. McKenna's work pays greater attention to issues of context, but is guided by the application of trauma theory which he then imposes as a lens through which not only the plays but the whole of Northern Irish society are viewed. He focuses on the literary and psychological structure of a range of plays and on their theatrical components, a range which intersects with many of the productions discussed here. However, while McKenna traces the trauma he identifies to its roots in 'the violence inflicted on colonized territories' (2003: 10), the result is to pathologise Northern Ireland and its stage representations, and to repeat the ideological assertion that the conflict is primarily about identity. This is something which I would regard as a particularly unhelpful strategy in the discussion of an essentially political situation.

Individual dramatists and plays have been written about at much greater length. Brian Friel is the most discussed contemporary playwright across the island, with numerous books and articles devoted to his work and life (Dantanus 1988; Pine 1990; Andrews 1995, for example). Of his plays dealing most directly with the politics of Northern Ireland, *Translations* and *The Freedom of the City* have received most attention. Again, however, the emphasis has been on close readings of the text, although the context and reception of *The Freedom of the City* have been attended to much more closely (Zach 1992, for example). Frank McGuinness has become an increasing object of study with Eamonn Jordan's full-length study appearing in 1997 and a collection of essays edited by Helen Lojek published in 2002. Such a concentration of critical focus on the work of a limited number of writers has skewed the sense of theatre history and has overlooked the experience of a range of other productions by actual audiences. This book is one attempt to address this effect of distortion.

Theatre, Ideology and Propaganda

The central foundation of this project is that all forms of art are conditioned by an ideological perspective, conscious or not. I use ideology to refer to 'the set of ideas which arise from a given set of material interests, or more broadly, from a definite class or group' (Williams 1988: 156). Moreover, I accept, as Holderness argues, that

All culture. . . contains or expresses or implies a political view: all art whether consciously or unconsciously, is tendentious, polemical, partisan; all literature and drama speak on behalf of an admitted or unacknowledged belief that one order of things, one set of social arrangements, one structure of political relations is better or worse than another.

(1992: 17)

This emphasis on the ideological functions of all art forms seeks to refute any sense of art being separated from or superseding its context. This is particularly crucial when art is being put to the service of re-imaging selected parts of the state of Northern Ireland (Neill 1995; Murtagh 1995): a subject which forms the background to Andrew Hinds's *October Song* (1992) and Derry Frontline's *Threshold* (1992). Art may be itself the expression of an individual vision, but it is articulated within and has its reception conditioned by ideological perspectives.

If it is accepted that art works are conditioned by and contribute to the functions of ideologies, then it is clear that they all do not operate in relation to their contexts in the same way. This follows Kershaw's aim which is, 'not to deny that "all performance is political" but to encourage discrimination between the different ways in which, and degrees to which, particular kinds of performance may be more or less politically efficacious' (1996: 134). To this end, I refer to the formulation provided by Szanto (1978) in classifying three broad ways in which a work of art might function in relation to its context. They may be agitational, integrationist or dialectical. Szanto provocatively describes each function as a form of propaganda since 'they are the result of processes of collection, editing, revealing and concealing of information about or experiences of reality. Thus, they are the product of an ideology that assigns significance and meaning to the world' (1978: 6–7). In this, he is removing from the concept of propaganda any necessary condition of conscious intention, whilst retaining the connection between the ideology of the work and the ideologies with which it might interact. Furthermore, he focuses the sense of propaganda on the relationship which is established between the ideology of the work and the ideologies of the audience in context, rather than on merely matters of content or form.

Thus, works which function as agitational propaganda oppose dominant ideologies. Szanto argues that,

It participates in raising the audience's consciousness to a point where social and political problems take on a shape and immediacy. It excites audiences to an awareness that they previously had lacked. It has the power to render in concrete form circumstances which up to that moment have remained parts of quietly undifferentiated, general daily reality.

(1978: 73)

By contrast integrationist propaganda encourages the audience to accept that,

> all is as well with the world as it is ever going to get; that the best way for
> an audience or society to cope is within carefully delineated boundaries,
> clear-cut channels and categories; that one should accept the ideological
> precepts of the society within which one functions even to the point of
> never understanding there is a created ideology within the precepts.
>
> (1978: 74)

In terms of drama, Goodlad terms such work as 'the drama of reassurance' which 'shows potential social problems being resolved and discord turned to harmony' (1971: 177).

Szanto's final category is that of dialectical propaganda which 'attempts to demystify, by depicting separately, interactively and always clearly the basic elements which comprise a confused social or historical situation. . . [It emphasizes its own partiality in order to] emphasize that reality is far more complex than any single view of appearances' (1978: 75).

This function is perhaps the most crucial in a context in which reality and history are continually being assimilated into apparently mutually exclusive and monolithic narratives to support opposing political positions and in which assertions of truth and authenticity have underpinned particular senses of identity.

The Shape and Approach of the Book

What is being explored, then, are the ways in which dramatists and theatre makers *and* the audiences for their work have responded as creative agents to the structural impositions of the conditions of Northern Ireland. It is equally important to recognise that the efficacy or otherwise of a work of art is tied closely to its situation of utterance and that its function is bound to the context in which it is produced and received. Kershaw makes the case that 'anything which appears to make absolute theoretical sense needs to be tested against the specifics of practice, especially when we are dealing with the political potential of performance' (1996: 144). Clearly the context of the audience has a large part to play in this. I adopt Bennett's model of the audience's experience of theatre which uses two frames:

> The outer frame is concerned with theatre as a cultural construct through
> the idea of the theatrical event, the selection of material for production
> and the audience's definitions and expectations of a performance. The
> inner frame contains the event itself and, in particular, the spectator's
> experience of production strategies, ideological over-coding, and the
> material conditions of performance. It is the intersection of these two

frames which forms the spectator's cultural understanding and experience
of theatre. Beyond this, the relationship between the two frames is always
seen as interactive. Cultural assumptions affect performances and
performances rewrite cultural assumptions.

(1991: 2)

So, this book will compare the strategies by which different productions have
engaged with specific elements of the political crises and the responses at play
in their reception. The aim is not to arrive at any sense of a single definitive
reading of the productions, but to demonstrate the ways in which the social
event and process which each production called into being involved the interplay of divergent engagements, analyses and responses, an interplay which
need not begin or end at the door of the auditorium.

The categories under which the plays in each of the main chapters are
discussed have been chosen to allow both a detailed discussion of each play
and a diachronic comparison of how a similar approach has been undertaken
in different historical moments. These categories are: in Chapter 2 issues in
representing the immediate reality of a conflict situation; approaches to
history in Chapters 3 and 4; the use of myth in Chapter 5; the representation
of gender in Chapter 6; the development of community theatres in Chapter
7; and, attempts to negotiate with a post-conflict context in Chapter 8. The
final chapter draws together aspects of the earlier discussions. Of course, there
are countless variations of theme under which the material might have been
grouped, any of which might have been just as illuminating. One such might
have been the foregrounding of a discussion of dramaturgical strategies (such
as the use of monologue) or consideration of formal characteristics (such as
dramatic genre). Instead, such discussions are contained in relation to the
function of the plays as produced within specific contexts. By relating these
productions to their actual conditions of performance and reception, the aim
(based on Kershaw 1996) is to discriminate between these strategies and to
identify how they may be considered to have been efficacious in context. This
sense of efficacy extends beyond discovering the meaning of the script, itself
a translation of the performative into the literary. What is being attempted is
a delineation of both the meanings of a performance and its significance for
its audience which extends beyond signification into the realms of the
emotional and affective.

The selection of particular plays was no less vexed than the selection of
categories under which to group them. Within the discussion and the playography, my choice focuses on plays in which the political conflict is a dominant given, rather than an incidental backdrop; which had their original
production on the island of Ireland; and which were written by people from
or with a close association with Northern Ireland. Exceptionally, Rona
Munro's *Bold Girls* (1990) is discussed on the basis of the contribution which

it has made to both internal and external conceptions of the relationship between gender and nationalism in Northern Ireland. For the rest, each production is chosen as an exemplar of a particular kind of intervention: in the process by which it was composed; in its dramaturgical strategies; or, the event which its performance constituted. In this sense, each production is in some sense typical. Each has also been selected for its particularity too, a particularity arising from the precise contours of its engagement with its context. Inevitably, there is a bias towards productions of which I have had first-hand experience, though equally inevitably the discussions focus predominantly on works for which there is a published script, providing access for readers who have not shared in their performance. Nonetheless, for other reasons I have included discussion of productions such as JustUs's *Binlids* (1997), Martin Lynch's *The Stone Chair* (1989) and Tim Loane's *Caught Red Handed* (2002), for which there is no widely available play script. The selection process has also had a negative dimension: I have largely avoided discussion of productions around which have been generated wide-spread critical histories and discourses. As discussed above, this book is intended as a means of redressing the imbalances of the weight such works exert within existing criticism. Thus, plays such as Friel's *Translations* and McGuinness's *Observe the Sons of Ulster Marching Towards the Somme* in particular serve as an assumed backdrop to which I refer, rather than displacing other works at the centre of these discussions. There are other omissions too, of works for which there is little or no archival record, an inevitable consequence of the difficulties of retrieving the past from the shards of theatre history. These are accepted as regrettable but inevitable. A final omission is that of Irish language theatre which is due entirely to the limitations of my own knowledge of the language: its history requires a more accomplished grasp than I can provide currently.

In the following chapters, then, I hope to expose the range of approaches to engaging with the Northern Ireland conflict in and through the theatre. In so doing, I hope to open up to the reader some unfamiliar territory and to effect a re-evaluation of the familiar. This involves introducing new approaches and performances to critical scrutiny; exploring alternative ways of thinking about theatrical representation; and suggesting alternative conceptions of Northern Ireland. Ultimately, its aim is to provide a space in which to rethink the relationships which are possible between each of these elements.

2
Direct Engagement

DIDO: Tell me the truth. Isn't it just like real life?
(Silence)
Did yous like it?
HARK: I'm searching for words to describe it.
DIDO: Do you think it was too short?
HARK: It's not short. It's shite.

(Frank McGuinness, 1988, *Carthaginians*, 43)

In the intensity of a conflict situation, there are difficulties in representing the events outside the theatre in a dramatic form onstage. In only a few instances have there been issues of personal security and safety, such as the dangers from loyalist gunmen and harassment by the security forces faced by the Derry Frontline company members during their preparations for *Threshold* in 1992 (Baron Cohen and Pilkington 1994; Baron Cohen and King 1997). In more secure circumstances, two inter-related factors militate against such theatrical representation. The first is the familiarity of such events in the consciousness of the audience, both through direct experience and through representation in the press and broadcast media. Such representations will have been formulated and viewed within discourses which vie for authority and legitimacy and diverge according to already established divisions within the society itself. The second factor is the difficulty of finding a form of representation which fulfils the function intended by the theatre makers. As Dido discovers in the extract above from *Carthaginians* by Frank McGuinness, audience criticism can be damming. For example, Richards (1995) criticises representations of the conflict in the form of tragedy which figure the society as doomed to play out a predestined fate. By contrast, Cleary argues that the 'very elements of domestic tragedy usually deemed to be those which hinder the genre from adequately dealing with social and historical problems. . . may, paradoxically, have the potential to contribute to the development of an authentically radical materialist critique of the Northern Irish social system' (1999: 506). The issue of form focuses attention on the ways in which the resources of live performance are marshalled to engage with the theatrical audience's relationship to its reality, what Holderness has called 'the politics of function' (1992: 7). Szanto argues that 'the aesthetic forms of an artwork are themselves functions of the work's ideology. . . . To suggest the opposite, that a preconceived formal arrangement should order the idea or the experience, implies an artificial relation between the content and its artistic shape, a relation that would deny a great deal of a work's validity, or truth-value, even before a consideration of either its form or its content has begun' (1978: 6).

Ian Hill suggests that 'there has indeed been little written in Irish theatre which tackles the reality of The Troubles head on' (1993: 46). A brief overview of the theatres in Belfast in the early 1970s would have supported his conclusion: while other theatres closed, a staple fare of uncontroversial Irish classics at The Lyric offered respite from the imploding civil society and collapsing state outside. Nonetheless, the necessity of representing the reality of the Troubles has been keenly felt by many playwrights and theatre makers over the course of the conflict from as early as the Lyric's 1971 production of John Boyd's *The Flats*. Problematically, Boyd's work seemed to have provided the precedent for a separate genre of 'Troubles plays' which rapidly degenerated into hackneyed representations, summarised by Mark Patrick,

> Protestant boy meets Catholic girl meets terrorist bomb, with an insubstantial sub-plot featuring various re-incarnations from Ireland's bloody past. While an easy target for ridicule, I believed (as I still do) that this type of play had a more serious and insidious side—perpetuating the myths which prevail outside Northern Ireland and fuelling the parochialism and self-obsession which reign within.
>
> (1989: 20)

The exploration here seeks to identify plays which engage with the challenge of tackling the Troubles head-on without resorting to the clichés Patrick describes. The aim is therefore in part to mount a corrective to those who would dismiss such work out-of-hand and to explore the choice of formal responses which theatre makers have undertaken. Moreover, I wish to ask questions about the nature of the responses from audiences which were in contest during the performance of these works.

There has been a long tradition of realist dramas that have engaged with the Troubles on stage and screen. The model of O'Casey's Dublin trilogy has provided a potent precedent and it was embraced by working-class writers such as Sam Thompson and subsequently by numerous dramatists of the Troubles. This has not, however, produced a uniformity of style, and the form has yielded variations of genre such as Gary Mitchell's police thriller *Trust* (1999) and Joseph Crilly's comedy-farce *On McQuillan's Hill* (2000). At its historical roots in naturalism (the terms are often used interchangeably), realism had concerned itself with how individuals act under environmental pressures, offering a critique of how society determined the conditions under which its members lived, particularly in extending the focus of drama beyond the aristocratic and upper classes (Williams 1977a; Styan 1993). However, classic realism was to develop very quickly a focus on individual agency and psychology which superseded this social critique. An alignment with classic narrative structures created in classic realism a model in which the narrative focuses on an individual journey from disruption to resolution. Moreover, this narrative journey is offered in its dramatic form as a transparent mode of performance, unbound by ideological leanings which might affect its claims to representing the world as it is objectively. Müller-Schöll argues that, 'It mixed up referential potential and reality and thereby hides the performativity of its performance. Thus it reduces theatre to its plot, forgets the difference between plot and what is being presented in it and replaces the presented—the 'real' in its continuing 'retreat'—by its concept' (2004: 43).

As a consequence of these characteristics, however, the form has been seen as incompatible with radical social change by a range of practitioners and critics, not least where it is focused on the personal at the expense of the social and political.[1] The empiricism which underpins realism restricts the engagement with the social knowledge which can be provided,

> Knowledge of social and political relations, for example, does not derive from any simple observation of what is visible but also from an understanding of what is, in effect, invisible. . . . To take an example, it is possible to show how the poor live on the screen. It is rather more difficult, if not impossible, while remaining within the conventions of 'realism' to demonstrate how such poverty is the effect of a particular economic system or socially structured pattern of inequality.
>
> (Hill 1986: 60)

Stephen Lacey identifies a restricted narrative scope as the source of the limitations of realism: 'The tight narrative focus that realist plays adopted placed restrictions on their ability to represent directly the society they were trying to explore, for how much actual social reality can be shown, rather than simply talked about, when the action is confined to a single location and a small group of characters?' (1995: 104).

Morally, realism asserts the primacy of individual humanity over political structures or social pressures. Clearly, such a view has a value in a violent political conflict. Atrocities cannot be traded against each other to justify further violence; nor can the motivations for actions or the context in which they happen excuse the perpetrator of these actions from their responsibility for carrying them out or the consequences which result.[2] Dramatically, this concern with the individual allows the creation of points of empathy for the audience and it is in the deployment of such empathy that the theatrical power of emotion can be harnessed in the performance. Realism, then, derives its power from the proximity of the representation to the world with which it engages and in its ability to draw its audience into its illusion.

If realism is the most illusionist of forms, the form which relies on the recognition of proximity, its antithesis is performance which signals its own theatricality, distancing the audience from what is represented. This form of representation creates frames of reference outside the unifying perspective of the drama and draws attention to the problems of representation (Bleeker 2004). Such performance allows the audience to 'distinguish two actions taking place at the same time in any theatre, the presented action and the very act of (re)presenting, in other words, discourse and address' (Müller-Schöll 2004: 44). The foregrounding of this distinction between stage action and what it represents in the dramatic world seeks to relocate the perspective of the spectator, who, thereby distanced from the events depicted, becomes alert to the ideology of the representation and the limitations of all representations. Holderness argues that

> The kind of theatre (such as that of Brecht) which lays bare the device, exposes the mechanisms of its own construction, encourages in the spectator a critical and questioning alertness towards all ideological naturalisation, can be regarded, whatever its ostensible political content, as politically more progressive—because it targets the most powerful weapon of social control, ideology—than a theatre which collaborates in form and content with a hegemonic ideology and with dominant cultural forms.
>
> (1992: 9)

This laying bare of and drawing attention to the device therefore is offered as a metatheatrical commentary on the performance itself as a form of representation.[3] Such metatheatrical performance has its own tradition within Northern Irish theatre where the performance seeks a separation of character, actor and role; and to distinguish what is done onstage from what is imagined. Brian Friel's *The Freedom of the City*, which will be discussed in detail in Chapter 3, includes a number of formal elements to signal the ways in which experience is mediated ideologically. Arden and D'Arcy had brought *The Non-Stop Connolly Show* (1975) around community venues in Belfast, in a tour which Martin Lynch helped organise. Patrick Galvin's *We Do It For Love* (1975) used a non-naturalistic revue-style performance mode. Frank McGuinness's *Carthaginians* (1988) contains a play-within-a-play which parodies dominant representations of the Troubles. Scenes within Stewart Parker's *Northern Star* are modelled on the theatrical styles of various Irish dramatic writers (see Chapter 4). Christina Reid uses the role of the stand-up comedian in juxtaposition to the main action in *Did You Hear the One about the Irishman?* (1985), a device to which she returns in *Clowns* (1996). *At the Black Pig's Dyke* (1992) sits squarely within this tradition in its attempts to deconstruct 'the unitary dramatic framework in terms of the multiplication of frames' (Bleeker 2004: 30).

So, in representations of the Troubles, there have been two dominant poles between which theatre makers have steered. One pole is constituted by performances which have sought to confront the audience with a reality from which they have been protected by their own strategies of reception or by the intervention of forms of censorship and propaganda by those responsible for the mediation of that reality in print and broadcast media. Such performances have emphasised the proximity of their representation to the actuality beyond the performance. The second pole is the mode of performance which has sought to alienate the audience from its experience of actuality and its own strategies for selective perception and reception. By creating a distancing effect through its subject matter (Chapter 5 examines the use of myth in this respect), its form or its context, such performances have tried to break down the habituated response of the spectator. Two productions have been chosen for detailed analysis, Martin Lynch's *The Interrogation of Ambrose Fogarty* and Vincent Woods's *At the Black Pig's Dyke* in the following discussion. Each exemplifies the particular approach to the relationship of form to function in representing the Troubles which each of these poles represents. Each is also distinctive in its deployment of this form within the particular context of performance which I will discuss.

The Plays in Context

Martin Lynch was raised within a politicised Republican and socialist working-class Belfast family, initially in Moffet Street in the York Road area and later in Turf Lodge when his family—he is one of twelve children—were relocated in a larger house.[4] Without the advantages of either grammar school or university education which other playwrights of his generation enjoyed, he is in many respects a model of the working-class autodidact in the same tradition as Sam Thompson before him. Having left school at 15, he trained as a cloth-cutter, worked as a casual docker, but spent a long period of unemployment. Active in working-class politics from an early age, he was a founder member of Turf Lodge Socialist Fellowship. Inspired to work in theatre after having seen both Patrick Galvin's *We Do it For Love* and Arden and D'Arcy's *Non-Stop Connolly Show*, Lynch wrote plays for the Fellowship as well as a series of sketches which were performed on Sunday nights in local clubs based around a character Billy Maxwell.[5] The plays included *Is There Life Before Death?* (1975), which excited controversy when a local priest condemned it from the pulpit after an excerpt was broadcast on television by BBC Northern Ireland. When the Group Theatre in Belfast's city centre reopened to amateur companies, Lynch decided to take the work there. With *They're Taking the Barricades Down* (1976), *A Roof Under Our Heads* (1976) and *What About*

Your Ma, Is Da still Working? (1976) he was able to attract a working-class audience from across the city eager to see their lives represented on the stage.[6] So, although Lynch's professional career as a playwright began in 1981 with the Lyric Theatre's production of *Dockers*, he already knew from direct experience what worked with his audience in performance. This was recognised too by his appointment as playwright-in-residence at the Lyric in 1980 after John Boyd, Sam McCready and Pearse O'Malley (Board Members of the Lyric) had seen *A Roof Under Our Heads*. Lynch followed the success of *Dockers* a year later with *The Interrogation of Ambrose Fogarty*. He was appointed as writer-in-residence at the University of Ulster in 1985 and was to go on to write for radio and a variety of professional theatre productions. These have included his contribution, *What Did I Know When I Was Nineteen?*, as part of Tinderbox's highly acclaimed *Convictions* (2001) at Crumlin Road Courthouse. In 2002, he and Mark Dougherty co-wrote *The Belfast Carmen*, a large-scale opera at the Grand Opera House, Belfast. In 2003 *The History of the Troubles (accordin' to my Da)*, a collaboration with Alan McKee and Connor Grimes was a major success in its initial run as part of the Cathedral Quarter Arts Festival in Belfast; on a subsequent Irish tour; in revivals at the Grand Opera House, Belfast; and at the Tricycle Theatre, London. He also contributed to the screenplay (along with Edmund Ward) for Mike Hodges's (1987) film adaptation of the Jack Higgins novel *A Prayer for the Dying*. A founder member of Belfast's Community Arts Forum, he has combined this work for the professional theatre with a series of community theatre projects, including *The Stone Chair* in 1989 (see Chapter 7), and a collaboration with Jo Egan to conceive and co-write with Marie Jones and the company, *The Wedding Community Play* (1999).

The Interrogation of Ambrose Fogarty was staged under the direction of Sam McCready at the Lyric, then under the overall artistic direction of Leon Rubin.[7] It opened on 27 January 1982 and played for an extended run of seven weeks. It was produced later at the Peacock in Dublin and at the Irish Arts Centre in New York; it was revived by the Lyric in 1984. In interviews, Lynch was explicit about what he was trying to achieve in the play, as he makes clear in an *Irish Times* article, 'I want Catholics to have a better understanding of the police and I want Protestants to have a better understanding of how people end up Republicans' (Wren 1982).

Set in Springfield Road Barracks, a police station in West Belfast, the play traces three days during which two men from neighbouring streets in nationalist West Belfast are held and intermittently interrogated by members of the Special Branch of the Royal Ulster Constabulary (RUC). One of the prisoners is Ambrose Fogarty who has been involved in republican activities, though never convicted, and whose guilt or innocence is never made clear for the audience. The second prisoner is Willie Lagan, a crackpot Country and Western singer who was inadvertently caught up in a riot on his way home

Figure 2. *The Interrogation of Ambrose Fogarty* by Martin Lynch, Lyric Theatre, Belfast. Photographer: Chris Hill

from an afternoon gig and arrested.[8] By setting the action simultaneously in multiple locations, a sharp contrast is able to be drawn between the day-to-day routine workings of the police station and the brutal methods employed during the interrogation of Fogarty. At the end of the play, Fogarty is released while Lagan is remanded in custody to face charges of which he is patently innocent.

Inspired by Lynch's own experience of being held in custody by the police—he has been held on five occasions—*The Interrogation of Ambrose Fogarty* breaks down any sense of homogeneity within the ranks of the police in its characterisation. Sergeant Knox adheres to an old-fashioned sense of duty and the aspiration that some day he will be able to undertake a normal policing role. Policewoman Yvonne Lundy has only joined up because she was expected to and is looking for a way out of the backwater that for her is Belfast. Davy McFadden is a police constable because it represents a step up the social scale from his working-class roots. None of the three is directly involved in the interrogation of Fogarty. The three Special Branch officers are characterised distinctively too. We are given least background detail about Stanley, the most experienced of the three and the senior officer, who has a long experience of the conflict stretching back to the 1950s. He is a staunch Paisleyite, seeing his role as the last bastion between criminals of all shades and decent people.[9] Jackie occupies more stage time, but his actions onstage are dominated by his short temper and proclivity for violence. For him, joining the RUC was a more effective means of attacking the IRA than becoming a loyalist paramilitary. These two most closely conform to the stereotypical nationalist view of the RUC as bigoted thugs. Their static characterisation enhances this stereotypical view of their representation. In contrast Peter shares much in common with Fogarty's experience of growing up (though he is from middle-class Bangor), and his approach to the violent interrogation of prisoners is more psychologically sophisticated. His characterisation too is static since the apparent changes in his behaviour are merely further revelations of what is continuously present. Pfister's conception of static characters suggests that 'the receiver's perception of them may gradually develop, expand or even change under the influence of the inevitable linear process of information, transmission and accumulation' (Pfister 1988: 178). All three accept that the violence is an inevitable and necessary instrument in their work.

The production questioned the role of the state in the conflict, most overtly in its treatment of nationalists held in custody by the RUC. It was notably one of the first plays staged in Northern Ireland to raise this question. Almost immediately after the introduction of internment in 1971, reports emerged of the maltreatment and torture of people held by the British Army. In September 1976, the European Commission of Human Rights ruled on a case taken to it by the Irish government that Britain was guilty of 'degrading and inhuman treatment' in cases where it had employed sensory deprivation techniques (McKittrick and McVea 2001: 68). Moreover, allegations of direct brutality by the RUC on suspects were rife amongst nationalists, although rarely reported or taken seriously by the British press and media. Peter Taylor, a journalist on Thames Television's *This Week*, wrote that 'If Northern Ireland is the most sensitive issue on British broadcasting, interrogation techniques are its most sensitive spot' (cited Curtis 1984: 57). Not only was there direct censorship of news and current affairs material from within and from outside media organisations (Curtis 1984), but even dramatic output was affected.[10] In 1979, an official investigation of police brutality at the RUC's Castlereagh detention centre confirmed the findings of an earlier Amnesty International report of ill-treatment. Nonetheless, any play which dealt overtly with the treatment of prisoners by the RUC was likely to be radical in its impact. For example, a letter to the editor of *The Belfast Telegraph* attacked the staging of *The Interrogation of Ambrose Fogarty* argued that the play was,

> The Lyric's most bigoted production of the year. . . One would be naïve
> to expect that in a war with terrorists who commit such horrific and
> depressing outrages on fellow human beings interrogation methods are

Dixon of Dock Green affairs. The consequence of terrorist activity is that suspects are subjected to treatment designed to extract information about atrocities. The production does not seriously attempt to examine and develop this scenario, however. . . It is tribal propaganda which will repel Protestants and Catholics and drive yet another wedge between our two communities.

(cited Byrne 2001b: 63)

While the interrogation techniques of the RUC are the ostensible subject of *The Interrogation of Ambrose Fogarty*, a larger issue hangs over it. This concerns the relative moral and political positions of the agencies of the state and those it deems terrorists. By 1980, a long-running dispute over the treatment and categorisation of prisoners held on terrorist charges had come to a head. In 1972, such prisoners had been granted special category status, equivalent in treatment if not in name to that of prisoners of war (McKittrick and McVea 2001: 137–8). This was ended in 1976, provoking what became known as the 'blanket protests' where Republican prisoners refused to wear prison uniforms. This escalated, firstly to a no-wash or 'dirty' protest, then eventually to the hunger strikes of 1980 and 1981. By the end of the second hunger strikes in October 1981, ten prisoners had died.[11]

At stake were not just the privileges of the prisoners, but claims to legitimacy. Seamus Deane has argued persuasively that 'the language of politics in Ireland and England is still dominated by the putative division between barbarism and civilisation' (1983: 11). This division is particularly focused in relation to violence, whereby 'violence is understood as an atavistic and disruptive principle counter to the rationality of legal constitution as barbarity is to an emerging civility, anarchy to culture' (Lloyd 1993: 125). Such a discourse promotes a stereotype of the terrorist as barbarian criminal: he is Irish; Catholic or extreme Protestant; from a working-class background; unemployed but dependent on the state he despises; violent; and drunken (Deane 1983). Within the play, this stereotype is partly distributed between Fogarty and Willie Lagan, and attention is drawn to aspects of it by their interrogators. Fogarty is unemployed and has been politically involved in the past. In his case the stereotype is, however, confounded since he is calm and rational during his interrogation, and concerns himself with his wife and family, worrying over the domestic rather than his supposed acts of violence. Lagan is a harmless buffoon, the comic stage Irishman, and in demonstrating the ways in which he is made to inform falsely on Fogarty and then remanded unjustly on charges, the play indicts the system of justice in which he is caught up. Certainly he appears unhinged and with a fondness for alcohol; yet, just as with Fogarty, he demonstrates no tendency to violence. However, it is the policemen (Jackie and Stanley) who fly into the rages which result in the brutalisation of the prisoners.

Within this discourse, those who oppose terrorism can operate or 'kill with impunity, because they represent, they embody the Law' (Deane 1983: 12). However, if the gap between this discourse and the actions of the state agencies is exposed, the ideological bias of its implementation is made overt and its system of values discredited. If it could be demonstrated that the state was operating in its own interest or the interest of only part of its population and not on the basis of a moral position, then its own legitimacy would be suspect. Equally, if the state ceased to be recognised as the embodiment of the law, then those contesting its authority could themselves claim legitimacy, moving from the position of criminal barbarians to be recognised as political dissidents with as much claim to the law as the state (see Elliot et al. 1996). Peter Sheridan, writer of *Diary of a Hunger Striker*, captures succinctly the issues at the heart of the hunger strikes and underpinning *The Interrogation of Ambrose Fogarty*,

> The basic proposition was 'are these guys criminals or are they politically motivated?' To me there was no argument they were politically motivated. . . These people were trying to change the society in which they found themselves. . . And we've a British Prime Minister telling us that these people are criminals. And you go and live in Belfast, and everybody to a man on the nationalist side is saying these people are political.
>
> (Sheridan and Mulrooney 2001: 453)

Whilst Fogarty's insistence on legal procedures defined under the Emergency Provisions Act 1973 in the opening scenes of the play is regarded by his Special Branch interrogators as an act of bravado, it emphasises for the audience the legal framework within which the subsequent events take place. For the audience, there is a question to be answered, a question articulated in Fogarty's musings to himself on finding himself alone in a cell for the first time, 'Maybe I'll be all right. You never know. On the other hand, I might end up throwing myself out of an upstairs window like your man from Ballymurphy. Or the fella they *said* hanged himself in his cell at Castlereagh. Jesus Christ! What would have to be going on to allow that to happen?' In then comparing his situation to Chile, Fogarty and the audience have to confront whether or not he can trust his treatment to 'British justice and all that crap' (2003: 20).

Ten years on from *The Interrogation of Ambrose Fogarty*, the violence appeared to have worsened. Following the murder of ninety-four people in 1991, the first two months of 1992 saw twenty-seven deaths in the conflict making it the worst period since the early 1970s. Unionist politicians were clamouring for tighter security measures, including the return of internment. Simultaneously, security force collusion in loyalist attacks against nationalists was being revealed in the trial of British intelligence agent Brian Nelson. By the time *At the Black Pig's Dyke* reached Derry in July 1993, there was heightened tension around the possibility of a cessation of Provisional IRA violence, following talks between John Hume of the Social Democratic and Labour Party (SDLP) and Gerry Adams of Sinn Féin. Accusations of collusion were given further substance following Yorkshire Television's *First Tuesday* investigation into the Dublin and Monaghan bombings in 1974. Of course, few of these immediate factors could have been known by the writer or the company at the time at which the play was written and rehearsed. However, they identify the wider context in which the play's ideological alignment and the reaction to it by at least some of the Derry audience might be considered.

The play was the result of a commission from Druid Theatre Company in Galway to Vincent Woods, a former RTE journalist and presenter, poet and playwright.[12] The commission had arisen from a chance meeting between Woods and Druid director Maeliosa Stafford in Australia where Woods was taking time out to develop his writing career. It engages with Woods's own background in the border counties of Leitrim and Fermanagh; the darker side of the mumming tradition; and was a response to the PIRA bombing of a Remembrance Day commemoration service in Enniskillen in 1987 in which eleven Protestants were killed. Woods has explained that he was involved in campaigning for Sinn Féin and 'was involved in campaigns around the hunger strikes of 1981' (Woods and Barry 2001: 487). His growing disillusionment with republican violence is part of the motivation for the play, although he suggests that 'I also feel that I did not set out with an agenda, I simply told things as I perceived them' (ibid.: 487). Despite this disclaimer, the play was viewed as a very directly political intervention by reviewers. I refer again to Ian Hill who suggested that, 'there has been little written in the Irish theatre which tackles the reality of the Troubles head on. . . this harrowing examination of two women's lives in the killing fields of the Fermanagh borders, where ethnic cleansing has been a sour and cold reality for 200 years, has put the record uncomfortably straight' (1993: 46). It is in this area of setting the record straight that the first production of the play entered the conflict over representation and politics in Northern Ireland.

This production opened at Druid's home theatre in Galway on 28 September 1992, before undertaking a tour across Ireland, including Armagh, Coleraine, Enniskillen and Belfast on the northern side of the border. The tour was supported by the island's two Arts Councils. The production was awarded the Best Theatre Production in the *Belfast Telegraph* Entertainment and Media Arts Awards in March 1993, with Frankie McCafferty picking up the Best Actor Award for his role as Tom Fool and his work with Charabanc. It transferred as part of the London International Festival of Theatre to Kilburn's Tricycle Theatre in July 1993. Tours to Australia and a further revival by Druid secured the play's status as a landmark in contemporary Irish theatre. It was published in Fairleigh's edited anthology of new Irish plays, *Far from the Land*, in 1998.

The play traces the lives of three generations of one family brought together by the marriage of the Catholic Lizzie Flynn and her Protestant husband Jack Boles. The couple sought to live out of the reach of the determining hands of their respective communities, but get caught up, nonetheless, in a cycle of violence which engulfs them; their daughter Sarah and her husband Hugh Brolly; and, ultimately, their grandchild Elizabeth. The play is distinguished formally by the use of performance conventions from the mumming tradition which is extant in the border area in which the play is set. These mumming rituals are used to counterpoint the 'continuity of guiltless violence in the Irish countryside' (Barry 1998: xiii).

The controversy over the play shares much of the ideological context of *The Interrogation of Ambrose Fogarty* in its characterisation of republicans. In the play, the role of Frank Beirne is that of a brutish thug. The role combines an ingrained hatred of the Protestant English and Planters and their descendants with an unswerving republican interpretation by which Beirne justifies the violent working out of his own sexual jealousy.[13] Played by Peter Gowen in the original production, the role earned him praise for the menace and passion he brought to 'the savage and psychotic Frank Beirne, rejected lover and chief terrorist' (Murphy 1992: 46). At a performance of the play in Derry's Rialto Theatre in July 1993, a group of protesters mounted the stage to produce an unannounced alternative ending to confront what they saw as the misrepresentation at the heart of Woods's work. According to James King's account, what occurred was that one of the protesters, 'Adam', mounted the stage and in mummer's role at the end of the final speech of the play

> removed his straw headgear to reveal a union-jack bag mask. . . in a butcher mummer costume. Adam was now in the role of the symbol of British state violence. When the union-jack mask was removed, a clown make-up identical to that of Tom Fool in the play was revealed, the third role. 'Who's fooling who?' he called. A woman now came on stage, cut the string attached to Adam's meat cleaver and pronounced the words, 'Peace is not the absence of war, it is the absence of the conditions which create war.'
>
> (2001: 92–3)

The production was thrown into chaos, with some actors leaving the stage in the belief that they were being threatened. As the subject of a report and a number of letters to the editor in the *Derry Journal*, and the subject of a discussion in the *Galway Advertiser* and *Irish Press*, for example, in July 1993, the incident became a focal point for a debate on the relationship between theatre and politics, and the boundaries between them. In a letter to the editor of the *Derry Journal*, the rationale for the intervention in *At the Black Pig's Dyke* was explained by the members of Derry Frontline (see Chapter 7 for further discussion of the company):

> [A] storyline loosely based on fact is moulded through lines "It was long ago, and it was not long ago," into a metaphor. This attempts to depict in sophisticated naivety the reality of the ongoing conflict in the six counties as an irrational consequence of evil borne in the hearts of men. We are asked to collude with the author's view that it is disturbed psychology rather than social injustice that fuelled and still fuels the conflict. Any reference to the British involvement was peripheral and ultimately obscured by the main focus of the play.
>
> The danger of such sophisticated Irish theatre offering tabloid representations of the present situation contributes to a manufactured consensus and debate that marginalises the rational voices of opposition and produces endless talks about talks which ultimately talk about nothing. Additionally the play makes a significant contribution to the cultural revisionism which is rampant in the south.
>
> (Gargan et al. 1993: 2)[14]

Reviews of the play seem to support the analysis of the protesters, variously describing the action of the play as 'lunacy', 'savage', 'primitive' and 'tribal'.

The objections raised by the protesters should not be seen in isolation. First, as Imelda Foley has noted, the company had already aroused controversy with the nationalist community of Derry with its production of Frank McGuinness's *Carthaginians* as part of the IMPACT '92 festival. On seeing a performance of the play in Galway, members of Derry City Council which was organising the festival 'declared it to be a travesty of Bloody Sunday and called a special council meeting to consider whether or not to cancel the Derry event' (Foley 2003: 121). Secondly, while there is much to which Republicans can object in the presentation of Beirne in its own right, it is in the reiteration of a narrow range of stereotypical traits that the characterisation is most repugnant to them. John Hill argues that there has been a consistently racial conception of the Irish as uncivilised across a range of filmic representations. In such figurations, Irish characters demonstrate a proclivity for violence which 'was not to be accounted for in terms of a response to political and economic conditions but simply as a manifestation of the Irish "national character"' (1987: 149). Similarly, Patrick Magee's survey of the representation of republicans in prose fiction reveals that 'the composite Irish republican to materialise was of a Mother-Ireland fixated psycho-killer, aka a Provo Godfather, readily discernible with recourse to an identikit indebted to Tenniel's "Irish Frankenstein" and other images from *Punch* redolent of

Victorian racism' (2001: 2). The representation of the composite republican was to reach its nadir in McDonagh's *The Lieutenant of Inishmore* (2001) where the deranged Padraic is too mad for the IRA, but attempts to set up a splinter group within the INLA while mourning his dead cat.

Magee explains why such misrepresentations require to be challenged, 'To read these works uncritically is to accept at face value many assumptions that continue to hinder a resolution of the divisions in Ireland. Gross negatives of the IRA gunman, like the Irish joke or the Cummings' cartoon, offer non-explanations that have befogged the issues central to the conflict and detract from the ongoing search for a just and lasting peace settlement' (2001: 2). Likewise, as Rolston points out, revisionist critiques, such as the one contained within the play, are not politically innocent, 'despite the value of an approach that seriously questions myths and conventions, the revisionist argument reveals its political bias by confining its critique to nationalism and republicanism' (1999: 33). Thus, at a time when at least some republicans were seeking to move towards a negotiated settlement, this production appeared to repeat the misrepresentation which would later bedevil the negotiations themselves, that they were mindless self-serving barbarians beyond the rule of law and unfit to be involved in government.

Discussion: Form and Perspective

The discussion of the form of these plays is an attempt to delineate how they seek to organise the audience's perspective on the violence outside the theatre. Clearly they are formally distinct in their approach to representing directly the conflict. There are, however, points at which they converge in engaging their audience in the dramas they present, specifically in the confrontation of their audiences with the responsibilities of the individual in relation to acts of violence. This issue has been a perennial one since the actor playing the British soldier in Boyd's *The Flats* turned to the audience to ask 'Who's responsible?. . . Who done it?' (Boyd 1973: 85). In general terms this might be seen as a radical strategy by which each audience member is implicated in the politics of the conflict. However, within the context of each of the productions it becomes more vexed. The objective of confronting the audience with issues of personal responsibility prompts a number of dramaturgical decisions from which the function of each of the productions followed.

For *The Interrogation of Ambrose Fogarty* the key dramaturgical decision is in the choice of realism as the mode of presentation. Much was made of the play's authenticity in reviews: the play was described as 'fiercely realistic' (Rosenfield 1982: 10) presenting what the *Gown* reviewer described as the 'raw reality of the situation' (cited Byrne 2001b: 63). In performance, there was a high level of verisimilitude in the behavioural codes, costuming and the recreation of the set and props typical of a police station. The play benefited too from the casting as part of the Lyric company of a number of local actors able to handle the sophisticated social codes by which place, social class, age and religion are signalled through accent. This capacity in itself helped to individuate the roles of the policemen, moving them beyond crude stereotypes. This was welcomed by at least one reviewer who commented that, '[Lynch] pleads that an understanding by all sides of the views and feelings of others must preface a settlement here. He contributes to the birth of such understanding by humanising the drama being enacted on our streets daily' (O'Brien 1982: 9).

The main focus for empathy is in the role of Fogarty. Not only does he occupy the largest amount of stage time, including a number of monologues, but qualitatively the role is distinguished by the lucidity of Fogarty's thinking and the access granted to the audience to his state of mind and emotional journey. However, Fogarty is not the locus of the issue of individual responsibility; instead that is located in relation to the actions of the policemen. Different figure perspectives are advanced between the uniformed officer roles and the roles of the Special Branch interrogators. Among the uniformed officers, the primary figure perspective is that of Sergeant Knox. The role might be conceived of and played as a sympathetic picture of a career policeman who longs for normalcy. However, for an audience which has experienced vicariously the vicious beating handed out to Fogarty, the interpretation of Knox's role as standard-bearer of decent policing is untenable. In his strict adherence to procedure he acquiesces in the violence while he knows that it is underway. His presence onstage during the beatings, albeit unlit, implicates him in them physically. His response is bureaucratic not moral as the final interchanges with Fogarty after his beating reveal:

> AMBROSE: How many innocent people have been beaten up in here
> through mistake or suspicion?
> KNOX: That's impossible to tell. I just look after my end of things by
> filling in any complaints that are made and sending them on.
> (Lynch 2003b: 79)

The procedures which Knox follows clearly separate out the roles of each of the individual policemen and their place within the hierarchy of the RUC. He does what he is expected to do within the strict confines of these procedures, he does exactly his duty and no more.

By contrast, the interrogators all seek to justify their methods not in terms of their designated duties, but in terms of the role with which they are commissioned by society. Their illegal actions to defend the law-abiding result from the inadequacies of the structures within which they find themselves, as Stanley explains to Peter:

PETER: But is there no other legal way of getting convictions against the
          wild men?

STANLEY: Quite simply, no. Most of them are hardened operators who
          come in here knowing the whole set-up inside out. While we
          can't get witnesses to stand up in court, these jokers know it's
          only a matter of sitting the three days out. Peter, what's a few
          slaps around the face if it keeps the likes of the Shankill Butchers
          safe from the community, behind bars?

                                                       (Lynch 2003b: 79)

What are juxtaposed here are figure perspectives informed by different
understandings of the nature of responsibility. The members of the Special
Branch are compelled to act outside the law by the nature of the conflict and
thus their actions flow from the political structures of the conflict. The actions
of Knox are determined by his role as defined by the bureaucratic structures.
None of the policemen, however, elucidates a perspective in which personal
responsibility is raised as an issue.

It is left to Fogarty to question the relationship between the individual and
their actions: 'Sergeant, what sensible, level-headed person would work at a
job which entailed punching other human beings on a daily basis? "I had a
hard day at work today love, is the tea ready? I punched the fuck out of ten
people today." Who would do it?' (ibid.: 79). The juxtaposition of the banal
domestic detail and the brutality in the role makes Fogarty's point eloquently.
Moreover, the positions articulated by the policemen are intercut with
Fogarty's conversation with Knox, as the focus flits back and forth between
Fogarty's cell and the interrogation room. This technique allows each of the
contributions made by the policemen to be undermined by Fogarty's questioning of Knox. His questions rest on the liberal assumption that individuals
hold responsibility for their actions in a way that resists the attempts of the
policemen to exculpate themselves. In this respect then, the play seems to be
approaching Williams's characteristic of a radicalised form of realism which
is 'consciously interpretative in relation to a particular viewpoint' (1977a: 68).

The discussion of responsibility follows the staging of Fogarty's beating
and is therefore viewed in the light of it. It is in this scene that the realist mode
is most critical within the play's proposition. The stage directions indicate the
ferocity of the violence accompanied by a running commentary by Jackie that
is almost equally disturbing, as his opening involvement demonstrates,

Where is the bastard? I'll soon knock the nonsense out of you, mate! Get
on your feet! Get on your feet, I said! [*He trails* AMBROSE *to his feet.*] You
won't sign, eh! [*He punches* AMBROSE *fiercely in the stomach.*] We'll soon see
about that. [STANLEY *grabs* AMBROSE's *arms from behind.* JACKIE *repeatedly
punches him and yells abuse.*] Bastard! Cunt! Cunt! Bastard! [AMBROSE

finally falls to the floor, taking blows from both JACKIE *and* STANLEY. PETER
sits calmly at the table.]

(Lynch 2003b: 77)

The placing of the scene towards the end of the play and its resolution of the
suspense about what will happen to Fogarty make it the climax of the action.
Its affective impact should not be underestimated as Aleks Sierz's survey of
the British theatre of provocation in the 1990s notes: 'Unlike the type of
theatre that allows us to sit back and contemplate what we see in detachment,
the best in-yer-face theatre takes us on an emotional journey, getting under
our skin. In other words, it is experiential, not speculative' (2001: 4). The
effect is borne out in the comments of the reviewer who noted that 'The final
scene in which Fogarty is subjected to severe physical and verbal abuse is
necessary and excellently executed. It left me drained and it is not for the
squeamish' (O'Brien 1982: 9). The commentary by Jackie is shocking in itself
since, as Sierz notes, the use of sexual swear-words contravenes general
cultural taboos:

> Because they refer to sex, but are violent in intent, those words pack a
> double punch. Unlike euphemism, which is a way of defusing difficult
> subjects, of circling around a meaning, the swearword aims to compact
> more than one hatred, becoming a verbal act of aggression, a slap in the
> mouth. In the theatre, 'bad language' seems even stronger because it is
> used openly.
>
> (2001: 8)

Another reviewer draws attention to how, in representing the violence of
police methods, the production 'exposes its crudity and horror with passion
and some humour too, in a succession of scenes [that] rise to a frightening
crescendo of brutality, sending shock waves right into the audience'
(Rosenfield 1982: 10). What the audience sees is far in excess of the 'few slaps
around the face' to which Stanley refers in his justification of his techniques.

Witnessing the enactment of a brutal assault within a realist mode of presentation is intended to be a shocking confrontation of the audience's sensibilities, a means of confronting who they really are (Sierz 2001). Ellis
discusses the effect of witnessing in relation to mechanical modes of representation, but his central idea is relevant here:

> by the very act of looking, individuals in the witnessing audience become
> accomplices in the events they see. Events on a screen make a mute appeal,
> 'You cannot say you did not know.' The double negative captures the
> nature of the experience of witness. At once distanced and involving, it
> implies a necessary relationship with what is seen. The relationship is one

of complicity, because if you know about an event, that knowledge implies a degree of consent to it. With this complicity comes an aching sense that something must be done.

(2000: 11)

The play therefore sets out to confront the audience with the direct and live experience of a set of contradictory circumstances to which it must respond, a fundamentally political contradiction (see Rabey 1986: 3). In so doing, it goes beyond a use of the realist form to merely authenticate its perspective or to add depth to embodied debate of abstract principles. Instead it requires of the audience an engagement in which its own judgements and sensibilities are placed into crisis in the face of what it sees on the stage as witness to the event. Etchells suggests that 'To witness an event is to be present at it in some fundamentally ethical way, to feel the weight of things and one's own place in them, even if that place is simply, for the moment, as an onlooker. . . The art-work that turns us into witnesses leaves us, above all, unable to stop thinking, talking reporting what we've seen' (1999: 17–18). Matthew Goulish presents a further gloss on this sense of witness when he suggests that 'we may consider the Etchells' event ethical exactly because of its initial ethics-defying nature, forcing the Witness, at a loss for an immediate 'correct' response, into a position of choice, either dismissal of the event, or an unsought worldview adjustment. This adjustment may at first appear aesthetic. . . but with the passing of time, it inevitably becomes ethical' (2000: 147–8). Lynch articulated this function of creating the audience as witness as being to ensure that 'People have to take a political decision going out the door' (Wren 1982: 5). The play's function is agitational therefore: the *Belfast Telegraph* reviewer suggested that 'Those who believe that anyone who is taken in for questioning deserves whatever is coming to him will have second thoughts' (O'Brien 1982: 9). This assumption articulates what Pfister has termed the 'idealised receiver implied in the text itself' (1988: 39).

The responses of actual audiences may be very different from such an idealisation, however. In facing such a contradiction, audience members need not passively follow the lead of the dramaturgy and may invoke a range of strategies of resistance or avoidance. One such strategy is to attack the authenticity of the actions taken, as in the *Belfast Newsletter* review: 'The violence. . . is the violence of frustration rather than the more sophisticated techniques practiced by modern inquisitors. . . The playwright had first-hand experience of Castlereagh, but was it THAT crude?. . . The Interrogation of Ambrose Fogarty has the makings of a classic, but not in its present lumbering and sometimes hard to accept form' (cited Byrne 2001b: 63). While apparently aimed at the artistic quality of the representation as much as the action represented, such a comment points up the inherent problems in the choice of the realist form which Ellis identifies:

In the end, judgements about 'realism' come down to judgements about
the relation between the object and its representation. And as most of the
time, knowledge of the object concerned is usually gained through the
representation anyway, the argument becomes rather speculative. In any
case, arguments about realism ignore what many viewers of the representation bring to the experience.

(2000: 13)

Ellis's case is reinforced in a critical letter to the *Belfast Telegraph*, which points
up a second strategy which audiences might deploy 'Oh yes, the audience
laughed—even at the sight of a torturer standing on his victim's head; one wit
at the front increased the volume of laughter by enquiring in a loud voice
during this scene if he "should get the peelers?" ' While it is not clear from
this account why the audience laughed, the effect of such laughter is to
diminish the effect of the violence represented, aligning it with the perspectives set up in the rest of the play in the presentation of Willie Lagan. Thus,
the potential of the play's realist mode to ask questions of the audience, to
exercise an agitational function, depends as much on the disposition of the
audience prior to the performance as it does on their experience of the
performance itself, a point to which I will return later.

If the realism of *The Interrogation of Ambrose Fogarty* does not of itself secure
a specific audience response, one might expect that other forms might prove
to be more efficacious. *At the Black Pig's Dyke* was self-consciously theatrical
in both its scripting and performance under the direction of Maeliosa
Stafford, from the opening prologue in which Lizzie enters 'carrying a half-
made straw wren and a knife' (Woods 1998: 3) and begins her story: 'It was
a long time ago, Elizabeth, and it was not a long time ago', a speech which is
taken up and extended by the ghostly figure of the adult Elizabeth. Fragments
of three of the narrative strands which intersect in the play are interspersed
in this prologue: the present moment of the adult Lizzie; the adult future of
Elizabeth, her granddaughter; and the performance of the mummers, which
in its repeated ritual seems to stand both within and outside of each moment
of history within the other narratives. The playing-out of the mummers' plays
within the production serves as a metatheatrical commentary on the action
within the other narratives. It juxtaposes the ritualised struggle over and
within the performance space of the kitchen with the violence within the other
narratives, for which there can be no symbolic Doctor's remedy.

The juxtaposition of the drama within the mummers' play and the drama
of the main action might be considered to alienate this main action, framing
it in a way that seeks to overcome the resistance of audiences in the theatre
to seeing yet another representation of the Troubles. The repetition of their
appearance at different points of the linear historical narratives serves to
emphasise the cyclical and apparently ineluctable nature of the violence they

re-enact. The possibility of progress and development within these narratives is suspended by the interruptions of the mummers. The dual roles of the mummers as members of the mumming troupe and members of the local community suggests, moreover, a communal complicity in the violence, since it is they who carry out the stage ritual from which the dying Jack emerges and who surround Sarah's husband Hugh before he is shot. This complicity was extended to the audience in consideration of the death of Lizzie. As Angela Kerr noted, 'when the Captain Mummer swings his lantern and asks "Did any of you have a hand in this?" it is us he's looking at' (1992: 11).

In performance the role of the mummers was theatrically impressive. Fintan O'Toole welcomed the play as 'an important achievement for Irish theatre. It doesn't just represent a remarkable piece of Irish theatrical invention, it reinvents the categories of Irish theatre. It reaches back beyond the Creation, grasps hold of the elements and puts them together in new combinations' (1994: 12). O'Toole's approbation is based on the ways in which the play appropriates a traditional form which is rural but neither Catholic nor Gaelic in origin and makes from it a new yet recognisably Irish form of performance. Problematically, however, the integration of the Mummers' performance and role within the dramaturgy and performance of the play as a whole is incomplete. The mummers' roles are divided between the fools, Tom Fool and Miss Funny, and the main group. Tom Fool and Miss Funny take forward transitions and changes within the main narrative in their direct address to the theatre audience. They enter the action in other roles (such as the bride and groom at the wedding). They stand outside the action to comment on it, for example, contextualising the history of mumming before the mummers appear. They direct the audience's perspective on the main action,

> Bite the bullet, Tom, shut your mouth,
> The play is what we're here about.
> Not the rantings of a fool about
> The bomb, the gun and foreign rule.
> Play your part, Tom, play it right
>
> (Woods 1998: 15)

Here they vocalise the playwright's expressed intention that the play be viewed outside of the political context in which the action is set and be regarded instead as the working-out of a long-standing feud.

The primary role of the main group of mummers is as members of the community within the same narrative frame as the main action. It is in this role that they perform the mummers' plays and the killings of Jack, Hugh and Lizzie. But their function is not clear, and there are inconsistencies in the narrative. As the *Irish Times* reviewer noted, 'Too much is asked of the audience in terms of sorting out the various symbolisms of generation changes, traditions and wilful murders for this to be an easy night in the theatre' (Nowlan 1994: 10). If the mummers who kill Hugh are not the same mummers who discover the bodies of Sarah and Lizzie, this is not obvious from within the performance. (Indeed it is not clear precisely how, where and by whom Sarah is killed.) Equally there is no indication as to whether or not these are the same mummers who killed Jack Boles, years before. Further, if mumming is itself a non-denominational or inter-denominational cultural practice, it is not clear why it takes on this specifically republican dimension in relation to the killings. These ambiguities might provoke a desired response in which the spectator is forced to resolve contradictions for himself following recognition that this is not a representation of the world as it is. What emerges from the repetition of the actions of the mummers, however, is a sense that there is something deep within Irish identity which prompts the killings, evacuating the representation of any reference to political, social or economic conditions.

These narrative inconsistencies are echoed in the performance. When the mummers performed their first play in Act One, it was performed to include the theatre audience as the spectators of the dramatic world. The mummers then have to shift performance modes to respect the fourth-wall convention while they engage in dialogue between themselves. The mummers' formations are used to indicate the dimensions of the *mise-en-scène* as in Act One, where it is their circle which establishes the exterior walls of the kitchen where the bodies of Lizzie and Sarah lie. However, in Act Two, when Beirne enters to carry out the killing all he need do is to bang the floor three times to indicate he is outside.

Such transformations may well be characteristic of a mode of performance which draws attention to its own construction and relishes its own theatricality. However, I suggest that instead of promoting a rational critique of the politics of form, the use of the mumming tradition encourages a visceral response that distracts from (and resists) the critical distancing which an engagement with the politics of form invites. The presence of the mummers might be regarded, therefore, as disruptive to a naturalistic presentation but it does not create a dialectical relationship to the action for the audience. Holderness notes that 'The formal devices of political drama can be readily assimilated into a theatre with a very different political inflection' (1992: 9). Thus, audiences might feel powerfully moved by the experience of the performance of the mummers, yet this arousal is not matched to an engagement with the representation of the dramatic world as itself ideologically constructed. Instead, the power of the mummers' performance lends a sense of authority to the proposition of the main action. They are reminders of a primitive, tribal tradition with which violent reality is intertwined and it is only by rejecting all such ties to the past that progress to a new future can be made.

Their presence then is a sharply visual embodiment of the didactic proposition at the heart of the play, summed up thus by one reviewer, 'The author's thesis is clear, there is a vicious cycle of violence, bred from the history of earlier generations, which is fuelled by the personal envies and jealousies of those who, today, cover their misdeeds under the straw head-masks of tradition and against whom those whose lives today break against the myths of the past have no defence' (Nowlan 1994: 10).

A further criticism of *At the Black Pig's Dyke* may be made also of *The Interrogation of Ambrose Fogarty*. Each of the plays produces a politically significant omission from the scope of their representation, that of the role of the British state and its security forces. Even in *The Interrogation of Ambrose Fogarty*, engagement with the role of the state is incomplete. It is incomplete because it is almost entirely limited to figures drawn from Northern Ireland. Indeed, it is one of a number of representations which have delineated police figures in the same terms by which terrorists have previously been stereotyped (as discussed earlier). This extension of the stereotype of the terrorist to members of the Northern Irish security forces reinforces the dominant narrative of the conflict as tribal, albeit one where the renegade *Northern Irish* agents of the state operate partially. *The Interrogation of Ambrose Fogarty* complements this omission in its reiteration of a second convention in representations of the Troubles, the introduction of a British figure to serve as a yardstick of the normal against which *all* Northern Irish figures are measured as irrational, psychotic and/or barbaric. The play has only one British figure, the soldier, Captain Levington. Whilst personally unreliable in his treatment of the young police woman, Yvonne Lundy, Levington has little part in the attacks on the prisoners, and is relegated to a minor role as the play's love interest. The stage directions for his entrance with Lagan whom he has arrested read that 'an army captain swings into view with the legs of the body, and proceeds to trail it across the floor, kicking it as he does so' (Lynch 2003b: 12). However, Lagan is 'grinning broadly', producing an effect of physical comedy rather than brutality. Crucially, the Captain is not interested in the politics of the context, regarding police and terrorists alike as Irish, his mind is set on the impending end of his tour of duty and returning to the family business and a normal life. This granting of 'psychological withdrawal' (Cornell 1999a) to the figure of a British soldier completely obliterated his role in the conflict, and by extension the role of the British state.

Of course, the reception of the performance of plays depends on the ideological situation of the spectators and is often not completed until long after the event, something overlooked in demands for balance within productions. Such demands are predicated on the assumption that the dramatic world is offered within the theatrical event as the primary site of contestation. Thus, the main dialectical struggle at the heart of the drama will be resolved within the dramatic world and offered to the audience, sitting in objective judgement. The audience are homogenised as idealised spectators in making such judgements. However, there are a number of objections to this assumption. For example, much of the preceding argument has been to demonstrate the ways in which the plays articulated pre-existing perspectives within received discourses, or the ways in which audience responses might involve a range of different perspectives dependent on their own mental luggage. This might give rise to a sense that the theatre then has been an arena in which pre-existing ideologies are contested in the engagement with live performance. However, institutionalised theatre rarely offers a facility where debates can contribute to the performance event (see King 2001).[15] Where audience members do respond directly to a performance within the event, as in the case of *At the Black Pig's Dyke* in Derry, this too is problematic for dramatic representations which seek to frame off the action of the play from the unacknowledged presence of the audience.

What was lacking from theatrical engagements with the Troubles, then, appears to be the influence of traditions of oppositional theatre which have operated on the assumption that the dramatic world is not self-contained and that the dialectic process is between the propositions of the dramatic action and the society in which it is experienced and which consequently have sought to promote and facilitate processes of dialogue. For such traditions, theatre is taken, therefore, as one of a number of activating linkages within wider political processes. Without such linkages, dramatic performances may just be another repetition of the known, an affirmation of an intractable status quo articulated as a plaintive lament.

3

Authentic History

LOMBARD: If you're asking me will my story be as accurate as possible—
of course it will. But are truth and falsity the proper criteria?
I don't know. Maybe when the time comes my first responsibility will be to tell the best possible narrative. Isn't that what
history is, a kind of story-telling. . .Maybe when the time
comes, imagination will be as important as information.
(Brian Friel, 1989, *Making History*, 8–9)

In many senses, the dilemmas outlined by Lombard, the chronicler of Hugh
O'Neill in Friel's *Making History*, face any playwright who chooses to use the
past as the basis of a play: there is a tension between fidelity to the past
moment, the public memory of it, and the necessity of refashioning the event
imaginatively for an audience. In the programme for the original production
of the play, Friel noted that 'I have tried to be objective and faithful—after
my artistic fashion—to the empirical method. But when there was a tension
between historical "fact" and the imperative of fiction, I'm glad to say I kept
faith with the narrative' (cited Murray 1991b: 62). It is in the satisfactory
resolution of such tension that authenticity is ascribed to the representation.
Thus, the representation of the past is no less contested than the engagement
with the present discussed in the previous chapter, particularly since for
colonised cultures the recognition of authenticity in representation has a
specifically political dimension. Lloyd has argued that 'On the side of the colo-
nizer, it is the inauthenticity of the colonized culture, its falling short of the
concept of human, that legitimates the colonial project' (1993: 112).
Likewise, Graham argues that 'Authenticity and claims to authenticity
underlie the conceptual and cultural denial of dominance' (1999: 8). Thus,
claims to authenticity for works of representation are subject to the relative
positions of power within colonial discourses. Nonetheless, those representations which contest dominating discourses may become significant acts of
resistance through which the dominated seek to claim for themselves a legitimacy that has been denied them. Actress Niamh Flanagan, a member of the
Binlids company in 1997, pointed out: 'We constantly have to keep proving
that we're real and that what we're doing is authentic, and that we have a place

in the scheme of things' (Hurley 1998: online).

A further dimension to the representation of historical events within the context of Northern Ireland is that the past functions as one more arena in which the conflicts of the present are played out, where divergent interpretations have been in competition to justify ongoing attitudes and actions. Fintan O'Toole has suggested that,

> There is no past tense in Irish history. The ideas by which we describe ourselves, republicanism, orangeism, Catholicism and Protestantism, are still in the process of forming themselves, still play a powerful role in the present. But equally those ideas do not mean the same thing now as they did when they originally became part of the political process on this island.
>
> (1984c: 18)

The past is continuous with the present, an "all-too-well-known past that will not go away" (Cummings 2000: 293) and to which Northern Ireland is tied ineluctably. This view is problematic, however. There has been a widely shared assumption that the Troubles are the result of an unhealthy fixation with the past and the interrelated narratives and memory. It should not be forgotten that for those directly involved in and affected by the violence, the Troubles have been an immediate, daily and experienced reality, albeit one explained by narratives of continuous and continuing historical traditions. Dealing with the apparently insistent presence of history, theatre makers have struggled to construct representations which are regarded as authentic. As noted in the previous chapter, realism has been the dominant mode in dramatic representations of the Troubles. Representations of history have adopted this mode or variations on it as one strategy by which to secure an authentic version of history, rooted in the potential it offers for apparently objective accounts of the past. Brian Friel's *Translations*, on the implementation of the first Ordnance Survey of Ireland, is largely realist, as is his *Making History*, for example. Gary Mitchell's account of the 1789 uprising, *Tearing the Loom* (1998) is a further example. Stewart Parker's *Pentecost* (1987) takes the form of a magical realism in which the naturalistic setting of a Belfast parlour house and the psychological rendering of character are disrupted both by the presence of the ghost of Lily Matthews, the previous owner, and the final passages in which the characters speak in tongues (see Chapter 5).

However, there is, as Friel's *Making History* argues, little reason to trust the possibility of any apparently objective representation of history such as that offered by realist representations (see previous chapter). Murray suggests that 'we have reached the position, then, where the Irish playwrights of today can deal with history only in a tentative, ironic, or self-conscious way. It is largely a question of style' (1988: 287). One of the strengths of much of the work cited is to push at the boundaries of the realist mode to question the

possibilities of its veracity. According to Fintan O'Toole, in the work of Brian
Friel,

> There is no stable point in the present from which one may look at the
> past and say with certainty: this is what happened. . . And if the past is
> unreliable, then not only does the naturalistic law of cause and effect
> become unworkable, but also the whole notion of character as the sum of
> all things that has happened to it becomes untenable.
>
> (2000: 52–3)

Friel's plays expose the ways in which the sense of personal and communal
identities is fabricated through incomplete and unreliable narratives. This
exposure emphasises the force of memory in the construction of a sense of
self in the contemporary moment. Memory supersedes history. In Parker's
Northern Star, Mary tells Henry Joy McCracken, 'They forget nothing in this
country not ever'. To which he replies 'No. It isn't true to say that they forget
nothing. It's far worse than that. They misremember everything' (Parker
1989b: 64).

    If the past cannot be relied on as stable and fixed, however, this need not
mean that consideration of it can or should be completely evacuated from the
present. Anne Devlin has offered an alternative vision to that proffered by
Parker in describing the relationship of her own writing to history:

> I do not think that history is a nightmare from which I am trying to awake,
> I think it is part of what I call memory and forgetting: before I can forget
> I have to remember and before we can put down this particular burden
> that is our history we have to recall certain things that have not been visible
> during a certain period. Because of the dominance of the ideological
> conflict between the particular political groups there have been lots of
> things that haven't been visible and have become almost part of the collec-
> tive psyche. I think we have got to identify those areas, that is why we are
> not finished with history: we have buried the body and we have seen the
> shape of their life, and now we have to go back and explain.
>
> (Devlin and Cerquoni 2001: 117–18)

Thus, for Devlin memory rather than history takes precedence in her relationship with the past, not as a means of establishing an objective account of
what happened, but as a way of recovering a more complete sense of self that
is part of a process of moving on from the past. The possibilities offered by
such a process of remembrance have led a number of theatre makers to
explore the past as a means of interrogating the realities with which individuals and communities engage in the present. This shift from history to
memory is signalled most obviously where a largely realist representation is

framed within a subjective narrative so that the audience is confronted directly with a character or characters whose memories will constitute the subject matter of the play. Examples of this include Beth in Reid's *Tea in a China Cup* (1983), Pyper in McGuinness's *Observe the Sons of Ulster Marching Towards the Somme*, and Michael in Friel's *Dancing at Lughnasa* (1990). In other examples, realism is dispensed with in lieu of modes of presentation which offer more theatricalised processes of remembering such as the parade of theatrical styles in the staging of the memories of Henry Joy McCracken in Parker's *Northern Star*; or McGuinness's 'Bloody Sunday' play, *Carthaginians*. More recently, playwrights have been drawn to the intense performativity in story-telling performances of the past where narration within character becomes the primary mode of representation.[1] Such plays include Marie Jones's *A Night in November* (1994), Reid's *My Name, Shall I Tell You My Name* (1989), or Lynch, Grimes and McKee's *The History of the Troubles (according to My Da')*. As such plays demonstrate, however, memory is no more reliable than history and remembering may itself become a process of discovering the 'most acceptable narrative' as individuals and communities forge a sense of who they are. For playwrights who have explored the relationships between history and memory to find ways for audiences to re-engage with what is known from and about the past, their project has been to find ways through which both history and memory can be turned over to and by the imagination. In the two plays which will be discussed here, Brian Friel's *The Freedom of the City* and JustUs/DubbelJoint's *Binlids*, there is an exploration of the relationships between memory and public history. These are productions which were the result of very different processes of composition and which were staged in very different contexts. They exemplify different, perhaps even opposing, models of the possibilities for theatre's intervention in social life. These differences provide sharp contrasts. Nonetheless, they share a concern with the project of reconfiguring a sense of authenticity in representing the past, and a concomitant imperative to make that authenticity operative within the present.

The Plays in Context

Brian Friel has reached such an elevated position in the world of English-language theatre that it is sometimes necessary to recall that his plays have not always met with unequivocal success in production. *The Freedom of the City* is a case in point. Although Friel had been writing for the theatre full-time since 1960, with *Philadelphia, Here I Come* (1964) marking his first major success, the first production of *The Freedom of the City* had at best a mixed reception in Dublin (Murray 1997: 200) and was panned by the critics as an exercise in propaganda both in London and in New York. Dantanus includes the following snippets from English reviews:

'an entertaining piece of unconvincing propaganda' (*Daily Telegraph*); 'its bias against the English robs it of its potential power' *(Sunday Express)*; the play 'suffers fatally from an overzealous determination to discredit the means and the motives of the English in the present Ulster crisis' and the writer 'is also engaged on a Celtic propaganda exercise' (*Evening Standard*); 'Friel's case is too loaded to encourage much intelligent sympathy' (*Daily Express*).

(1988: 140)

Arguably the reviews were a complete misreading of the complex dramaturgical structures within the play which with the passing of time have become more generally recognised (Zach 1989; Etherton 1989: 167–73; Worth 1993). Such misreading has of course been helped by Friel's own sense of regret that the play was written 'out of some kind of heat and some kind of immediate passion that I would want to have quieted a bit before I did it' (O'Toole 1982: 22).

Schrank notes that Friel 'has always been uncomfortable with the explicitly political' (2000: 122). This might seem somewhat surprising given Friel's background and experience.[2] Born in Killyclogher, County Tyrone in 1929, he moved with his family to live in Derry in 1939. He was educated at St Columb's College in Derry, before attending St Patrick's College, Maynooth and teacher training in Belfast. He taught in Derry for ten years and was well aware of the effects of discrimination by the unionist majority in the city on his fellow nationalists (Dantanus 1988: 34). He started to work as a full-time writer in 1960, writing plays, newspaper pieces and short stories. He relocated to Muff just across the border in Donegal in 1967, later moving down the Inishowen peninsula to Greencastle. He was a co-founder with Stephen Rea of the Derry-based Field Day Theatre Company which he inaugurated in 1980 with *Translations*.[3] The company was supported by the Arts Councils on each side of the border. Lojek has commented that Friel's 'personal and professional lives then have involved a constant crossing of borders' (2004: 177). It is as if Friel has refused to observe the partition of the island, explained perhaps since his father had been a nationalist councillor in Derry and he himself was a member of the Nationalist Party for a number of years. Despite this, he has remained publicly wary of expressing a political agenda through his art.

Irrespective of this, *The Freedom of the City* was regarded by others as a highly political response to the events of Bloody Sunday and the subsequent Widgery Tribunal, opening less than a year after the Tribunal released its report. This was an investigation into the events in Derry on 30 January 1972 in which thirteen men were shot dead by members of the British Army, with another dying later of his wounds. The killings came at the end of a civil rights march which had been banned. At the tribunal the army argued that soldiers had only opened fire when they had come under attack and that each person shot had been holding either a firearm or bomb. This was contradicted by the many civilian eyewitnesses and the evidence from press photographs. The inquiry which was established by the British Prime Minister, Edward Heath, reported in April of the same year and largely exonerated the soldiers.[4] The inability of this process to call to account those directly responsible for the civilian deaths did much to alienate nationalists even further from the state and provoked a violent response which would make 1972 'the worst year of the troubles' (McKittrick and McVea 2001: 76). With the introduction of direct rule in March 1972, however, it appeared that the British press and public more generally were in no mood to accept anything other than that British soldiers were on the streets of Northern Ireland as a means of thwarting even more excessive violence than that which they witnessed nightly on their televisions. Moreover, the strengthening of the hand of militant republicans as a result of Bloody Sunday was viewed as a major threat in the Republic also (ibid.: 78).

The narrative of the play traces the events leading up to the deaths of three civil rights protesters, Lily, Skinner and Michael, who stumble into the Guildhall in Derry when the march in which they are taking part disintegrates into a riot. The play juxtaposes three sets of events: scenes within the Guildhall involving Lily, Skinner and Michael; scenes from the subsequent tribunal in which the events leading up to their deaths are reconstituted from a range of testimonies; and interspersed with these are scenes in which a variety of commentators appropriate the deaths for their own purposes. The events which the play represents are entirely fictitious and Friel is careful to distance it from the real events. Not only is the action set in 1970 instead of 1972, but the setting is removed to the Guildhall rather than the streets of the Bogside and the civilian victims are clearly distinguished from those killed on Bloody Sunday. Schrank suggests also that Friel attempted 'to talk his way around a too close identification of the play with Bloody Sunday' in an interview given before it opened at the Abbey (2000: 123–4).

The concern with public history in *The Freedom of the City* was expressed also in JustUs and DubbelJoint's *Binlids*.[5] The origins of the production lay two years previously in 1995 when DubbelJoint Productions assisted in the development of a play devised by a group of women to celebrate International Women's Day, *Just a Prisoner's Wife*. Around this production a new company was formed, JustUs Community Theatre, with the vision 'to empower our community to tell their own story, in their own words, through the medium of the dramatic arts' (JustUs Community Theatre 2000: 2). The company was awarded the Belfast City Council Best Arts Partnership Award for the collaboration with DubbelJoint on this project.

The company's second co-production with DubbelJoint was *Binlids—A Drama of West Belfast Resistance*, first staged as part of Féile an Phobail in

1997, before being revived in February 1998 and then transferring to New York in October of that year.[6] The play was scripted jointly by four members of JustUs: Christine Poland, Brenda Murphy, Danny Morrison and Jake MacSiacáis. It charts the experience of women in nationalist West Belfast through the eighteen years following the introduction by the British government of internment without trial.[7] The play's title commemorates the lids of the metal bins or trash cans banged on the ground to warn of the arrival of British forces in an area. With the initiation of this second project, director Pam Brighton had spent time with the core group of women talking through stories and together they worked out the main areas which they then set about researching. This research 'involved hundreds of interviews with individuals, or relatives of individuals, who would feature in the play, as well as collating articles and speeches to be used' (Scally 1998: 18). Thus, the production was rooted in the memories of the community whose history it charts. A script emerged from this process of research, with some scenes being written beforehand but much of the second act being devised through rehearsal. Four professional male actors were brought in to augment the amateur cast but the emphasis was on the experiences of women as mothers, daughters, sisters, soldiers and activists. Even with a large cast, several of the actors played more than one role. The production was mounted as a promenade performance with the audience surrounded by five stages between which the action switched. Sometimes this created interactions between actors and spectators: implicating spectators as part of the scene, for example when a British Army snatch squad arrests a character and drags him through the audience. In other scenes, the audience are situated as witnesses to the action. For example, they watch a group of British soldiers refuse to return a football to a young boy, eventually forcing him to say his prayers at gunpoint.

The decision to mount such a production was one marker of a turning point in the wider conflict for reasons concerned with both its location and timing. The production was first mounted at the Belfast Institute of Further and Higher Education theatre on the Whiterock Road in West Belfast, opening in August 1997. Nationalist West Belfast is defined and set apart by factors which are both natural and planned; socio-economic; cultural; and ultimately, political. Its positioning is articulated through physical boundaries: at its back to the west is the Black Mountain; to the north the peace-line separating it from the Shankill and other loyalist areas; to the east the M1 motorway; and to the south the town of Lisburn and its green belt exclusion area. Socio-economically, the area was characterised at that time by high levels of unemployment and deprivation, with related problems in areas of health and education. While nationalists in Northern Ireland in general had been structurally disadvantaged (see Ruane and Todd 1991 and Darby 1997), those within West Belfast have been among those who have endured the greatest levels of disadvantage (Murtagh 1995). Politically, the nationalist constituency of the area had resulted in the concentration of hostile British military forces there and its effective ghettoisation. These factors combined to disempower the community, particularly as the city sought to re-image itself (see Maguire 2000b). This provoked a number of responses from the nationalist communities in West Belfast, one of which was the inauguration of a West Belfast Community Festival, Féile an Phobail, in 1987. According to then Festival Director, Catríona Ruane:

> Féile an Phobail began as the direct response of the West Belfast commu-
> nity to the neglect and discrimination which the area suffered in terms of
> facilities and resources. . . The dual purpose of Féile was to create from
> within West Belfast the resources and facilities which had been withheld
> from it and to take control of its own image-making—to create a show-
> case of creativity, talent and energy.
>
> (1999: online).

Clearly, *Binlids* in its capturing and replaying of the community's reminiscences fitted with this strategy. It further fulfilled these functions since it was
also the occasion for a drama training programme:

> DubbelJoint Productions, The Training for Women Network and Féile
> an Phobail with assistance from the Open College Network and the Peace
> and Reconciliation Fund have all assisted in the project, one of whose aims
> is to provide training and employment for women in non-traditional skills
> such as script-writing and technical production thus enabling them to gain
> entrance into what has traditionally been a male dominated profession.
>
> (Ó Broin 1997: 15)

If the play's production was one demonstration of a growing self-confidence within the nationalist community, the timing of its staging could hardly have been more propitious. Following the general election in May 1997, the new Labour Prime Minister Tony Blair almost immediately sought dialogue between government officials and Sinn Féin. The party itself had campaigned in the election that a vote for it was a vote for peace. By July 1997, this promise appeared to be fulfilled when the PIRA announced a cessation of military activities. By August, the Sinn Féin leadership had been invited by the Secretary of State for Northern Ireland, Mo Mowlam, to join all-party talks. Thus, as republicanism was itself turning from a military to a political engagement (for a second time), the play offered a possibility of reviewing and testi-
fying to the journey which this particular community had undertaken to reach this juncture.

Discussion: Authenticity and History

At the outset of this chapter I suggested that in dealing with the past the play-wright has to mediate between fidelity to the past, memory and imagination. In doing this an interplay is created between what Burns has described as rhetorical and authenticating conventions. Burns describes rhetorical conventions thus:

> Between actors and spectators there is an implicit agreement that the actors will be allowed to conjure up a fictitious world. . . This agreement underwrites the devices of exposition that enable the audience to understand the play. These devices. . . can be described as *rhetorical*. They are the means by which the audience is persuaded to accept characters and situations whose validity is ephemeral and bound to the theatre.
>
> (Burns 1972: 31; cited Kershaw 1992: 25)

These conventions refer therefore to those codes which the audience has to accept because this event is a play, in order to make sense of what they witness before them. Such conventions point up the specifically dramatic and theatrical aspects of the representation, tying it to its medium. Each of the plays contains specific conventions, for example, in their use of space, through which the theatrical here and now becomes not just one but a range of other places. *The Freedom of the City* establishes the spatial frame of the tribunal within which the Guildhall scenes are enacted, and in so doing divides the space both horizontally and vertically. Schrank comments that 'whereas the horizontal divisions speak primarily to differences in power and status and their associated languages, the vertical partitioning between soldiers and civilians reveal differences (British vs. Irish), but also unacknowledged commonalities (class, language)' (2000: 137). Likewise *Binlids* shifts between the five stages and the promenade space between them as its action moves across time and different locations. In both plays, these shifts are achieved also by transitions between lighting states, an obvious marker of theatricality which the audience must accept.

Burns contrasts such devices with authenticating conventions which she argues

> 'model' social conventions in use at a specific time and in a specific place and milieu. The modes of speech, demeanour and action that are explicit in the play. . . have to imply a connection to the world of human action of which the theatre is only a part. These conventions suggest a total and external code of values and norms of conduct from which the speech and action of the play is drawn. Their function is, therefore, to *authenticate* the play.
>
> (Burns 1972: 32; cited Kershaw 1992: 26)

Thus, such conventions point to the closeness of the match between what is being represented and the extra-theatrical actuality. Such authenticity provides a sense of authority for the play as a means of knowing not only a fictional dramatic world but also of knowing the world outside. There is a tension set up therefore between these authenticating devices and the careful rhetorical structuring conventions which require the audience to review their own roles and ideas. Examples of such conventions within the plays include the setting and use of references to well-known parts of each of the cities in which they are sited; and, the capturing of the precise nuances of the language of each of the characters. Lojek comments of the protesters in *The Freedom of the City*, for example, 'incapable of discerning motive or meaning in their own experiences, they are nevertheless blessed with voices which ring with vigour, authenticity and individuality' (2004: 182). Within the productions, careful attention was paid to reconstructing appropriate costumes and props (including guns). Sound effects are used within both plays as iconic indications of the world beyond that which is visible to the audience.

A third set of conventions is at work in both *The Freedom of the City* and *Binlids*, conventions which are specific to the genre of documentary theatre. It is perhaps remarkable that these two productions are examples of the relatively few attempts to pursue a documentary approach to theatre-making within Northern Ireland. Filewod notes that:

> The documentary theatre seems to thrive in periods when new cultural imperatives cannot be expressed within the framework of traditional dramatic forms. . . At the core of the documentary impulse is an implicit critical statement that the conventional dramatic forms of the culture in question no longer express the truth of the society, usually because those conventional forms cannot accommodate rapid social change. The documentary approach provides a way for artists to realign the theatre to these changes.
>
> (1987: 14)

One might therefore have expected more practitioners to have engaged with the form in the context of violent civil unrest. Peter Weiss outlined the characteristics of documentary:

> Documentary Theatre is a theatre of reportage. . . Documentary Theatre refrains from all invention; it takes authentic material and puts it on the stage, unaltered in content, edited in form. On the stage we show a selection based on a definite theme, generally of a social or political character. . . This critical selection and the principles by which the montage of snippets of reality is effected, determines the quality of the documentary drama.
>
> (1971: 41)

Weiss's definition emphasises not only the external referentiality of the material of documentary theatre, but also its formal emphasis on montage as the principle of dramaturgical structuring. Moreover, it points up that such organisation is fundamentally polemical rather than balanced. As Favorini notes, 'If the historian can play the role of virtual prince, in educating and mobilizing, so too may the documentarian' (1994: 33). To this definition Filewod adds two principles of documentary theatre: 'It is a genre of performance that presents actuality on the stage and in the process authenticates that actuality, and it speaks to a specifically defined audience for whom it has special significance' (1987: 16).

Each play demonstrates a number of these documentary conventions. Schrank notes that there are a number of aspects to *The Freedom of the City* which are drawn directly from the experience of Bloody Sunday. The most obvious is the use of an almost verbatim reproduction of the findings of the Widgery Tribunal within the play's fictitious tribunal. Other elements are directly reproduced from the events of Bloody Sunday such as the figure of a priest waving a white handkerchief as he ministers to the bodies, directly recalling the role of Father (later Bishop) Edward Daly; and the inclusion of the words attributed to march leader Bernadette Devlin on the day, shouting to the protesters to 'Stand your ground'. Dramaturgically, the play demonstrates sophisticated devices to set up the montage characteristic of documentary theatre. These include: switches between different settings and time periods; the implication of the theatre audience at various points within the dramatic action (including direct audience address by a variety of characters); and the technique of backtracking (see Fo 1985) whereby the outcome of the action is known from the outset.

Moreover, there is a complex interaction between the modes of representation which the play uses. Within the naturalistic scenes set within the Guildhall, the audience are privy to the interactions of the characters of Lily, Michael and Skinner in exploring this bastion of unionist domination. The audience view also other forms of acting out within other scenes, enactments in which they are implicated: as members of public at the inquiry, the congregation at the chapel and viewers of the television broadcast, for example. However within both forms, enactment gives way to a third form of representation: narration. This is the focal point of the play since, as Worth (1993) has argued, the play is an exploration of the power of story-telling in which stories vie for legitimacy in explaining how and why these three civilians came to be murdered. Crucially even the enacted scenes in the Guildhall are driven by conflicts between the narratives of the three characters in trying to explain and understand each other. It is only finally in the monologues which open Act Two that the characters are allowed space and the lucidity to narrate themselves without contradiction.

The interplay between the modes of presentation within the play is complex. Since the audience see the Guildhall scenes at first-hand, the action staged there becomes a direct experience against which its mediation in other modes of representation is measured. In the scenes beyond the Guildhall, the audience observes the gaps between this first-hand experience of the characters and the ways in which they are mediated in the different narratives of the tribunal and the witnesses who testify at it, the security forces, the church, the sociologist, the television reporter and the drunken republican singer. In foregrounding the incongruity between the reality of the characters as experienced by the audience, the actions against them and the recounting of these actions, Friel demonstrates the ways in which they become transformed within narratives serving powerful interest groups. For example, the same beginning is used for two sermons by the same priest, one which laments their brave loss, the other as a pretext for an attack on godless communism. None of the external story-tellers are shown directly to knowingly lie, merely to be subject to the power of the discourse within which they operate and thus view the world. As Worth comments:

> Rethinking the story, remaking the history; these revisionist emphases draw Friel's audience along a somewhat Brechtian line but not by an overtly Brechtian method. Friel's way is more oblique: doubts and questions are subtly insinuated into the gaps between one story or another or between story and live event.
>
> (1993: 77)

Likewise Dantanus comments that 'The whole structure of the play seems to be designed as a clinical and formal analysis intent on controlling the flow of emotions' (1988: 138). *Binlids* employs similar techniques. Although developing chronologically, the incidents it presents are carefully selected within its polemical frame. The final script included verbatim accounts, transcripts of political speeches, facts and figures, political songs from the period and choral chanting.

The use of such documentary techniques might suggest that there is an attempt to justify the dramatic representation by the invocation of its match to an objectively verifiable reality. Such a match might then be considered as a means of authenticating the perspective produced and bestowing authority on it.[8] This is problematic for *The Freedom of the City*, since although it is documentary in form, it documents the experience of an event which has never taken place.[9] Thus, although it captures the nuances of the narratives (and exact words in some instances) within which representations of the events of Bloody Sunday were contained for and by the Widgery Tribunal, these are articulated self-consciously within a fiction: an example of a lie which seeks to reveal a truth.

However, this fictional dimension did not figure in the critical reception of

The Freedom of the City. Rather the basis of the criticisms of both *The Freedom of the City* and later *Binlids* was that they were too one-sided to be authentic. As indicated in the previous chapter, this has been a perennial issue from early on: a tendency amongst reviewers has been to assume that if they must be staged, plays about the Troubles should exhibit an approach which is balanced. The reviews of *Binlids* echo the criticism cited earlier of *The Freedom of the City.* In the nationalist Belfast-based *Irish News,* Webster suggested that 'Given their concern over media distortion, it is strange that the authors did not give equal treatment to their depiction of republican violence' (1997: 5). This was echoed in other reviews including those in Irish-American newspapers: 'No matter how justified the arguments may be, it's still just a noisy, primitive commercial, overemphatically making its pitch' (Marks 1998: online). Even otherwise favourable reviews declare, for example, that there is 'an unashamed political bias to Binlids' (Marlow 1997: 41). The production's director, Pam Brighton, mounted a strong rebuttal of these criticisms in a response article to Webster's review:

> *Binlids* is criticised for its one-sided approach, yet with all the resources at their disposal when have the media given us a play or film that whilst it attacks republicanism, carefully reminds itself about the nature and degree of its own brutalising behaviour?. . . *Binlids* was not seeking a balance within itself but seeking a balance in the overall perception of what makes West Belfast tick.
>
> (1997: 8)

Brighton argues that there is a wider context within which the production must be viewed. As such, it is a corrective to what has passed for the facts of an objective history within existing discourses. In this she is following Weiss's prescription for documentary theatre: 'Many of its themes inevitably demand and assume judgement. In such a theatre, objectivity is likely to be merely a concept used by a ruling group to justify its actions. The call for restraint and understanding is seen as coming from those who do not wish to lose their privileges' (1971: 42).

The disjunction between the experience of plays as authentic and an awareness of them as partial is derived from different understandings of authenticity where it is articulated either as a relationship between reality and its representation or in an ascription of agency and authority. So, in the same article Brighton argues that the authenticity of the piece did not lie in its match to an objectively verifiable reality:

> The events in Binlids were selected on the basis of what had most affected people in the community. Internment, obviously, because the experience of the wholesale onslaught on the homes and families of the area was crit-

ical in shaping people's sense of vulnerability and their anger and outrage
at the British army.

(Brighton 1997: 8)[10]

Thus, the basis of the production's claim to authenticity is shifted, rooted
in the authority of individuals and communities to speak from and act out
(of) their own experience. This is a shift from a concern with *histoire* to a
concern with *discours*. Elam summarises Benveniste's distinction between
histoire,

> the 'objective' mode dedicated to the narration of events in the past, which
> eliminates the speaking subject and his addressee. . . and *discours*, the
> 'subjective' mode geared to the present, which indicates the interlocutors
> and their speaking situation. *Histoire* abstracts the *énoncé*—the utterance
> produced—from its context, while discours gives prominence to the *énon-
> ciation*, the act of producing the utterance within a given context.
>
> (1988: 144)[11]

This shift promotes a different conception of authenticity: one in which
agency rather than accuracy to actuality is the validating criterion. Graham
invokes Golomb's proposition in this respect: 'One is historically authentic
when one creates one's own history by utilizing and recreating one's past and
the past of one's people. . . [Authenticity] is the loyalty of one's self to its own
past, heritage and ethos' (Golomb 1995: 117; cited Graham 1999: 11). The
play is not concerned with the positivist enterprise of discovering an objectively testable match between the totality of reality and the representation;
rather, it is concerned with the preservation of the sources used as a recognition of the authority of ordinary people in remembering their own lives. It is
in this sense that the work is authentic: 'Authenticity here becomes rooted in
"the people" and in the bond between the self and the group; and additionally, authenticity relies on the ability to "utilize" and culturally employ such
"loyalty" ' (Graham 1999: 11). The production's authenticity is therefore a
way of validating the experiences of different individuals within the context
of a community, articulating for them the right to be heard. It is on this basis
that Schaefer (2003) categorises *Binlids* as a testimonial play, suggesting that,
'These monologues succeed as raw idiosyncratic testimony. They capture the
essence of what is powerful about oral history: it can teach those who hear it
something about the lived emotional reality of a historical event' (2003: 12).

The Freedom of the City too presents the experiences of the three victims in
their own words and actions within the Mayor's Parlour, contrasting these
with the ways in which they are recuperated by others. Even where there is
uncertainty, ambiguity or disagreement in the accounts that the three have of
themselves or each other, the empathetic relationship set up between these

characters and the audience raises the authority of their accounts over those presented by outsiders. Moreover, in the monologues which each gives at the start of the second act, Friel bestows on them a lucidity and awareness which cannot be captured by anyone else and is presented as singularly authoritative because of this. According to Murray, 'History in itself, as a means of recording the truth is, in Friel's drama in general suspect because its formal, objective methodology is too presumptuous to understand the experience Friel values most, namely the inner, the subjective, the lyrical' (1988: 283). The play's argument then is fundamentally a democratic one: suggesting that the best interests of people are served by giving voice to their concerns, allowing them to speak for themselves.

In drawing attention to this act of speaking, the productions thereby sought to provoke a different relationship for the audience to that of traditional theatrical spectatorship. To explain this relationship, I want to develop further the concept of 'witness' which was introduced in Chapter 2. Peggy Phelan notes that 'To solicit an ethical witness in a theatre event requires one to trust that the border of the performance exceeds its spatial and temporal boundaries' (1999: 13). Unlike *The Interrogation of Ambrose Fogarty*, the spectator is not required to act as witness to an act (the beating of Fogarty) as if it were happening in the here-and-now, emphasising the division of spectator as witness and the stage action witnessed. Rather, the spectator in these productions is cast in the role of witness to the act of speaking by the actors/characters in the roles which they enact. The spectator's presence testifies to the authenticity of the stories which are told by granting authority to the tellers. In *The Freedom of the City* the characters of Lily, Skinner and Michael and the stories they tell about themselves are framed within the dramatic structure, apart from the direct audience address at the beginning of the second act. Nonetheless, the voices which Friel is articulating are those of the real victims and their families who had been so clearly omitted from the Widgery findings. It is their experience which lends authenticity to the representation for audience members who are able to recognise the validity of what they have to express.

A further dimension is set up for spectators in watching *Binlids* insofar as they are aware of the external identity of the amateur members of the cast, simultaneously present with the identity of the dramatic character. In watching someone whose own life experience is the basis of the dramatic role or who is acting on behalf of a family member, friend or neighbour to tell their story, spectatorship becomes a powerful act of solidarity with the teller of the story, either directly present or represented by someone else. Witnessing the performance becomes an expression of *communitas*, what Turner defines as 'a direct, immediate and total confrontation of human identities' (Turner 1982: 47; cited Kershaw 1992: 28). Such *communitas* is 'the foundation of community cohesiveness' (Kershaw 1992: 28). This is a fundamental difference between the two productions: whilst *The Freedom of The City* received an unsympathetic reception in Dublin, London and New York, *Binlids* was staged for the kind of 'specifically defined audience for whom it has special significance' which Filewod described as a fundamental characteristic of the form (1987: 16). It may explain, moreover, the exclusion felt by those critics from outside the community who felt the play to be too one-sided.[12]

The proximity of the material to the audience initiated a series of processes within that audience which exceeded the boundaries of the performance in the ways which Phelan describes as important to the process of witnessing. The first of these is the recognition that authenticity is not about fidelity to fact but about the right to tell your story and for it to be heard. As such the performance was an assertion of a fundamental political right. Secondly, it provided an opportunity to confront those events which had conditioned the community's internalised sense of self without necessarily being acknowledged as such at the time. One of the actors, Máiréad Uí Adhnaill, commented that 'My mother came to the dress rehearsal. She said that it wasn't that you had forgotten any of these things, but when she was living through it there was always another crisis. You went through internment because there was something else happening after that, and now all of a sudden it was back in your face' (Scally 1998: 18). Being able to externalise these experiences is important, as Day comments in relation to Playback Theatre: 'without the chance to speak and externalize the insights that emerge from our angle of vision, we are unable to experience our own positioning, far less to make any sort of comparison or negotiation with other people who are positioned differently' (1999: 85). A third, related, process is that of a release from the past, almost as an act of catharsis, as at least one review picked up: 'Passion and fury are the hallmarks of this production; passion because all the elements of the drama are combined in a powerful expression of real genuine feelings; the fury vented during *Binlids* seems like the inevitable unburdening of anger after a long and frustrating confinement' (Ó Liatháin 1997: 31).

Finally, by demonstrating the ways in which the community has evolved in response to its changing context, there is a differentiation between the past and the present. This is a way of showing both that the present is not inevitable but the result of specific historical processes and that the present moment is not the same as the past and therefore presents an opportunity for doing things differently. By making manifest the changes within the community and in the community's external relationships, it articulated the possibility that the conflict is the product of specific historical circumstances which now can be changed. On this basis, the play can be seen to have had a role in the process of peace-making for this community at the precise point of its staging in 1997. This was the moment when fresh negotiations were being initiated by Sinn Féin with the Ulster Unionists and the British government in anticipation of the declaration of a second cease-fire by the Provisional IRA.

4

Failed Origins

COMEDIAN: Good morning. This is your captain speaking We are now
approaching the city of Belfast. Will all passengers please
fasten their seatbelts and turn their watches back three
hundred years

(Christina Reid, 1997,
Did You Hear the One About the Irishman?, 69)

In the previous chapter I argued that the past is an arena in which projections
of present circumstances contend together, following Croce's dictum that 'all
history is contemporary history' (cited Peacock 1991: 9). Such projections
have given the conflict an air of inevitability, particularly within specific narratives in which it is alternatively the result of eight hundred years of colonial
domination, of centuries of sectarian rivalries, or of the ongoing effort to
defend the faithful from the apostasy of Papism. It should not be forgotten,
however, that at the outbreak of the Troubles many people experienced a
sense of bewilderment that their society, for all its failings, could have erupted
into such horrific violence. The ensuing years of violence may have only exacerbated this initial bewilderment. Certain theatre makers have looked to the
past for moments when the situation might have led to a different outcome,
turning over the 'polluted origins to search into the roots of a society so
impregnated with strife and division' (Richie 1985: 5). It is as if by understanding moments when events might have turned differently a way might be
discernible to bring their consequences to an end, playwrights might be able
to supersede politicians in mapping the future. In attempting to do so, they
have been able to play out the reasons why events have turned out as they
have, and to interrogate those unyielding conceptions of the past and the
present which have become ossified under the pressures of the subsequent
conflict. Such productions have been engaged both in excavation (revealing
a past which has given rise to the present moment) and projection (of present
concerns on to past moments). This is literally the case in Friel's *Volunteers*
where political prisoners are set to assist an archaeological dig and argue over
the meanings of the objects and skeleton they unearth. Like Friel, other playwrights have sought to demonstrate that history is not fated to repeat itself

inevitably a second time. Stewart Parker's Henry Joy McCracken asks 'So what if the English do bequeath us to one another some day? What then? When there's nobody else to blame but ourselves?' (1989: 75) The question is posed for the contemporary audience to answer.

Asking such a question suggests that a shared dramaturgical aim has been to undertake a process of historicisation aligned with, though not necessarily derived from, the Brechtian tradition which Reinelt identifies:

> Brechtian historicization actually works in three modes simultaneously. In representing the past, the specificity of its conditions, its 'Otherness' from now, and the suppressed possibilities through which it might have been otherwise are presented. Then the relationship of the past to the present is shown to consist of analogous conditions, unchanged and/or unexamined legacies that make the latent possibilities of the past act as a springboard to present possibilities. Finally, the representation of the present must be such that it is seen from a distance similar to the way the 'past' is seen, that is historically.
>
> (1999: 87)

There are complications in invoking history in the context of Ireland. These arise from the assumption, repeated as a commonplace by both artists and commentators alike, that Ireland's past has a uniquely unhealthy hold on the present, retarding the emergence of a fully modern society, a retardation most obvious in Northern Ireland. For example, Taggart argues that 'While the rest of Europe has been able to look towards the millennium with relative confidence, Northern Ireland has been unable to wake from the nightmare of its own history' (2000: 67). The assumption is that a pathological fixation with history is the cause of the current conflict, rooting the society firmly in the past. It is against the back-drop provided by this assumption that certain productions have provided counter-examples to the present from moments in Northern Irish history, moments which might be reworked with positive outcomes within the contemporary setting. Thus in their exploration of what might be called 'failed origins', Martin Lynch's *Dockers* and Stewart Parker's *Northern Star* demonstrate the mutability of the historical moment and the opportunities which, missed once, need not escape again.[1]

The Plays in Context

Dockers was Martin Lynch's first professional play and his first success as playwright-in-residence at the Lyric Theatre, Belfast. Directed and designed by Sam McCready, the production earned Lynch favourable comparisons with Sam Thompson and Thomas Carnduff (see, for example, R. Rosenfield 1981 and McAughtry 1981). McCready was directly influential in the development of Lynch's understanding of dramatic form, encouraging him to move scenes out from the single, often domestic, setting for which Lynch had been accustomed to write; and to flesh out the characterisation of John Graham in particular.[2] One of the achievements of the production was to give a sense of the whole world of the docks: the quayside, the pub and the family home. According to Lynch's own account there were around seventy dockers at the opening night of the play (Triesman and Lynch 1983: 3) and reviewers felt that the production would bring working-class people into the theatre: ' "Dockers" should bring, if I may use the term, working-class people to the Lyric who have never been there before, especially dockers who will recognise the language and the atmosphere as being of their world' (O'Brien 1981: 13). This presence in the audience was crucial to the response to the performance: 'the presence of a goodly contingent of actual workers in the Belfast docks did much by their quick response to illuminate some incidents or gestures that might otherwise have gone unregarded' (R. Rosenfield 1981: 8) and Lynch himself commented that 'One of the greatest compliments paid to me was that the working-class were coming to see it. It would've been pointless if it had been the normal crowd' (Cassidy 1981: 11). As an act of occupation, then, the staging of the play marked a radical departure for the Lyric and in what might have been seen as acceptable dramatic material on the Irish stage.

The play is set in Belfast's dockland area of Sailortown in 1962. Its central narrative concerns John Graham, an idealistic docker who, as a newly elected shop steward, tries to overturn the practices of the system whereby employment on a day-to-day basis depended on being selected from the throng of men who might present themselves for work. Such selection was carried out by foremen appointed by the employers, endowing them with disproportionate power and an unaccountable authority over their fellow workers. The trade unions colluded in the system despite its capacity for exploitation. Moreover, large numbers of casual workers could present themselves for work alongside union members, effectively allowing employers to maintain low wage rates due to the surplus of labour. At that time, two main trade unions operated within the docks: the Irish Transport and General Workers' Union (members of which were invariably from nationalist backgrounds) and the Transport and General Workers' Union within Britain (whose members were invariably from unionist backgrounds). This division of the labour force allowed it to be exploited by employers able to play off one set of workers against the others. In speaking out against the casual system and the sectarian division of the workforce, Graham falls foul of the foremen and the union bosses from both sides who work the system for their own benefit. He ends up being assaulted for singing 'The Red Flag' at a Labour Day meeting of the trade unions' joint committee. The incident is based on an actual event in dockland lore in which a young radical, Kipper Lynch, suffered in the same way as Graham for singing 'The Red Flag' at a union meeting (Triesman and Lynch 1983: 4). Graham's principled stand in the play echoes Sam Thompson's *Over the Bridge*, in which trade unionist Davy Mitchell is killed by a Protestant mob whilst standing up for a Catholic worker's right to work. Ironically, it is the rejection of Graham's socialism that unites his fellow trade unionists. While this is the central narrative, the play traces also a series of sub-plots concerning a range of characters and stories, including the battle of wits between the idler Buckets McGuinness and the money-lender Sarah Montague; the sibling rivalry of Hughie and Danny-Boy McNamara over who will take on their father's privilege of union membership; and the domestic relationship between Graham and his wife, Theresa. Thus, it is able to mine a variety of experiences and situations familiar to anyone connected to the docks.

Reviews of the first production lauded both the authenticity of its writing and the ensemble playing of a cast which included many Lyric regulars.[3] Such authenticity derived from Lynch's own family background, since his two older brothers and his father worked in the docks (as had Lynch's grandfather).[4] However, Lynch became a cloth cutter as a result of the same arcane regulations about who could work in the docks which are explored in the play, instead of following the family tradition.[5] His experience of the shop-floor in the garment industry in the 1960s helped to form a class-consciousness which went beyond sectarian divisions: 'There was certainly a marginal difference as to whether you were a Catholic or a Protestant, but your class was more important. I found that as I grew up—I didn't realise it then, I know it now—I was discriminated against on the basis of what class I had come from' (Thompson 1984). His involvement with the Republican Clubs further developed this class-consciousness.[6] In 1976 as a representative of Turf Lodge Housing Action Committee, he attended a socialist conference in Leeds where he encountered other working-class activists from across Northern Ireland and Britain. From this came his first play in which he explored working-class solidarity, *We Want Work, We Want Bread* (1976) about the 1930s Outdoor Relief Act riots in which Catholics and Protestants came together in protest in Derry and Belfast.

The possibilities of co-operation across sectarian divisions are explored too in Stewart Parker's *Northern Star*. The setting of the play is a derelict cottage on the slopes of the Cavehill, overlooking Belfast, on the evening after the United Irishmen have been defeated at the Battle of Antrim in 1798. There, Henry Joy McCracken, one of the leaders of the uprising, contemplates why it failed and the fate that awaits him. This temporal focus allows the character of McCracken to reflect on his own deeds in ways which are not open to Graham in the dramaturgy of *Dockers*, and the framing of the play in this way allows the development of a self-conscious critique of his actions which is absent from Lynch's play. Haunted by the memories of those with whom he

Figure 3. *Northern Star* by Stewart Parker, Lyric Theatre, Belfast.
Photographer: Chris Hill

planned the rebellion, McCracken is accompanied by his lover, Mary Bodle, and their illegitimate daughter. Crucially, McCracken is a Presbyterian and his appeal in inciting the rebellion has been to unite Catholics and Presbyterians against the established order to bring about a republic of equals. In many respects the play is a riposte to the claims of nationalists to a unique republican heritage and a reminder to Protestants that they have an obligation to own their role in the past. Stephen Rea (himself a Protestant nationalist), who directed the 1998 production, suggested that: 'There is an amnesia amongst Protestants in this town about their part in the creation and preservation of so much of the culture of modern Ireland' (Coyle 1998: 1). Parker himself was very open and specific about his motivations in writing the play:

> The technique allowed me to march the play throughout the decades towards the present day and say to the audience, forget about historical veracity, forget about realism, I'm going to tell you a story about the origins of Republicanism and I'm going to offer you a point of view on what's gone wrong with it and why it's become corrupt and why it's serving the opposite ends to what it set out to serve, and I'm going to demonstrate this like a ventriloquist, using a variety of voices.

(Carty 1985: 19)

According to Marilyn Richtarik's notes for the programme of the 1998 production, Parker's idea for a play about Henry Joy McCracken had emerged first in 1967 while he was teaching at Cornell, the idea at that time informed by his experience of the campaigns against the Vietnam war and for Black liberation. However, despite approaching the BBC with a view to producing a radio play on the matter, it was not until the Lyric Theatre, Belfast, commissioned a production in 1984 that his concept was to be fully realised. *Northern Star* opened there on 7 November 1984, the first of what would be Parker's 'triptych' of plays dealing with figures from the margins of Irish history (Parker 1989: 9), and the first of Parker's plays to be premiered in Belfast. Both the play and the performances by Gerard McSorley as Henry Joy McCracken and Emer Gillespie as Mary were warmly received during the run at the Lyric (Bell 1984; Nowlan 1984c; O'Toole 1984c), although Murray notes that the production was 'a dismal failure at the Dublin Theatre Festival' (1988: 286). The timeliness of that original production in the context of the Anglo-Irish Agreement led Fintan O'Toole to comment that: 'One of the reasons why *Northern Star* is such a fine play is that Parker manages to maintain a constant tension between the past—the events that McCracken was involved in—and the present—the audience in Belfast in 1984' (1984c: 18). However, it was when the play was revived under the direction of Stephen Rea in November 1998, that it 'took on resonances which could hardly have been anticipated previously' (Byrne 2001b: 130). 1998 was the bi-centenary of the 1798 rebellion, and the year in which both the Good Friday Agreement had been reached and Omagh was bombed by dissident republicans. Rea himself suggested that 'It could be that the context for *Northern Star* has finally come. The ideals of 1798 were wiped out by sectarianism and 200 years of bigotry and discrimination followed' (Coyle 1998: 1). Byrne reflected that 'In the midst of the turbulent peace process, capacity audiences flocked to see a play deemed both wonderfully joyful in its depiction of a brief moment of political possibility, and prescient in its warnings of the consequences should such a possibility be accorded a "botched birth"' (2001b: 131). For this reason it is this revival by Tinderbox and Field Day, in a co-production with the Belfast Festival at Queen's, which will be considered here.

This production was staged at the First Presbyterian Church in Belfast's Rosemary Street with a design by Bob Crowley and lighting by Conleth White, opening on Saturday 14 November as part of the Belfast Festival. The production could hardly have had a more apposite setting since a plaque outside the church declares:

> The members of this congregation believe in the freedom of individuals to form their own opinions and fashion their own faith, free from compulsion or coercion from any ecclesiastical or civil authority. We do not seek to exclude persons because of their beliefs nor do we seek to impose ours

upon them. We welcome all who are seeking to work out and understand
the purpose of life, with freedom of thought and without constraint of
uniformity.

(Coyle 1998: 1)

The radical individualism embraced by this statement is a key feature of the
Presbyterian tradition and one of the informing principles of the United
Irishmen. The building itself was erected in 1783 and members of the congregation were notable contributors to the developing city of Belfast. At the time
of the United Irish rebellion, its membership was split into the opposing
factions (Playfair 1998). The choice of this location by Stephen Rea was
therefore quite deliberate and Rea commented that 'the church was built to
hear ideas; its ideology is shot through with debate and discussion. . . The
setting itself has the potential for cultural combustion. We have a licence to
explore ideas in the very place where they were introduced and then wiped
out 200 years ago' (ibid.). Michael Billington suggested that 'Short of seeing
Hamlet at Elsinor, you could hardly find a play that comes closer to home'
(1998: 12). Crowley's design made full use of the space, with a long central
ramp projecting into the audience, and the action dispersed across the aisles,
pews and balconies of the church. Within this arrangement, as Satake notes,
'Just as the medieval audience followed the footsteps of Christ by moving
from stage to stage, the audience of *Northern Star* are led through the course
taken by the United Irishmen with a certain sense of inevitability until they
see the idealistic movement end in further deepening of the divide they set
out to bridge' (2000: 177). The playing allowed the audience to be both spectators of the action and crucially to be interpellated as the citizens of Belfast
of 1798 when addressed directly by the actor as McCracken. The challenge
could hardly be more direct as Stephen Rea would note: 'To set the play in
that church, to stand up and remind people that two hundred years ago there
were these revolutionaries, these thinkers and artists who had made this stand;
and hanging behind the pulpit was the flag of the United Irishmen' (Rea and
Pelletier 2000: 57). The effect was to provoke an 'uneasy quiet among the
middle-class Presbyterians in the audience' (Hill 1998: 8).

Born in 1941, Stewart Parker was to win scholarships to both grammar
school and university, lifting him outside of the working-class unionist background of the East Belfast areas of Sydenham and Ballymacarrett in which
he was brought up. He went to Queen's University in 1959 to study English,
becoming a keen participant in both the drama society and Philip Hosbaum's
poetry group where he encountered Seamus Heaney and Seamus Deane. In
his second year, he contracted a form of bone cancer which resulted in the
amputation of a leg. He left Ireland to pursue postgraduate study in poetic
drama in the United States, where he would go on to teach at Hamilton
College and Cornell University. Having published two pamphlets of poetry,

The Casualty's Meditation (1966) and *Maw* (1968), in 1969 he returned to Northern Ireland to begin a professional career as a writer, his return voyage coinciding with the outbreak of the Troubles in Belfast and Derry in August of that year. He went on to write a number of plays for BBC Radio and a music column, 'High Pop', for the *Irish Times* from 1971 until 1976. His first successful stage play was *Spokesong* (1975) which was premiered at the Dublin Theatre Festival. This was followed by *Cathchpenny Twist* (1977) which was staged at the Peacock, Dublin. In 1978, Parker again left Northern Ireland to live first in Edinburgh and later in London. He worked across different media, writing for radio, television and film, while continuing his successes as a stage dramatist.[7] On 2 November 1988, Parker succumbed to cancer at the age of 47, according to the *Irish Times* obituary having 'established himself as one of the most versatile and imaginative of the current generation of Irish writers for the theatre and television' (3 November 1988: 8).

The play demonstrates the deft handling of a dramatist able not only to structure the representation of McCracken's last night, but to do so through seven 'ages' in which the events leading up to that point are styled after a particular Irish playwright. Thus, the Age of Innocence draws on Farquhar; Boucicault is the model for the Age of Idealism; Wilde is imitated in the Age of Cleverness; Shaw is the source for the Age of Dialectics; the Age of Heroism is modelled on Synge; O'Casey is imitated in the Age of Compromise; and finally Behan and Beckett are the models for the Age of Shame.[8] This might be seen as a flaunting of the writer's cleverness running 'the risk of distracting the audience into a literary guessing game in which the point of his citational mode is missed' (Andrews 1989b: 20). However, there is a serious intent here underpinning all of Parker's writing and expressed in 1984 in his tribute to his former teacher, John Malone.[9] Seeing theatre as a means of imagining an alternative reality, he argued that, given the lack of vision from politicians

> if ever a time and place cried out for the solace and rigour and passionate rejoinder of great drama, it is here and now. There is a great culture to be achieved. The politicians, visionless almost to a man, are withdrawing into their sectarian stockades. It falls to the artists to construct a working model of wholeness by means of which this society can again begin to hold up its head in the world.
>
> (1986: 19)

Discussion: The Actual and the Symbolic

Two key issues from the immediate context and the past of Northern Ireland were treated within the scope of each production. The first is the power of language to establish or operate within reality (and the related issue of who is given authority to speak). The second is the nature and justification for individual self-sacrifice in pursuit of political aims.[10] These two are connected by the relationships in politics and in theatre between the actual and the symbolic, particularly where the latter is taken to substitute for the former. Yeats expressed his anxiety about the power of language to transform the actual into the symbolic in his 'Easter 1916'. Indeed, much of Anglo-Irish relations and of Irish political life has consisted of a substitution of the actual for what it has come to stand for, so that people have fought and killed over the words of treaties and agreements which have sought to establish particular political realities. That dying for a cause has been a recurrent part of Irish political culture indicates the transformational powers of discourses across the political spectrum.

In *Dockers* Lynch's own fascination with language and his ear for the speech of Belfast's working class find expression in the naming of the characters and the patterns of dialogue throughout the play and, in performance, marked it as an authentic expression of working-class culture. According to Judith Rosenfield 'At the opening night, 40 dockers were present and when I spoke to some of them they vouched for its truth not only of situation but of dialogue and characterisation' (1981: 4). Lynch himself noted that 'the middle-class people got their eyes opened to an insight into life which I presume they don't very often see. Apparently quite a lot of people didn't know what was being said. Belfast middle-class people didn't know what Belfast working-class people were saying to each other' (Triesman 1983: 3). Parker likewise enjoyed deploying the richness of demotic Ulster speech with which the dialogue is peppered. Moreover, his imitation of the styles of other dramatists demonstrated an engagement with all forms of language. Each age deploys a distinctive rhetorical style such as the malapropisms of Peggy Barclay, including 'Your fancy words won't butter no parsimony, not with me' (1989: 22); and the reverse logic of the Wildean exchange in the Age of Cleverness wherein Tone says of Bunting, 'What a disagreeable fellow, I do hope we shall see more of him' (1989: 41).

However, it is in the interrogation of the power and limitations of language that the productions engaged with the politics of their contexts. One of the central actions of *Dockers* focuses on Graham's commitment to speaking publicly against the injustices to which he is witness and on behalf of the socialist values which he espouses: talking the 'red talk' (2003a: 31) against which he has been warned. Ranged against him are forces which prefer to hatch deals quietly and will silence him and anyone else who suggests change. The power of language is enacted through naming which is a key part of the action. From the opening scene ritualised name-calling is a taken-for-granted element of colloquial exchange, 'sleggin' between mates. Name-calling can also serve as a proxy for more open conflict in which the antagonists are reluctant to engage: Graham 'has words with' Jimmy Sweeney for an accident to Danny-Boy, takes action against him by 'raising his name' with the committee and castigates his fellow shop steward McKibben by calling him 'a lickspittle' in public. More significantly, however, name-calling is the means by which power is exerted when it is exercised by figures who have the authority to make their words count as deeds, to fix reality by the names they give to those around them. This is most potent in the naming by the foremen of the men who will work in each crew, as Graham finds out when Sweeney and Henry conspire to leave him uncalled for work at the beginning of Act Two. Further, the powerlessness of many figures is expressed in the ways in which their words are disregarded by those around them (relegated as 'slabberin''), or the ways in which they have to conform to other people's accounts. Legs defends his hypocrisy by arguing that: 'Trade unions, militancy, fightin' talk and all the rest is only for buck-eejits. At the end of the day, it's all about puttin' bread on the table. The childer can't eat speeches' (2003a: 29).

This concern with the power of language is central to *Northern Star* too. McCracken demonstrates his consciousness of this from the opening scene in which he is practising the speech which he will make from the gallows in an attempt to provide a context for the actions which have led to his execution. He cannot resist the temptation to show how easily this rhetorical power can be undermined as he deviates into the clichés of the death notice and the advertising bill:

> I go willingly to my death in the true faith of a Presbyterian, confident in the blind belief that you will all unite together in freedom this week next week sometime never and I hope you folk at the back can hear me, then and not until then let my autograph be given, R.I.P., no flowers at the house please, notice the rope, by the way, best quality sisal, sixpence the yard, from my father's own ropeworks, orders to be taken immediately following the execution, thanks for nothing.
>
> (1989: 15)

The speech demonstrates the two extremes between which McCracken has had to struggle in his campaigns: the ideal and the banal. The whole action which the play re-enacts focuses on the mismatch between the language which is being used and the functions which it is intended that it fulfil; a mismatch which is the source of McCracken's eventual disillusionment. Too often language is inadequate to the task or used by people unable to live up to its demands. The Declaration of the United Irishmen read out in the Age of Innocence is full of noble rhetoric, but the language is incapable of transforming the members of the Mudlers' Club from drunken dilettantes. Even performative language such as taking the oath of the United Irishmen at the end of Act One does not prevent contradictory actions, as when McCracken is sworn in as a deputy leader of the sectarian Catholic Defenders later in Act Two. A promise likewise is rarely kept, whether it is for an investigation into attacks by Catholic Defenders against Protestants in County Armagh or for 7,000 Defenders to join the United Irishmen at Antrim. The written word too is equally unreliable. The Declaration of the United Irishmen whilst a laudable document would lead to the arrest of the Mudlers if Belle Martin were a more successful spy. Papers can be forged to provide a new identity for McCracken, while Gorman and McFadden fall out over the authenticity of the papers Gorman holds for the horses he sells on. Just as in *Dockers*, naming has an important role too. McCracken's own name has a number of permutations depending on the context: from Harry to Henry Joy, to Henry Joy McCracken. With false papers, he can become Owen Pollock, Master Carpenter. Importantly, McCracken names his various antecedents in a declaration that Ireland is not a name for a select and racially pure nation, but an idea in which distinctions can be dissolved:

> My great grandfather Joy was a French Huguenot, my great-grandfather McCracken was a Scottish Covenanter, persecuted, the pair of them, driven here from the shores of home, their home but not my home, because I'm Henry Joy McCracken and here to stay, a natural son of Belfast, as Irish a bastard as all the other incomers, blown into this port by the storm of history, Gaelic or Danish or Anglo-Norman, without distinction.
>
> (1989: 17)

Naming also has a more sinister role given the plethora of spies and informers who seek to undermine the cause of the United Irishmen, including Belle Martin and John Hughes. The inclusion of a scene in Act Two in which members of the United Irishmen are subjected anachronistically to the torture methods associated with the abuse of contemporary republican prisoners by the security forces until they name McCracken as the leader of the rising emphasises the importance of this naming function.

In both plays the central character repeats the mistake of accepting speech as a substitute for action: each accepts saying the right thing as an equivalent for doing the right thing and thus the realities of the situation in which he is placed escape him. If, as Graham's wife says 'There's a thin line between idealism and blindness' (2003: 72), both Graham and McCracken cross that line in ignoring what is going on around them. Graham seems fixated with the rhetoric of class struggle, believing that truth will itself be a sufficient weapon to liberate the workers. McCracken realises ultimately the inadequacy and unreliability of language when refusing the promise of his sister Mary-Anne that he will become a model for others: 'Christ forbid, what an example! Pious phrasemaking over a butcher's shambles, valiant defeat, maudlin self-pity—"we wuz robbed!"—defeat!' (1989: 36). For a man who has built his life around reason, the realisation that the world can be shaped neither by nor to the patterns of Enlightenment logic is devastating. For both Graham and

McCracken, then, their struggle is as much rhetorical as anything else and, in pursuing this, each fails to see the material basis of the situation or the political tactics by which power is manipulated. Thus, Graham believes that the purpose of committees is 'So people can talk and avoid trouble' (2003: 35), disregarding the politics by which committees are manipulated through the exercise of power. Moreover, his commitment to speaking causes him to reject Hughie's offer of physical reinforcement in Act Two, leaving him open to the beating he receives at the end of the play. As Theresa says 'John, you're all fancy talk' (2003: 59).

In *Dockers*, Graham's central role is juxtaposed with that of Buckets McGuinness. At the bottom of the dock hierarchy since he refuses work at every opportunity, Buckets survives on his wits, expressed in his ability to manipulate others through language. Never stuck for an excuse, Buckets is the supreme improviser and story-teller. His ultimate success comes in the second act where, having been pursued for mounting debts by Sarah Montague for the bulk of the play, he manages to convince her not only that the debts have been paid, but that she in fact owes him money. He thereby demonstrates the power to change reality through his words. Despite his apparent success, however, Buckets stands in contrast to Graham, since he knows better than to trust to words alone and is endowed with a clear-sightedness which Graham never achieves. It is Buckets who (in an echo of Shaw's Mr Doolittle) undercuts the ethic of honest labour:

> BUCKETS: If work was any good, the wealthy would be doing it.
> MCKIBBEN: You're only a drunkard.
> BUCKETS: A happy drunkard. And I'd rather be a happy drunkard than
>   a sweat-arsed, work-drunk, mealy mouthed, nothin'-to-show-
>   for-it dock labourer.
>
> (2003a: 16)

Likewise it is Buckets who counsels Graham about the nature of the struggle with which he is engaged:

> And would you tell me what union hasn't got problems? Just never let that divert you from the real thing—the struggle with the employers. On every issue luck [*sic*] to put the onus on the employers. They own you, me, the newspapers, the city, the dock, everything. Ownin' means responsibility. Don't take it off them for the wages they pay out.
>
> (2003a: 41)

In *Northern Star*, the function of external commentator is fulfilled by McCracken himself in his narration around the recollected events and the discussions he has with Mary and Mary-Anne.

This external commentary in each play helps to draw the attention of the audience to the inadequate grasp both central figures have on the material basis of his own existence and the existence of the people each seeks to lead. This is expressed most clearly in the relationships of each to the women around him. Like Juno Boyle, Theresa Graham cannot afford the luxury of principles: her pragmatism is an expression of gender politics (although there are problems with this as discussed in Chapter 6). This is an area into which Graham's political language does not extend and he falls back on the received language of his own gender when he feels under threat. McCracken too relies on the women around him to look after the practical details of every day life. Mary has found the unfinished dwelling in which they are staying, and Mary-Anne has made all the arrangements and provided the wherewithal for McCracken's escape to America. Women are left on the periphery of his focus, distractions from the cause, until he realises belatedly his own inadequacies.

Just as both productions mark moments in history when the opportunity for communal solidarity was missed, they were staged too out of a deep engagement with their present circumstances: a reminder that the same mistakes should not be made again. Despite an inauspicious start to the decade, the context in which *Dockers* was staged allowed for the possibility that some way out of the political impasse might grow through political dialogue. Following the 1979 election, the Secretary of State for Northern Ireland, Humphrey Atkins, attempted to generate cross-party discussions, and there was a gradual reduction in the overall levels of violence. A first hunger strike by H-block prisoners was called off in December 1980 and a joint summit was held by Prime Minister Margaret Thatcher and Taoiseach, Charles Haughey, to discuss cross-border co-operation in the same month. The largest nationalist party, the SDLP, had already lost two of its most prominent leaders who had argued for cross-community working-class politics, Paddy Devlin and Gerry Fitt, as the party realigned itself in a more nationalist mode. Notably, Fitt also proffered as a reason the initial refusal of the SDLP to accept the invitation of the Secretary of State to engage in a convention between political parties on power-sharing devolution.

Despite the failure of these talks, Dixon (2001) suggests that they were a foundation on which the later peace process which resulted in the Good Friday Agreement would be built. The Agreement was the direct fruit of a talks process which lasted from September 1997 until April 1998, but was rooted in the earlier dialogues initiated between the Provisional IRA and the then Conservative government under Margaret Thatcher. Moreover, it was negotiated under the shadow cast by the failure of the Sunningdale Agreement in 1974, when the deal struck was defeated through the Ulster Workers' Council strike in that year. The similarities between the eventual agreement in 1998 and that of 1974 led SDLP Deputy Leader Seamus Mallon to characterise it as 'Sunningdale for slow learners' (cited Dixon 2001: 285). Much more attention was paid second time around, however, to the ways in which words were used in the negotiations, in the final agreement and in briefings by all parties to the media. The choreographing of the process to ensure no side would look to be losing led to forms of words which were sufficiently ambiguous to be capable of being interpreted in contradictory ways by the political leaders in selling the deal to their parties and voters. By November 1998, however, the peace processes were mired in difficulties over the meaning of the Agreement. The fixation then which both Graham and McCracken display with the relationship between rhetoric and action echoes precisely divisions within Northern Ireland politics over the necessity for dialogue through which to enact a new dispensation rather than political posturing and demagoguery. Both plays served as timely reminders of the consequences of the failure of talking and the possibilities which meaningful dialogue might bring as regards a political settlement.

This relates closely to the second characteristic of the contexts in which both plays were staged: individual self-sacrifice in pursuit of political aims. Self-sacrifice is deeply embedded within the political cultures of Northern Ireland as a result of the longevity of the violent struggles here. It is perhaps this longevity and the internecine aspects of the violence which distinguishes attitudes towards dying for the cause from the glorification of military deaths in other societies. The tradition of violent resistance to the British presence

Figure 4. *Observe the Sons of Ulster Marching Towards the Somme* by Frank McGuinness, Lyric Theatre, Belfast. Photographer: Chris Hill

in Ireland has promoted its own history of martyrdom (Harris 1988; Kearney 1997), whilst the blood-sacrifice of the 36th Ulster Division at the Battle of the Somme in 1916 is deeply embedded within Ulster unionist ideology as both an historical mark of fidelity of the Ulster Protestant people to their British identity and a symbol to be honoured by successive generations. Murray suggests that Frank McGuinness's *Observe the Sons of Ulster Marching Towards the Somme* 'illustrates the death-wish inherent in the Unionist mentality in the glorious year of 1916' (1988: 286–7). In each case the actual life and death of the individuals are transformed into symbols of the wider cause for which they have been sacrificed. Harris locates this passage by which the individual is transformed by martyrdom within a process of 'victimage' which she suggests is a 'pervasive element in Irish political life as well as in Irish theatre' (1988: 252). However, Kearney stresses that the Republican ideology of martyrdom is not

> some irrational reflex action. . . it is a highly structured and strategic method of combining contraries which secular reason keeps rigidly apart. The IRA's ideology is sacrificial to the degree that it invokes, explicitly or otherwise, a 'sacred' tradition of death and renewal which provides justi-fication for present acts of suffering by realigning them with recurring paradigms of the past and thus affording these acts a certain timeless and redemptive quality.
>
> (1985: 65–6)

This process is explored in each of the plays in different ways.

In *Dockers*, John Graham's engagement with words in lieu of action culmi-nates in his singing of 'The Red Flag' at the union meeting.[11] Graham chal-lenges the fragile unity which has been cemented within the committee on an issue of individual honour through the symbolic gesture of the song. In contin-uing despite warnings and the beating he receives eventually, Graham loses sight of the larger struggle in which he is supposedly engaged. His sole moti-vation for his action is 'I could never answer to my conscience if I lived out thirty years at the dock in silence' (2003: 36). He was reminded earlier by Buckets to 'Stick it out, kid, stick it out. The future depends on you. You wouldn't like to think that in twenty years time, things were just as bad for the dockers, just because you got fed-up and made a pig's arse of things' (2003: 41). Crucially, Graham mistakes the assertion of his individual integrity for an action that might lead to class solidarity and structural change. It is Graham's inability to turn the world to fit the ideals of his words which leads him to the symbolic but futile gesture of the song. He entertains the beating 'as a form of martyrdom or tragic sacrifice which consecrates the ideal of principled working-class solidarity while simultaneously acknowledging the sorry gap between that high *ideal* and the compromised mundane reality'

(Cleary 1999: 512). Whilst the entrance of Theresa into the bar to demonstrate her support for her husband and to assert that his resolve is undiminished appears to be an endorsement of Graham's position, this is not unproblematic. True, Theresa's lines fit with Harris's argument that it is the actual sacrifice which redeems all previous faults. However, the audience has to balance these out with both the beating itself and the remainder of the scene after Theresa leaves. The beating (as with *The Interrogation of Ambrose Fogarty* discussed in Chapter 2) is brutal and disproportionate to Graham's actions. Nevertheless, his continuing with his gesture is itself out of place given the ferocity of the reaction meted out to him. Moreover, the conclusions reached by the other figures on the scene when Theresa leaves demonstrate the futility of his actions. His political epitaph is performed by Buckets in removing the union photograph which had previously symbolised hope. Graham is doomed to failure because he did not heed Buckets's earlier advice about playing the long game.

This reading of the scene as a rejection of the martyr paradigm as a means of defending working-class interests was not, however, shared by either Lynch's intentions or by reviews of the first production. Lynch himself sees it as a demonstration of what were then his own beliefs in radical socialist politics in which such a grand gesture might precipitate a working-class revolution in the traditions of James Connolly and Che Guevara.[12] Notably, Lynch adopts a much more critical perspective on the self-sacrifice of the hunger strikers in his later play *Minstrel Boys* (1985). The character of John Graham arose from Lynch's own experience of idealistic young men who had been beaten down by the system at the docks, and the play was intended as a tribute to what Lynch viewed as their heroism. Contemporary critics responded to this: the *Belfast Telegraph* reviewer described Graham as a young idealist, trying 'to improve working conditions for his older lackadaisical and more pragmatic colleagues' (O'Brien 1981: 13). This sense of a system crushing the good (rather than the good choosing the wrong weapon) was enhanced by the casting of Oliver Maguire in the role of John Graham. According to Judith Rosenfield, he played the role with 'a quiet sincerity, rarely raising his voice even in anger and always believing that in years to come there will be a better work structure' (1981: 4).[13] The *Irish Times* review commented that 'Oliver Maguire brings to the role of John Graham a convincing earnestness overlaid by a calm assurance. His is not the doctrinaire approach, for all his commitment, for Lynch has cleverly allotted him a fair share of humour and shows him in his domestic as well as his work environment' (R. Rosenfield 1981: 8). Even the comments by the *Sunday News* reviewer that 'Oliver Maguire as John Graham looked more like a squire and spoke too well by half, and imparted an impression of being extremely well-fed' did not detract from her view that the audience saw 'how soul-destroying, divisive and demeaning such a system is' (McQuaid 1981: 10). Harris's view that 'martyrdom has become an Irish cultural root paradigm' (1988: 255) appears to be borne out by such reviews which laud the fact that 'in plays with strongly socialist viewpoints, the martyrs seem to recognise that their sacrifice is for the greater good, and they approach their role with courage and fortitude' (ibid.: 266).

Parker's McCracken is in a position to identify the futility of his actions retrospectively, and yet he toys incessantly with the prospect of the transformation which he is aware his death might bring him. Despite Mary's constant appeals that he refrain from the talking which invokes the ghosts that haunt him, McCracken persists in raising the dead. Mary asks him, 'So, you actually want to be hung, is that it?' (1989: 15) and he envies the child that sleeps 'dead to the world' (ibid.). He realises that 'All I saw was my own life, as a forfeit, willingly offered' (1989: 28). Like Graham, therefore, he supposed that his own self-sacrifice might itself be the spur for the radical change he was trying to bring about. It is in realising that his leadership not only failed to accomplish his dreams, but led to the deaths of countless others, that his disillusionment grows. Death seems to offer a welcome relief from responsibility for this slaughter, which he can no longer see as heroic or ennobling. Thus it is that his recollection of the taking of the oath of the United Irishmen at the end of Act One is consummated with the entrance of the Phantom Bride, the figure of death who haunts the unfinished cottage.

The pervasive view (particularly within republican traditions) that martyrdom in the name of the cause is justified as an honourable weapon of war, used as a last resort when dialogue is impossible, is therefore being interrogated in both productions. *Northern Star* makes specific reference to the hunger strikers in Act Two when McCracken, imprisoned in Kilmainham Jail, dons the emblematic blanket of the protest. Graham's decision to continue his gesture when he recognises the failure of his rhetoric, and McCracken's embrace of death as the ultimate resort mirrored the processes through which the republican prisoners in the H-Blocks had gone in the first hunger strike, and which would ultimately lead to the deaths of ten of their number when the strikes were resumed. Those ten men starved themselves to death for the right to name themselves political prisoners, to define their struggle in specific ways. Although the British government later granted most of the concessions demanded by the strikers, it reserved to itself the authority to make its narrative of the conflict the reality.

Thus, at moments where language and the act of speaking were crucial to the development of alternatives to violence, both plays explored the powers and limitations of words to (re) construct reality. By juxtaposing the rhetorical prowess of the central characters with their ultimate physical abjection, these productions suggested that the price of not 'putting the right words in the right order' would continue to be exacted in the death and destruction of the citizens of Belfast whom McCracken had sought to address two hundred years previously.

5
Utopian Myths

MARIAN: We have committed sacrilege enough on life, in this place, in
these times. We don't just owe it to ourselves, we owe it to our
dead too. . . our innocent dead. They're not our masters, they're
only our creditors, for the life they never knew. We owe them at
least that—the fullest life for which they could ever have hoped,
we carry those ghosts within us, to betray those hopes is the real
sin against the christ, and I for one cannot commit it one day
longer.

(Stewart Parker, 1989, *Pentecost*, 208)

In his discussion of the history play in Irish drama, Murray includes the category of myth, suggesting that 'in Ireland history tends always towards myth,
for what shapes political attitudes are the versions and images of the past
standing as symbols rather than as factual records of experience' (1988: 273).
Thus, I want to follow the discussion of the theatrical representation of history
in Chapters 3 and 4 by focusing now on the use of myth in dramatic representations of the Troubles.

Myth has a number of related characteristics. Primarily, myths operate
within an imaginary where the values and beliefs associated with a particular
communal identity are held as part of a symbolic order through which the
world is comprehended. There may be considerable asymmetry in the ways
in which an ostensibly communal mythology is operative within the lived
experience of individuals (such as Christian mythology within largely secular
Western societies), particularly where myths from one context or culture may
be known to, shared by or adapted alongside indigenous myths. Thus, mythological values may contradict one another, or exert a variable influence on
how people live their lives, from individual to individual and from time to
time. Myth may operate at the level of the unconscious, remaining uninter-
rogated but no less powerful or compelling in its logic. Myth may take a particular narrative form such that the identity of the community in the here and
now is expressed and justified by relationships within a story or collection of
stories. These narratives take on a performative dimension when expressed
in ritualistic re-enactment through which communal identity may be
mobilised.

Myth has two crucial functions in relation to groups or communities: maintaining or developing collective identity. According to Kearney, these two aspects may be considered to be in tension, which he characterises in the contradictions between ideological and utopian myths:

> Ideology refers to that complex of myths and images which serve to maintain the status quo; utopia refers to the deployment of myths and images to challenge and transform the status quo. Utopia can accordingly be equated with that unconquered power of imagination, that surplus of symbolic desire which resists the closure of ideology. Utopia has to remain critical, lest it congeal into a new ideology subordinating the catalysing power of dream to the literal demands of propaganda.
>
> (1997: 123)

Given this tension, myth would appear a fruitful area through which playwrights might seek to represent a state in crisis, inviting an imaginative response to the ideologies provoking conflict within the society at large. Fintan O'Toole noted in an article on the staging of Derek Mahon's *High Time* and Tom Paulin's *The Riot Act* (1984) that, 'The area where myths and modern realities meet is the territory Field Day has staked out for itself' (1984a: 16). The company staged two of the plays which will be discussed later in this chapter. Northern Irish society is replete with myths, some particular to specific communities of identity, others more general across the society. Many of these have arisen in relation to Ireland's colonial relationship to Britain (such as the loyalist siege myth or the republican myth of martyrdom). These may be considered to be ideological myths and much of the rest of this book explores their dimensions in dramatic representation. What is of particular interest within this chapter is the use of myth for utopian purposes. Kearney argues that

> Utopian myth is thus predicated upon an operation of estrangement. It alienates us from the inherited state of affairs and engages in the imagining of an alternative community, other ways of seeing and existing. This commitment to radical otherness sometimes produces an experience of 'uncanniness'. While mythology generally provides us with what is most familiar, utopian myth re-presents stories in an unfamiliar guise, with a twist in the tail, a shock of alterity at the heart of the habitual.
>
> (1997: 123)

This utopian use of myth is particularly apparent in the appropriation by dramatists of mythic narratives which have arisen outside of the immediate circumstances of the conflict. In this sense, one specific dimension of myth is more prominent than the others outlined above: its narrative form. In this dimension, myth has become a source story rather than an encapsulation of a fundamental belief. These mythic narratives are not necessarily shared widely and may be considered to be at most residual within society. Notwithstanding this, such stories may be recognised as expressing something fundamental about human experience or relationships. Morrison declares, for example, that

> Classics escape the prison of time. Whichever their era, they belong to every other era. People talk of 'contemporary classics' but the phrase is tautologous: classics are contemporary by definition. The bad director of an ancient Greek tragedy batters us with parallels to the present day; the good director lets the echoes reverberate for themselves. The classic doesn't have a sell-by date. If it did, it wouldn't be a classic.
>
> (2003: online)

Irrespective of this, the distance which mythic stories have from immediate circumstances lends itself to a utopian deployment, causing a reassessment of both the immediate context and the source myths themselves. The three examples of such use of myth which will be discussed in this chapter are: Greek in Tom Paulin's *The Riot Act*; Christian in Stewart Parker's *Pentecost*; and Irish in Big Telly's *The Pursuit of Diarmuid and Gráinne* (1999). In these examples the mythic originals function less as an operational belief system or structuring force within contemporary reality than as a metaphor for that reality, through which to expose aspects of it that are otherwise hidden or rendered impenetrable by familiarity.

The Plays in Context

Tom Paulin's adaptation of Sophocles' *Antigone* is one of many examples of Irish dramatists turning to ancient Greek sources.[1] 1984 was particularly notable for three stage versions of the Antigone myth: by Paulin, Aidan Carl Matthews and Brendan Kennelly. Pat Murphy's film *Anne Devlin* was to be the fourth version of the year. Later Irish adaptations were also undertaken by Conall Morrison for Storytellers Theatre Company in 2003 and Seamus Heaney for the Abbey in 2004. A number of displacements have been enacted in these uses of Greek myth: not only have the source stories been adapted by the Greek dramatists, but the Irish versions have been themselves predominantly adaptations from existing English versions of the Greek originals, rather than new translations.

The relationship between contemporary Ireland and ancient Athenian culture which may explain this fascination with Greek tragedy is complex. It owes something to the positioning of Irish culture in relation to British imperialism. Kiberd notes the prevalence of Classical references in bardic poetry and suggests that, in the period following the outlawing of the bardic schools in 1600, 'Analogies drawn by writers with ancient Greece often carried just the same sort of subversive implication to be later found by township audiences of Athol Fugard's plays' (2002: viii). It has been suggested too that the Irish invocation of Greek culture has been a measure of resistance to constructions of the Irish as barbaric within British imperial discourses (M. McDonald 2000; Kiberd 2002). Moreover the adoption of Roman culture as a model by the British empire provoked Irish constructions of Irishness as a more ancient culture in a relationship analogous with that of Greece to Rome in antiquity. In Friel's *Translations*, much is made of this by the figure of Hugh O'Donnell, suggesting a direct link between Ireland and the Classical world which the English do not enjoy, and at one stage drawing a parallel between Ireland as Carthage and England as Rome.

There are aspects too of the source plays and their contexts which might attract contemporary writers. Athenian theatre was a place of public debate on issues of politics, religion and ethics. Walton has suggested that Irish theatre offers the same arena for its society: 'Ireland has the last English-speaking contemporary drama that still sees the theatre as the natural place to juggle ideas' (2002: 8). Marianne McDonald similarly notes that 'Greek tragedy with its emphasis on ethics also appealed to the Irish for religious as well as political reasons' (2002: 40). The Greek tragedians' concern with the relationship between personal morality and public duty, focused often on conflict within families, has resonances too with Irish history and the contemporary Northern Irish conflict in particular. Moreover, Walton notes that the oral source of the myth narratives offers a malleability which is attractive to writers wishing to address a contemporary situation (2002: 8).[2]

The Riot Act was Paulin's first play, although he was to go on to write *The Hillsborough Script: A Dramatic Satire, Seize the Fire: A Version of Aeschylus's Prometheus Bound* and the radio drama *All the Way to the Empire Room* (BBC 1994). The play was revived to critical acclaim as part of a season of Greek tragedies at London's Gate Theatre in 2003. Born in Yorkshire to an English father and Northern Irish mother, from the age of four Paulin was brought up within the Protestant Unionist community in Belfast.[3] However, while his maternal grandparents were staunchly Ulster British, in time Paulin's own politics leaned towards a socialism imbued with a radical Presbyterianism sensibility. He left Northern Ireland to read English at Hull and Oxford, and at the time of the production was lecturing at the University of Nottingham. His sense of identity was transformed further by his marriage to an Indian. Paulin's first publication in 1975 was a critical study of Thomas Hardy, and his first collection of poetry, *A State of Justice*, was published in 1977 and was awarded a Somerset Maugham Award. This first volume marked an engagement with the Troubles in Northern Ireland which would recur in much of his writing. As a director of Field Day Theatre Company from 1980 he contributed to its print output as essayist, poet, playwright and editor. His concern with the relationships between ethics, politics and culture has continued in his own creative work and in his critical works.

The Riot Act was the result of an approach by Stephen Rea in January 1984 to write a version of *Antigone* for Field Day while Paulin was teaching at the University of Virginia. According to his own account, he completed the script within three months (Paulin 2002). Paulin had already come to the play as a sixth former through a modern Greek film version and Bradley's essay 'Hegel's Theory of Tragedy', but it was the writing of Connor Cruise O'Brien which focused for him the play's possible relationship to Northern Ireland (Paulin 2003).[4] Cruise O'Brien had compared the Antigone story to the Northern Irish situation, suggesting that like Antigone, the civil rights movement generally, and in the person of Bernadette Devlin specifically, had brought on itself the troubles which resulted from its protests. According to Paulin 'He misinterpreted the play, and in doing a version of it I set out to try and prove him wrong again' (2002: 167).

The history of Field Day has been well documented elsewhere (Richtarik 1995; M.W. Harris 1995, for example) so I will touch only briefly on it here. The company developed from the relationship between Stephen Rea and Brian Friel who had first met when Rea was playing Skinner in a production of *The Freedom of the City* at London's Royal Court (O'Toole 1984b). When Rea discovered that funding could be made available by the Arts Council of Northern Ireland (Rea and Pelletier 2000) to produce new work he approached Friel. The result was Field Day's first play in 1980, *Translations*, and that initial production established a number of characteristics of the company's subsequent work. One key decision was to premiere the work in Derry and then to tour across Ireland. Both aspects were the result of a conscious political decision-making. Premiering the work in Derry's Guildhall was intended as a means to reclaim the city from its history of unionist domination:

> Using the Guildhall was important, it had a huge symbolic value because it was the Unionist headquarters and we were doing this play about identity, language and domination. It was important also because of Derry being a city which had been denied so much. . . Derry had been the focus for the Civil Rights movement and as John Hume said, Derry actually reflected the demographics of Ireland as a whole in term of the number of Catholics and Protestants.
>
> (Rea and Pelletier 2000: 54)

Friel himself had noted the symbolic importance of the Guildhall in *The Freedom of the City*, where the justification for the killing of the protesters refers to their desecration of the Mayor's Parlour, and where the protesters can only share in the symbolic power of the city council in a transgressive charade in which they don the robes of the aldermen.

Touring across the whole island was likewise a political choice: 'we were northern but we belonged to the whole country, whatever we were talking about we wanted to address the whole country' (Rea and Pelletier 2000: 52). Touring also represented Rea's own vision of himself in 'a romantic throw-back to the fit-up days' (O'Toole 1984b: 16). The itinerary for these tours depended on the invitations which the company received, but they are marked by their reach to areas and communities with little tradition of receiving professional theatre.[5] It was as if the company had taken on the function of a national theatre in representing the nation to itself, in contrast to Rea's view of the Abbey as a reflection of 'The Twenty-Six County Fine Gael State' (ibid.: 16). The subject matter of *Translations*, the decimation of the Irish-language community during the imperial enterprise of mapping Ireland, like-wise located the company at the intersection of culture and politics, a locus which would be expanded once a Board of Directors was selected following the success of the production.[6] Spurred by Seamus Deane, the company spread beyond its theatrical focus to become a crucible for debates on the relationship between culture and society. These debates were made public through the company's productions and its publications. Although the Board was nominally mixed in terms of the community of origin of its members, it became the target of recurrent criticism of a narrow nationalist cultural agenda (Longley 1984; Richards 1991; McIlroy 1998: 12–13). The criticism was able to point for evidence to the rejection of two plays by the company which dealt with alternative perspectives on Northern Ireland: David Rudkin's *The Saxon Shore* in 1983 and Frank McGuinness's *Observe the Sons of Ulster Marching Towards the Somme* in 1985. In each case, the company's ostensible reasons for the rejection of the work did not stand up to close scrutiny: particularly in the case of Rudkin who had been commissioned by the company (Richards 1991).

One core concept that was developed was that of the 'fifth province' which originated with Richard Kearney in the editorial of the first edition of *The Crane Bag* (1977). Kearney wrote later that the fifth province 'is not a fixed point or centralized power. . . We are not speaking of a power of political possession but of a power of mind. The fifth province can be imagined and reimagined; but it cannot be occupied. In the fifth province, it is always a question of thinking *otherwise*' (1997: 100). Friel suggested that it was 'a province of the mind through which we hope to devise another way of looking at Ireland, or another possible Ireland, and this really is the pursuit of this company' (Quilligan 1984: 10).

The use of a Greek myth, then, as the source for its production is one way of rethinking conceptions of Ireland. The play is set in the aftermath of a civil war in the city-state of Thebes. Polynices has raised an army against the city while his brother, Eteocles, has fought to defend it. Both brothers are killed but Creon, their uncle, issues an edict that while Eteocles be given a hero's funeral, the body of Polynices is to be denied a burial, to be left to the elements. This contravenes the customs and laws regarding burial. Antigone, sister to the brothers, disobeys Creon's edict and sprinkles dust on the body. Some of the central debates of Paulin's version are in the discussion between Antigone and her sister Ismene over her actions. Creon commands that Antigone be walled up in a cave, despite the interventions of his own son Haemon, Antigone's betrothed, and the blind prophet Tiresias. Although Creon eventually relents, it is too late to save Antigone who has taken her own life, prompting the suicides of both Haemon and subsequently Creon's wife Eurydice.

Rea characterised the production as essentially political: 'There is a sense in Antigone that if you respond to a fixed position by a Government, in this case Creon, your response is in some way evil or subversive; she is unable to do anything else but to react in this way because the gauntlet has been thrown down. This play applies not only to Ireland but has a universal message' (Quilligan 1984: 10). Paulin argued that 'I didn't want it to be a straightforward conflict between state (bad) and individual (good), nor simply between Unionism and Nationalism. I wanted Ismene to argue back at her sister' (2003: online). However, Murray criticised the production suggesting that it was 'necessarily political, but surprisingly tentative in its application to Northern Ireland, if it could be said to have any real application at all' (1988: 285–6). This was despite the fact that Paulin's adaptation was distinctive in using a recognisable Northern Ireland vernacular, albeit in verse form.[7]

With a cast of eight, the production opened at Derry's Guildhall in September 1984 before touring across Ireland, as part of a double bill with Derek Mahon's *High Time*, a comedy after Molière's *The School for Husbands*. Antigone was played by Veronica Quilligan; Creon by Rea; Tiresias by Des McAleer; with Ciaran Hinds in the role of the Chorus Leader.[8] The production process had been troubled, with both the original director and set designer leaving early. Stephen Rea, already cast as Creon, took over as director and the final set design was by Brien Vahey. Paulin provided the inspiration for the revised set design, 'a disused Presbyterian church. It was a perfect, neo-classical meeting house' (2002: 168). What emerged eventually was a bare stage with the action played 'in stern greys and silvers, with a claustrophobic stage-set intensifying the sense of inescapable tragedy' (Deane 2002: 156). The production's reception was mixed at best. While it made for a contrast with the highly physical comedy of *High Times*, few reviewers of the original production felt that the play achieved the kind of dynamic conflict contained within Sophocles's original. Fintan O'Toole's *Sunday Tribune* review argued that '*Antigone* works as a play because we are also interested in Creon as a man, concerned with his dilemma and the way he tries to cope with it. Sophocles' Creon is a tragic hero as well as a villain. By satirising him from the start, the drama of his conflict with Antigone is rendered impossible'(1984a: 16). David Nowlan's *Irish Times* review concurred that the problem was a lack of emotional engagement from Rea as Creon: 'Mr Rea's Creon starts well, a cynical businessman turned rigid ruler, but fails to break emotionally under the weight of tragedy' (1984a: 12). Undoubtedly the responsibility on Rea to take two parts and direct one of the productions on the tour had a large influence on his playing of the role.

Rea was to receive a much better reception for his role in Stewart Parker's *Pentecost*, three years later. While *The Riot Act* was one of a number of versions of Greek myth, *Pentecost* was one of the few Troubles dramas to draw directly on a Christian myth other than the sacrifice of Jesus. Cleary, for example, traces the use of the crucifixion narrative within St John Ervine's *Mixed Marriage* (1911), Thompson's *Over the Bridge* and Paulin's *The Riot Act* in which 'the life of one good man, then, is offered up equally as an example to and an indictment against, and perhaps an act of atonement for, the rest' (1999: 513). The Pentecost story, rather than focusing on self-sacrifice, stands for the renewal of hope at the darkest hour when the apostles are cowering in fear after the crucifixion. The Holy Spirit is visited upon them, empowering them to overcome their fear and enabling them to proclaim the news of the resurrection in words which the diverse peoples of Jerusalem can understand. In using this narrative, *Pentecost* differs from the other two plays discussed here in that the source narrative may have functioned, for at least some of its audience, within an active belief system.

Parker's adaptation of the Pentecost narrative is set appropriately during the Ulster Workers' Council Strike of May 1974, an event mounted as an act of loyalist resistance to the then Sunningdale Agreement. That agreement made provision for a power-sharing devolved government for Northern Ireland and the creation of mechanisms for cross-border co-operation. By closing down the power stations and controlling access to and through the province with blockades and barricades, loyalist paramilitaries demonstrated the power of militant loyalism to control Northern Ireland, outwith the authority of its elected political representatives. Moreover, according to McKittrick and McVea, 'whatever the initial reactions of the Protestant middle class to an exercise so clearly enforced by paramilitaries, many of its members came to endorse the strike' (2001: 105). Neither the police nor the army took any concerted action to maintain the rule of law or to bring the strike to an end lest they provoke a second front in their battle against terrorism (Dixon 2001). The strike achieved its aim in bringing down the power-sharing executive and terminating the agreement, ending all hope of a negotiated political settlement to the conflict for over another decade.

While set thirteen years previously, Parker explained that the play 'is really about now, about the process started then which is continued by the Anglo-

Irish Agreement. That was the beginnings of the serious rift between the loyalists and the English. The beginning of the feeling of rejection on their part, and the hurt—the feeling of being lost' (Purcell 1987: 1). The Anglo-Irish Agreement had been signed by the British and Irish governments in November 1985, as a means of addressing the 'threat of Sinn Fein to security and political stability' (Dixon 2001: 191) and allowing some acknowledgement of the interest of the Irish government in Northern Ireland. The principal points of the Agreement were that any changes to the status of Northern Ireland would require the consent of a majority of the people of Northern Ireland; that the two governments would meet regularly at an Intergovernmental Conference in which the Irish government would be allowed to represent Northern Irish nationalist interests; that there would be cross-border co-operation in areas of security, economics, social and cultural matters; and that an International Fund for Ireland would 'promote economic and social advance and encourage contact, dialogue and reconciliation throughout Ireland' (ibid.: 197). Importantly for the context of *Pentecost*, these provisions echoed closely the outline of the Sunningdale Agreement. Just as in 1974, the provisions of the Anglo-Irish Agreement were met with hostility by the unionist population, believing that despite her staunch rhetoric against terrorism, Margaret Thatcher was continuing the process of preparing for Britain's eventual withdrawal from Northern Ireland. Around one-quarter of the total one million unionist population took to the streets to demonstrate against the Agreement on 23 November (ibid.: 205), the first of what would be a prolonged series of protests both peaceful and violent. In March 1986 a loyalist strike was called against the Agreement and was marked by violence against the RUC, a symptom of the increasing estrangement between the loyalist population and the state.

The first production of the play was staged by Field Day under the direction of Patrick Mason. It opened on 23 September 1987 at the Guildhall in Derry to a capacity audience of more than four hundred and went on to win the Harvey's Award for the Play of the Year.[9] Its tour to twenty-five different venues across Ireland, including the Dublin Theatre Festival comprised sixty-six performances over twelve weeks. Field Day was, at least on ideological grounds, the most obvious company to stage a Parker play. Friel's belief that if a new vision of society is to mean anything 'then it must first be "articulated, spoken, written, painted, sung" and then perhaps the definition can be forged by legislators and politicians' (Quilligan 1984: 10) resonates with Parker's own views on the role of the playwright in society.[10]

The play is set in a terraced house on Hope Street in East Belfast where four refugees from the 1974 strike are trapped together: Marian who has inherited the house and is still grieving for the death of her child; Lenny Harrigan, the unemployed trombonist, who is separated from Marian but not divorced from her; trendy Peter, returning from London full of smart observations about the city he has left; and Ruth, the victim of violence at the hands of her policeman husband whom she continues to excuse. A fifth presence inhabits the house too, the ghost of the former owner, the recently dead Lily Matthews, a staunchly Protestant widow.[11] Born at the turn of the century, Lily had lived in the house since her marriage to Alfie in 1918 and the story of her life there is central to the play. Over the course of a single night together the characters explore their past and how they can come to terms with it and each other.

The set by Bunny Christie was a recreation of a typical East Belfast 'two-up, two-down' terrace house, with the main action set in the dark back parlour, its walls lined with prints from the Great War and bible texts. Of the three plays in his triptych, this is the most domestic and intimate of Parker's settings. It allows a concentration of the powerful public forces beyond the front door within the human dimensions of the inter-relationships between the characters. The attention paid to period detail in the set was matched by Parker's keen ear for the nuances of Belfast speech and eye for the behaviour of the characters he sets up. This sense of authenticity was continued in the direction and playing, recognised by the reviews of the performances commending the restraint in the playing and the tautness in the direction. Fintan O'Toole noted that 'The performances are of a very high calibre' (1987: 35). Cleary indicts the model which this play demonstrates in establishing an inside domestic world which is threatened by pressures outside: 'This Manichean construction of stage space, which pits a small and vulnerable "inside" community against a hostile and cacophonous horde "outside," encourages a paranoid and reactionary conception of the world, one that rests on a division of humanity between the civilized few and the brute multitude' (1999: 520). This effect is heightened also by the device of having middle-class characters displace the working-class Lily, thereby marginalising her concerns and attitudes and those of her class.

It would be hard to conceive of a setting less constrained by the domestic setting than Big Telly's *The Pursuit of Diarmuid and Gráinne*, with its epic scope and setting which ranges across ancient Ireland. The use of Celtic mythology within Northern Irish theatre may at first glance appear unsurprising; an inevitable part of the Irish nationalist enterprise. Such a view requires revision, however, for two principal reasons. The first is that the initial appropriation of Celtic mythology by the Irish Literary Renaissance movement of the late nineteenth century was not of itself a means of creating a politically, religiously and ethnically exclusive communal identity. According to Kearney, 'Yeats sought in myth an idealized Celtic paganism pre-existing the colonial rupture of Ireland into sectarian denominations' (Kearney 1997: 113).[12] Thus, the invocation of Celtic mythology may itself be a strategy to locate the dramatic action in a place where contemporary divisions do not resonate, or at least do not resonate in the same ways.[13] The

Figure 5. *The Pursuit of Diarmuid and Gráinne* by Zoe Seaton, Big Telly
Theatre Company, Riverside Theatre, Coleraine.

second reason concerns the generation of a body of thought within the loyalist community that Celtic mythology has as much to offer that culture as it may offer to Irish nationalists. McAuley (1991), for example, establishes the link between the development of the ideology of the UDA and this reclamation of Celtic mythology based on the works of Adamson:

> Adamson argues that the 'Cruithin', the original inhabitants of Ireland, were driven north by invading Gaels and their last foothold in Ireland was in what is now Antrim and Down. Many, however, fled to Scotland, strengthening the historical link between the Scottish and Irish popula-tions. The Plantation then can be seen as a 'homecoming'.
>   This interpretation of history has been associated with the adoption of a number of symbols and hero figures from Irish history and pre-history which previously had been seen as the property of Irish Republicanism. Of particular importance are the events of the Táin Bó Cuailigne which forms the centre-piece of the eighth-century Ulster cycle of heroic tales.
>   (McAuley 1991: 55)[14]

Thus, it may be seen that the use of a Celtic narrative can be far from straight-forward. On the one hand, Celtic myths would appear to be detached from the explanatory basis of everyday life, lost as a scheme of identification. On the other, they have become a terrain itself contested as a means of authen-ticating contemporary claims for rights. In this context, the use of Celtic myths by Big Telly Theatre Company represents an intervention in cultural politics with resonances unavailable to versions and adaptations in other situ-ations and not necessarily intended by the company.

Big Telly was founded in June 1987 by Zoe Seaton and Jill Holmes who, though both from Northern Ireland, met as students at the University of Kent.[15] Like many drama graduates they formed the company as a means of creating opportunities for themselves and they returned to work in Northern Ireland where they identified an opening for a 'theatrically inventive' touring theatre company.[16] The company's base on the north coast was established when they were offered office and rehearsal space at Flowerfield Arts Centre in Portstewart. In their first year they mounted nine productions, ranging from Willy Russell's *Educating Rita* to Dario Fo's and Franca Rame's one-woman shows, a choice dictated by economics rather than any specific ideo-logical bent. The company devised and toured its first play *Onions Make You Cry* across Ireland. Following this, they were commissioned by ACNI to produce *Crumbs* as part of events to commemorate the bi-centenary of the French Revolution. This was followed by a play for children, *Little Lucy's Magic Box* and then a specially revised version of John Godber's *Teechers*.[17] Having secured revenue funding from ACNI in 1992, the company has subsequently produced two shows annually. Although their work has continued to be as eclectic as these early productions in its subject matter, much of it devised, a company style emerged through it: resolutely non-naturalistic, energetic and physical. Certainly the company's work, for children and for adults, has paid close attention to the visual dimensions of performance, drawing on forms of physical theatre and dance, as well as being marked by the use of a musical soundtrack as a core part of the productions. Importantly also, the company has always endeavoured to tour across the island of Ireland using and helping to establish a burgeoning network of small and mid-scale venues. Although founded and run by women, the company has never espoused a particular feminist perspective, with its ideological outlook extending only as far as 'the performance of non-racist, non-sexist work with a distinctly local emphasis' (Meany 1993: 34).[18] To the extent that the company has an ideology, it is to do with the creation of work which engages with its audience in the moment of live performance and giving access to that experience to as wide an audience as possible. Its oeuvre has also been marked by collaborations with a range of creative contributors, including musicians, composers, choreographers and designers, producing work which has been stylistically eclectic and innovative in a theatrical context still largely dominated by script-based and naturalistic performance.

The decision to stage versions of Celtic mythology was in keeping with the characteristics of its previous work. The decision to explore Celtic mythology was largely motivated by a need to find an interesting story on which to work with a narrative sufficiently open to theatrical invention and with some relevance to the Irish touring context. Seaton had been impressed by the Galway-based Macnas's large-scale version of *The Tain* (1992) and selected the first narrative from the Ulster Cycle of myths, the legend of Cu Chulainn, which was created by Seaton herself, the musician John Leslie and Jools Beech as choreographer. With a cast of six, the production toured across Ireland in the winter of 1995. It was well-received for its invention, energy and visual impact. Reviewers were less prepared to note the relationship between the play and its context, although Jocelyn Clarke (1995) suggested that 'Cu Chulainn seeks allegorical parallels between the conflict of tribal and individual loyalty'. Robin Greer noted that 'The story has been enjoying a revival of late. It is celebrated in exhibition at Armagh's Navan Fort—the place of the tale's origin—in murals on the Newtownards Road and in animation by the young artists of Londonderry. It is something it seems everyone wants to claim ownership of' (1995: 14).

The company's second production of a Celtic myth was *The Pursuit of Diarmuid and Gráinne* in 1999.[19] The myth was staged using only four actors, augmented by the use of puppetry and masks. Debra Salem provided an electronic dance beat soundtrack and the stage was dominated by a geodesic dome climbing-frame. The source legend concerns the beautiful daughter of the high King of Ireland, Gráinne. She has been bequeathed in marriage to Finn

McCool, the leader of Ireland's warrior force, the Fianna, although he is much older.[20] This is a political arrangement in which the kingdom and its defenders are to be bound together through the match, despite Gráinne's personal objections to Finn. Diarmuid is one of Finn's most loyal, trusted and favoured soldiers, a man with whom Gráinne is secretly in love. By invoking the Fianna's heroic code, she induces him to help her to escape from Finn and together they flee his wrath for sixteen years. Finn dispatches his son Oisín to track the couple down. Oisín is torn between his loyalty to the Fianna and its future stability; his duty to his father; and his desire to protect Diarmuid from Finn's destructive revenge. Part of the epic is the completion of certain heroic tasks by Diarmuid, some of which are to allow their continued escape, some of which are set by Finn as a negotiation for their freedom. Diarmuid is able to demonstrate his prowess and nobility by meeting and overcoming these challenges. He tricks and kills three foreign sea-champions summoned by Finn to kill him. He bargains with the brothers of Morna to whom Finn has promised admission to the ranks of the Fianna in return for head of Diarmuid or a fistful of berries from the magic wood at Dubhros. Diarmuid kills the giant guarding the wood and gives the brothers the berries to give to Finn. When eventually Finn confronts Oisín over his aiding of Diarmuid and Gráinne, he challenges him to a game of chess, the outcome of which will decide Diarmuid's fate. Diarmuid helps Oisín by dropping berries on to the board from an overhanging tree to direct his moves. When Finn thinks that Oisín has betrayed him he kills him. In the aftermath of this death, Finn and Diarmuid are reconciled. Diarmuid sets out to kill a wild boar for a celebration feast, but is lethally wounded by the boar in the hunt. Since Finn has the power of healing, one sup of water from his hands will revive Diarmuid. Three times Finn struggles to give him a drink, failing to do so before it is too late.

This narrative is rich then with parallels to the contemporary situation in which three forms of loyalty contend with each other to dictate what it means to do the right thing: loyalty to the community (the stability of the Fianna and safeguarding Ireland); loyalty to an ideal (the Fianna law); and loyalty to the family (Finn and Oisín as father and son). The demands of each to be respected are infused with the possibility of violent retribution. Both Oisín and Diarmuid try to reconcile these demands but both die at the hands of Finn: the one by commission, the other by omission. In this, there are significant similarities with Gary Mitchell's exploration of the workings of loyalist paramilitaries gangs (see Chapter 6 and Chapter 8). Indeed, Passion Machine's version of the myth set it successfully in a gangland milieu, for example, although without the paramilitary structure or the political dimensions of the conflict in Northern Ireland. Even without such a transposition, in the Big Telly version, Gráinne, whose presence provokes the struggle between these forces, can easily be seen as a gendered embodiment of Ireland (see Chapter 6) so that the epic could become an allegory for the conflict. In such a reading the issue would be one in which Finn's capacity to forgive and to be reconciled with Diarmuid, despite the loss of both his wife and his son, poses a question to the audience to explore their own capacity for forgiveness leading to reconciliation with those who may have wronged them; a theme later explored in Michael Duke's *Revenge* (2004) for Tinderbox.

Such a reception of the performance was not Seaton's explicit intention and she has always been wary of using theatre for interventions in the politics of Northern Ireland. Certainly there were discussions with the cast about the ending of the play in which Finn takes possession of Gráinne, immediately after the death of Diarmuid and despite her obvious grief for him. Yet, as with many of the production decisions governing the performance, this ending emerged as a solution to the specific issue in performance, in this case, that of resolving the narrative. This pragmatic approach, governed by Seaton's interest as director in theatrical expression free from the restrictions of naturalism, was the underpinning principle of the production. Thus, for example, the climbing-frame set evolved as a means of demonstrating the travelling which Diarmuid and Gráinne undertake to escape the wrath of Finn, and served equally as a representation of the enchanted wood where the characters are able to engage in a kind of magical free fall. The financial restrictions on the cast size also motivated the use of puppets and masks. Such decisions emphasised a shift away from psychological characterisation and its associated dialogue in favour of a richly visual and sonic experience for the audience, in which the narrative receded in importance to be replaced by a sequence of highly theatrical moments which created their own emphases and rhythms. However, the diminished importance of the narrative had the effect of pushing the performance towards spectacle. It verged on becoming a display of theatrical invention and away from the central dialectic of the source story. A further dimension to this sense of spectacle came through the casting of the performance. The role of Gráinne was played by Briana Corrigan, who had returned to Northern Ireland having made her name as a singer with the band the Beautiful South. Cast as the most beautiful woman in Ireland, Corrigan was the focus of the company's pre-publicity posters and flyers and a recurrent story in newspaper previews. The effect was to put her sexually on display, despite attempts within the script to make her character a more feisty and active agent within the narrative than traditionally allowed for (see Chapter 6).

Discussion: Distance and Familiarity

The capacity of myth to be deployed as a means of distancing the audience from its present circumstances in order to encourage a reassessment of them has coincided with the concerns of playwrights to play a role in their society through their art. In the context of Northern Ireland, Ronan McDonald has described a pressure on playwrights to 'develop techniques of refraction. In other words, distancing strategies are often developed in drama that strives to present the Troubles and all its complexities in a fresh light' (2002: 233). However, a second factor must be present if the drama is to have any possibility of efficacy in the here and now: 'vitality'. Walton glosses vitality thus:

> It involves discovering a stage dynamic that allows objects to acquire resonance; that makes dialogue debate; that offers subtextual meaning, shared with, or, on occasions, exclusive to the audience; it means deciding whether the weight of a line in the original is better served by the same number of words in the receiving language, or more, or fewer.
>
> (2002: 30)

A tension exists then between the co-presence of estrangement and vitality. The successful maintenance of this tension, rather than its resolution, requires the audience to recognise in the handling of the mythic narrative the proximity of the myth to the contemporary circumstance and the distinctions between these circumstances, the current representation and the originating form. Kershaw suggests that the efficacy of performance resides in the provocation of a crisis within the dramatic action that through the authenticating conventions of the performance somehow establishes a 'more or less transparent relationship between the fictionality of performance. . . and the real world of the audience's socio-political experience outside theatre' (1996: 27). He notes also that 'the longer-term effects of a crisis of authenticating conventions will depend centrally on their success in engaging with the fundamental values of the audience' (ibid.).

In Big Telly's *The Pursuit of Diarmuid and Gráinne*, vitality can be discerned as a performance effect resulting from the highly energetic performance and its rhetorical conventions which emphasised its spectacular aesthetic. This aesthetic resisted the engagement with the stage figures as the kind of complex psychological characters which have predominated in Irish drama. Instead, a series of set-piece moments of theatrical effect were created in which the stage figure is only one of a multiplicity of stage elements, a mark of Seaton's pictorial style of directing. The adoption of such an aesthetic, while arousing visual and aural sensation, emphasised the distancing of the narrative source from the audience's personal experience. For example, there are few occasions on which to dwell on the violent events within the narrative as each new moment of spectacle follows hard on the previous. Indeed, while the deaths of Oisín and Diarmuid may be regarded as tragic, the other deaths are figured in melodramatic terms. Gould argues, for example, that in dramatic representations, 'one could point to violence and suffering by showing that it was clearly required—to make up for a wrong, for the public safety, or for the survival of freedom and democracy. That is, one could confine oneself to melodrama'

(1991: 3). Even in the case of Diarmuid, the focus shifts quickly to the effect of returning Gráinne to Finn. Analysis of the motivation, enactment or consequences of the violence was largely avoided beyond the exposition of the basic premises of the plot. This dramaturgical strategy established a clear distance between the political conflict and the performance of the myth. In his discussion of wrestling, Barthes drew attention to this dimension of spectacle in which the audience 'abandons itself to the primary virtue of the spectacle which is to abolish all motives and all consequences: what matters is not what it thinks but what it sees' (1972: 15).

Such distancing is also enhanced in the use of a myth which draws on esoteric knowledge or forms with which the audience is unfamiliar. This may be due to the conventions of the genre of performance or of the value systems of the source context. In *The Pursuit of Diarmuid and Gráinne*, the heroic code of the Fianna is referred to, for example, on a number of occasions, hardly something of which an audience would have a detailed knowledge. The role of Oisín as the guardian of the code is crucial nonetheless in demonstrating that Finn's desire for revenge has to be moderated by ethical principles which safeguard the security of the whole community. Likewise, as Antigone goes off to die in *The Riot Act*, Paulin retains references to ancient Greek mythology and cosmology with which the audience might have only passing acquaintance at best. As Marianne McDonald notes, 'These are names which are not familiar and many translators, including Kennelly, eliminate them. Other playwrights also eliminate the mythological details, perhaps considering them too foreign for the modern ear' (2002: 57). This raises questions about the nature of the knowledge which the audience must bring to understand the relationship between the source material and the contemporary performance. It is upon this that both distancing and vitality rest. Only by recognising the distinction between the original and the adaptation can the audience take on a *liminal* role somewhere between the real and the unreal. According to Kershaw, this connects to the ludic role of spectators which 'turns performance into a kind of ideological experiment in which the outcome has no necessary consequence for the audience. Paradoxically, this is the first condition needed for performance efficacy' (1996: 24).

This use of myth in performance as an 'ideological experiment' rests on the assumption that myths operate only as symbols: whatever resolution is proffered exists at only a symbolic level. According to Kearney: 'myths are concerned with wish fulfilment and reversal, with making possible at an imaginary level what is impossible in our real or empirical experience. . . In short, myth can serve as an ideological strategy for inventing symbolic solutions to problems of sovereignty which remain irresolvable at a socio-political level' (1997: 109). The use of myth functions to contain the performance within the rhetorical conventions of the drama, framing it off from the extra-theatrical world with which it seeks also to connect. This presents problems for the necessary vitality for which Walton argues. Fintan O'Toole identifies the contradiction between the authenticating and rhetorical conventions in *Pentecost* which lead to the containment of the performance from the extra-theatrical world: 'Having convinced us of the reality of these people and of the time and place in which they live, Parker then has to try to leap beyond realism into some kind of metaphor of transcendence. That leap has to be credible on the level of the real political world which he has delineated so sharply and it isn't' (1987: 35).

This is a particular problem for *Pentecost* due to the emphasis on authenticity in its setting and performance which constrains the capacity of that setting (and the characters within it) to yield to the power of the myth. O'Toole criticises Parker's solution to this difficulty, 'We have been led to expect some kind of apocalyptic deliverance at the end of the play. What we get is an evangelical sermon on the "Christ in ourselves" as the source of change. The problem is that this pentecostal image works only on the level of words. Change is evoked verbally, it doesn't happen on stage' (ibid.). This verbal change is better motivated by the choice of the source myth than O'Toole concedes. Pentecost is marked in the biblical account by the ability of the apostles to speak out the good news, having acquired the gift of tongues and lost their fear. It marks above all else the capacity of language to forge a renewed world, one in which speaking in new forms is a form of innovative action.

This capacity for speaking to be accepted as action raises issues for the performance of these plays. For example, O'Toole criticised *The Riot Act* on much the same basis as his criticism of *Pentecost*: 'There is little here besides talking heads and, however fine their talk, it is not enough in itself' (1984a). The criticism was shared by David Nowlan: 'We are told rather than made to feel, that Creon's state must fall because of the hates deep-rooted in it. We listen and nod, but do not weep' (1984a: 12). As *The Pursuit of Diarmuid and Gráinne* demonstrates, however, a more embodied mode of performance need not of itself produce the affective result which both critics identify as important in character-based drama. Indeed, the sparseness of the dialogue in that play is in marked contrast to the spectacular visual impact of the performance. Both critics of *The Riot Act*, and arguably Seaton as writer of *The Pursuit of Diarmuid and Gráinne*, underestimate the importance of words for Northern Irish audiences, an importance which has at least two dimensions. The first of these is an acute awareness of the powers of language to bring realities into existence (as has been discussed in Chapter 4). The second, which derives from this, is the acute attention which audiences in Northern Ireland demonstrate to the ways in which words are deployed. Thus, for example, a reviewer of the first night of *Pentecost* at the Guildhall noted that, 'When the Catholic characters spoke, you could feel people relax and breathe understandingly, as they listened to a language that they well understood. When the Protestant characters spoke, the concentration was palpable, with no one wanting to miss a word, particularly when religious belief was mentioned' (McCafferty 1987: 8). The reviewer for the *Independent* noted the same effect when the play went on tour, 'In Enniskillen last weekend the audience for Parker's Pentecost. . . was most remarkable for listening to the play. Afterwards, in the foyer, they discussed it with a vigour unimaginable in a London audience' (Renton 1987). This suggests that audiences in Northern Ireland are able to attend to language and consequently are quite willing to accept verbal resolutions on the stage. This capacity appears to be specifically conditioned by the political reality in which words count for so much. Whilst the work of Big Telly and other visually focused companies such as Kabosh may have developed an audience awareness of the dimensions of performance which are not driven by character or dialogue, it would appear also that they are working in a context in which words retain primacy.

The primacy of language need not rest in its representational capacity. In *Pentecost*, despite the realism of the form of the play until this point and its production mode, the final scene is resolved not in narrative terms, nor even in terms of any message in the dialogue; rather the resolution is sonic. If the dialogue is regarded at this point as an antiphonal arrangement rather than naturalistic speech, it may provoke both an alternative playing and reception. Peter has already invited Lenny to play his banjo and 'Give us a talking blues' (Parker 1989: 203). As a form of antiphony, the musicality of the dialogue rather than its meaning function comes to the fore. Listening to the grain of the voices jamming on the riff of renewal creates a structure of harmony which complements the message of 'the Christ within'.[21] This riff provokes and leads into Lenny's trombone-playing and Peter's banjo accompaniment. The effect is to create the experience of harmony and resolution, an effectively utopian moment in a different sense to that used by Kearney. Richard Dyer's discussion of entertainment and utopia notes that,

> Entertainment does not, however, present models of utopian worlds, as in the classic utopias of Thomas More, William Morris, et al. Rather the utopianism is contained in the feelings it embodies. It presents, head-on as it were, what utopia would feel like, rather than how it would be organized. It thus works at the level of sensibility, by which I mean an affective code that is characteristic of, and largely specific to, a given mode of cultural production.
>
> (1992: 18)

The audience experiences the sensation of communality towards which the performance has been moving through hearing the sounds of the human voices as part of the musical resolution. In this sense, the performance might be seen to have created a vitality with its audience to counterpoint the distancing of its governing mythic structure. Such a rendering of dialogue as a sonic experience is an assumed performance convention of ancient Greek tragedy. In his version of the *Oresteia*, for the National Theatre in London in 1981, Peter Hall commissioned a score from Harrison Birtwistle which accompanied Tony Harrison's dialogue throughout. In the case of *The Riot Act*, however, Paulin deliberately worked against this possibility in producing dialogue which was described as 'spare and staccato, seldom using three syllables where one would do' (Nowlan 1984a: 12). His linguistic restraint was tied to his concern with using Northern Irish vernacular, itself commended in a number of reviews of both the original production (Nowlan 1984a; O'Toole 1984a) and the revival under Alan Cox's direction in 2003 (Gardner 2003; Morrison 2003). It did not lend itself, however, to the experience of performance available within *Pentecost*.

Just as in the attempts to represent the violence on the streets directly which are discussed in Chapter 2, the use of myth in performance has to meet the dual demands of proximity and distance. These demands are complicated by the relationship of the audience to the myth and its acceptance of its applicability to its own context and vice versa. Vitality, the performative expression of proximity, need not be achieved however by a close matching of the stage representation to the current context. In the case of *The Riot Act*, the decision to use recognisable Northern Irish accents and the figuration of Antigone as an oppressed nationalist proved problematic in skewing the dramatic conflict at the heart of the play, despite Paulin's intentions. In the case of *The Pursuit of Diarmuid and Gráinne*, physical energy and dexterity, spectacular effect, and terse dialogue provided a literal physical vitality which nonetheless obscured the possible resonances of the play to its performative context. In *Pentecost*, it is not the recreation of a recognisable setting and authentic characterisation which make the play vital; rather, it is that the audience experiences a utopian sense of resolution in the moment of performance, even if this is not fully motivated by the plot or narrative. Thus, the deployment of specific performance strategies to produce a sense of vitality in the adaptation of myths has ensured that such adaptations have remained within the realm of symbolic representations, rather than arguments for social action.

6
Gendered Troubles

BETH: I'm getting married tomorrow, I'm moving from my mother's house
to Stephen's house. . . I've been my mother's daughter and now
I'm going to be Stephen's wife. . . I've never been just me.

(Christina Reid, 1997, *Tea in a China Cup*, 50)

One of the projects of this book has been to disrupt dominant representations of the Troubles, through and within which various political positions, narratives and identities are elided into simplified and obscuring discourses. Given this, an exploration of the intersections between representations of gender and the Troubles is in many ways an obvious topic, since dominant representations have tended to overlook the differential relationships of men and women to the conflict, or to situate such relationships within a narrow range of gendered stereotypes. As Rooney has noted, 'Women rarely receive a mention in the prodigious literature on Northern Ireland. . . They are either assumed to be included or they are invisible' (1997: 535). The approach here seeks to explore the ways in which dominant masculinist discourses have intersected with other discourses of identity and their political consequences in both the experience of the Troubles and the representation of such experience on the stage.[1] Such intersections have provoked divergent interpretations of both what the relationship between such discourses is in actuality and what it should be as resistant voices struggle to find articulation.

One example of the intersection of gender and nationalism is evident in colonial discourses, which have persisted in characterising British and Irish relations in gendered terms:

> In the nineteenth century. . . the Irish were racialized in two distinct ways, each strongly gendered. Masculine images were of uncontrolled subhumans incapable of self-government. Feminine images were of weakness requiring protection. Both representations justified continued British rule whilst bolstering images of the ruling centre as the antithesis of these negative characteristics.

> (Walter 2000: 81)

Irish nationalist discourses have been complicit in such gendering of national identity also insofar as Ireland has been figured variously as female: Mother Ireland, Cathleen Ní Houlihan, Roisín Dubh, or the Shan Van Vocht, for example. Kearney notes that this depiction of Ireland as motherland was reinforced in the late nineteenth century by 'the counter-reformational cult of the Virgin Mary. . . Indeed, it is interesting how elements in the Irish hierarchy—which offered women no real power—increasingly came to equate Ireland with a virginal motherland best served by safeguarding the native purity or "faith and morals" against the threat of alien culture' (1997: 119). This demonstrates the widespread process whereby 'the construction of a unified national ideology is frequently dependent on powerful gendered identities' (Dowler 1998: 162), although Hanafin characterises this as 'an example of recourse to myth in order to compensate for colonial domination' (1997: 251).[2]

These limited tropes of femininity in representations of the nation have been matched by the limited roles open to real women within nationalist cultures. Graham notes that 'a broad consensual view can be discerned among critics and writers who deal with gender and nationalist (and indeed unionist) ideology in Ireland, suggesting that nationalism and unionism encompass gender in their theoretical constructions and social workings in patriarchal, controlling ways' (2003: 154). Rolston notes the reproduction of a 1914 postcard as a wall mural on the Shankill Road in 1988 which 'portrays an armed woman. . . depicted as a stereotypical Irish colleen representing not Ireland, but Ulster' (1991: 45). The sense of the deserted woman forced to defend herself recurs in loyalist writing as Todd traces, suggesting that 'The Orangeman is both defender and defended, assertively male but behind the defences possessing a powerless female core. The defences are at once physical (walls, security forces) and symbolic (flags), both manned by the vigilant loyalist who spans the divide between the "rough"/male and "religious"/female' (1987: 6).

Given the prominence of such tropes of femininity in competing identity discourses, there has been a tension between them and emergent discourses, such as feminism, which intersect with them (Edge 1998). On a wall outside the University of Ulster's Magee campus in Derry, a piece of graffiti reads 'women unfree shall never be at peace'. This appropriation of the republican slogan, replacing 'Ireland' with 'women', captures the sense of divergence between the objectives of nationalist and feminist enterprises. Each seeks to prioritise one element of identity as the basis of collective experience, analysis or resistance: nation or gender. Pelan argues that 'the traditional polarisation of Irish politics and historiography into Irish/English, nationalist/unionist and revisionist/post-colonial, has meant that women, historically have not only been forced to choose between such binaries in terms of their personal politics, but have been represented as being contained within these political categories' (1999: 244). However, Edge takes issue with positions which suggest that 'women's interest in nationalist identity politics [are] "self-defeating" ' (1998: 221), arguing that such an interpretation of 'Irish nationalism as something inherently at odds with a feminist position was and still is used to dismiss women's involvement or interests in nationalist politics' (ibid.).

The discussion here investigates the ways in which gender has been bodied forth in productions which have engaged with the Troubles, without assuming any sense of contradiction in principle between the politics of nationalist or ethnic identity and the politics of gender. There are three inter-related outer frames within which the discussion will be mounted: the operation of masculinist ideologies within society at large; the specific articulations of such ideologies within theatre as an industry; and the ways in which gendered roles have been configured on the stage. The discussion will then be focused on Marie Jones's *Somewhere Over the Balcony* (1987) and Rona Munro's *Bold Girls* for 7:84 (Scotland). Each play stages the conditions in which republican women within West Belfast maintain their existence under the harsh conditions of the ghetto.

Foley has characterised the social landscape of Ireland as a 'panorama of patriarchy' (2003: 24) in which any 'challenge to the relegation of women as literal and cultural servants is a challenge to the hegemony of church and state and, more importantly in Northern Ireland, to deeply held senses of history and tradition on both sides of a religious divide' (ibid.). While there is much to her comments, rigid definitions of gender roles have come under pressure from a variety of sources in the last thirty years (including the women's movement, the media and legal challenges). Moreover, the impact of both the Troubles and masculinist discourses on women have been complex, dependent on variables of ethnic-national identity, generation, class and place, for example. Some commentators have suggested that 'the "troubles" are an added burden to the lives of women struggling with poverty and "armed patriarchy" ' (Rooney 1997: 535), while other women have enjoyed relative freedom from both the violence and the limitations of gendered politics.

Foley's analysis is indisputable, of course, in that each of the Christian traditions has contributed to the containment of women within limited definitions of acceptable femininity.[3] According to Sales, 'the dominant ideologies of Protestantism make a sharp distinction between male and female spheres' (1997: 65), with women relegated to the domestic domain supporting the male near-monopoly over public roles. The emphasis on the centrality of marriage to family life reaffirms these distinctions, particularly since 'views on family morality are. . . significantly more conservative than in Britain, with Protestants, particularly women, less liberal than Catholics' (ibid.: 66). Likewise, the Catholic Church has promoted rigid gender roles, notably through its influence in education, including single-sex schooling; the composition of its clergy; and its teachings on marriage, family life, sexuality and reproduction (Dowler 1998). The Irish Catholic hierarchy has appeared inured to debates over and changes in the position of women and has offered little by way of public role models for women. The conservatism of the Irish hierarchy has been challenged, however, on two fronts which are directly relevant to the work of Derry Frontline. Republicans have been highly critical because of the unwillingness of the church to endorse the military campaign. Similarly, radical activists for social justice have sought to develop the application of liberation theology within the church in its role in wider society.

The containment of women by the churches has been replicated in the formal political sphere (Roulston 1996; Sales 1997; Bairner 1999; McCoy 2000). The practice of exclusion begun under the former Stormont parliament has been continued at almost every level. While individual women have enjoyed occasional prominence in political parties, a 'pyramid of power can be discerned. Among the party rank and file there are large numbers of women, but their proportion decreases further up the hierarchy' (McCoy 2000: 5). In *Caught Red Handed*, the wife of the leader of the Alternative Unionist Party reiterates that she is a simple Ulster woman with no contribution to make to the discussions of the male leadership, except to make tea. The reality has been little different although political parties have responded in part to pressures to incorporate women more fully. Within the parties, women have themselves refused to comply passively with their relegation. Externally, legal changes, such as the formation of the Equal Opportunities Commission in 1976, have also forced change. Parties have also promoted female candidates as a means of broadening their appeal to the electorate.

Moreover, many women have taken up roles which have usurped any attempt to fix them as 'only' mothers, sisters or wives. The realities of living through economic deprivation and/or of absent husbands have pushed women into roles which might have been hitherto reserved for men. Roulston notes that 'although there is overwhelming evidence of gender inequality in Northern Ireland, the situation has not remained static. Women are far from confined to the domestic sphere, but have been entering the world of paid work in ever-increasing numbers' (1996: 140). She continues that 'discrimination and unequal treatment are not accepted with resignation by women. . . The number of complaints about pay and discrimination at work has risen steadily over the past 10 years' (ibid.). Women have played a significant role in alternative politics, for example. Women were active within the civil rights campaigns of the 1960s (Fairweather et al. 1984; Roulston 1996) and have been at the forefront of much community activism and grass-roots movements for development (Roulston 1996; Rooney 1997; McCoy 2000). A number of populist movements campaigning for peace have been led by women and attracted widespread female support, notably the Peace People in the 1970s (Fairweather et al. 1984; McCoy 2000).

There have been movements and forms of collective agitation also for the improvement of women's status as women (Roulston 1996). Since the formation of the Northern Ireland Women's Rights Movement in 1975 (Connolly 1999), women's groups have proliferated, organising around a range of causes and issues. The most notable engagement with constitutional structures has been the Northern Ireland Women's Coalition which was established to provide a women's perspective on and contribution to the unfolding peace processes in the wake of the cease-fires in 1994. Its core principles were formulated in 1996: 'support for inclusion, equality and human rights' (Fearon and McWilliams 2000: 121). Following elections in 1996, it was able to send two delegates to the all-party talks from which the Good Friday Agreement would emerge. It retained two seats in the first elections to the newly formed Northern Ireland Assembly which followed and it has been suggested that it 'had managed to do something that had eluded the women's movement in Northern Ireland for many years: unite and organise around an identity as women' (ibid.: 132).[4]

Women have been directly involved as combatants in the conflict. They have taken on roles within nationalist and republican protests and resistance in recognition that the operation of masculinist discourse within a colonised society has meant that while all women are oppressed as women, republican women are doubly disadvantaged since they suffer also from the discriminations of colonialism (Edge 1998). When internment was initiated in August 1971, it was women who stood guard over their districts, pursuing the army patrols in 'hen' patrols of their own and banging bin lids to warn of the arrival of arrest squads in nationalist areas (Dowler 1998). Women also have had a long history of involvement in armed struggle within Cumann na mBan and the IRA itself (Morgan and Fraser 1995; Dowler 1998). Likewise, women have played a role in a number of loyalist paramilitary organisations. Although according to Fairweather (1984), the women's UDA was disbanded officially as early as 1974, Gary Mitchell's *Loyal Women* (2003) depicts the Women's UDA as a well-organised parallel movement to the men's UDA, with continued responsibility for policing women within loyalist communities. Nor should it be forgotten that women have served as members of the RUC, the UDR, the British Army, as prison officers and as civilian security officers. Any suggestion therefore that women are essentially more inclined towards peaceful processes needs to be regarded with suspicion as a form of gender role stereotyping that denies the reality of such women's experiences and engagement (Morgan and Fraser 1995; Aretxaga 1997). This has nonetheless been a dominant representation. It has been suggested that 'terrorism is a man's game. The preferred qualities of violent activism, and willingness to make use of others all constitute terrorism as an extreme expression of militant machismo. . . Women, by contrast, can only ever be 'token terrorists', masochistic victims of this demon lover, who seduces them into an alien world' (Greenhalgh 1990: 161). It is ironic that feminist analyses which emphasise essential differences between men and women have coincided with the same kind of gender role-fixing in Northern Ireland within which actual women activists have been marginalised within masculinist discourses. One of the republican women interviewed by Dowler puts the point forcibly: 'There are a couple of songs about women but most of them are about the men. It is absolutely desperate it is, the bold Fenian Men. What of the bold Fenian *Women*?' (1998: 170). Josie in Anne Devlin's *Ourselves Alone* literally faces the difficulty of trying to sing songs which address a woman's experience of the conflict.

The marginalisation and containment of women within wider society has been mirrored within the theatre industry in Northern Ireland. There has been frequent criticism about the lack of opportunities for women trying to make a career within the business across the island as a whole.[5] The fundamental issue for many women then has been 'work and the right to work' (White 1989: 34). Often finding themselves excluded from work within the theatre industry, women have done much to change the theatrical landscape by founding their own companies and defining the nature of their own work. The observation made by Martin about Charabanc that 'the company was born out of frustration with the lack of employment opportunities for women in theatre and the few roles that were available to them' (1987: 88) could be applied to a number of initiatives in theatre in the last thirty years.[6] Certainly, in terms of individual achievement, women now occupy an unprecedented prominence in the institutions of theatre in Northern Ireland in both administrative and creative roles, in sharp contrast to the position in even the late 1990s.[7]

Initiatives which have created opportunities for women in Northern Ireland's theatre, however, have often rejected an overt espousal of feminist politics and in many instances the participants have remained 'adamant that their work should not be ghettoized as "women's" theatre' (White 1989: 35). While women are more prominent today in a range of key positions, this does not necessarily challenge the operation of hegemonic masculinist discourses. Kruger has argued against seeing the advancement of individual women within the existing institutions of theatre as a sign of liberation, since such institutions might 'absorb individual female success without in any way threatening the legitimacy of the masculinist and capitalist definition of that success' (1996: 50). While the provision of roles for women on the stage and within the industry is important, she cautions also that the staging of dramatic texts by women can be accommodated as 'trademarks of a new commodity, "plays by women" ' (ibid.: 50). Outwith the mainstream theatre industry, women have initiated alternative theatrical processes in working in community, educational and interventionist contexts. The work of Charabanc in this area was pioneering. From it grew companies like Replay working in the area of educational theatre; and DubbelJoint touring to and working with working-class communities, including helping to establish JustUs in West Belfast.

These initiatives notwithstanding, the representation of gendered identities on the stage has tended to be framed within the dominant discourses operative within the society, with women on the stage 'sexually on display as actresses' (Kruger 1996: 50). This potential remains even where roles for women have improved in quality, quantity and range. Indeed even where women have taken control over the theatre which they make, this is no guarantee that such work itself will be in any sense counter-hegemonic. For example, in Marie Jones's *A Night in November* which was produced by the company she co-founded, DubbelJoint, and directed by Pam Brighton, the central story of the male narrator almost entirely occludes his wife and children except insofar as they contribute to the dilemma experienced by this male character (see Chapter 8). Moreover, masculinist values remain perniciously persistent in the critical reception of plays, as Williams comments: 'One of the difficulties in this area is that we are so used to men's images of men, and men's images of women on the stage, that a play written by a woman is regularly criticized or rejected for not complying with these norms' (1993: 7).[8]

These norms are articulated within a narrow range of character types within which many roles for women both onstage and off are configured. Rolston provides a taxonomy of female figures within novels concerned with the Northern Ireland conflict which might be applied to dramatic and to some extent social roles also. The first and most dominant of these types is that of the mother. According to Rolston: 'Men come to represent violence and women peace with all the force of a Greek myth. The only proper acceptable role for a woman is that of a mother—both in the domestic sense of caring, and in the more global or mythical sense of peace-loving. Because they care for children, women care about peace' (1996: 406). Within the tradition of O'Casey's Juno, then, mother figures are primarily concerned with material reality and are resolutely against violence and the rhetoric which underpins it. In Troubles dramas, the type emerged in Boyd's *The Flats* in the figure of Kathleen Donellan. Like Juno she has been saddled with the responsibility of maintaining the household in the face of trouble on the streets and the predilection of her husband for alcohol. Her role as mother is fused with that of wife, with her husband functioning largely as a third child. She is sceptical of grand narratives and ideologies that divide people, with her values rooted in a humanist common sense infused with Catholic religiosity.

It is Kathleen who looks after her Protestant neighbours in the flats and ensures that the young British soldier on guard is supplied with tea and cigarettes. Crucially this nurturing role sees her confined largely to the kitchen or to the functions of feeding and providing for the rest of the household or her Protestant neighbours, evacuating the central playing area of the living room for the male roles. The men by contrast have the ability to go where they please and leave when they want. Being on the run from the security forces or from commitments to a wife and family is all the same to male characters more generally: it is not a question of whether or not they'll leave, just when. Marie in *Bold Girls* tells Deirdre, her husband's daughter by another woman: 'The thing about daddys, all the daddys, is they up and leave you; they go out with their friends, they go inside, they die, they leave you' (Munro 1993: 78). In *A Night in November*, Kenneth McCallister can jet off to America but it is his wife who will stay behind to minister to their children. In *Loyal Women*, Brenda accuses her husband Terry of pleading guilty to a murder committed by Brenda, because it is easier for him to be imprisoned than to take care of his daughter and invalid mother on his own.

Dowler has noted how this role intersects with a gendering of space whereby 'the confinement of women's identities to the domestic/private arena has promoted the development of gender tropes whereby women appear frail, vulnerable and become the protectors "only" of their immediate private spaces of the home' (1998: 163).[9] Thus, singularly lacking in discrimination, Boyd's Kathleen displays hostility only when her family or her flat are under threat from either the army, the local defence committee, or her husband's attempts to relocate her away from the flats. This figuration of the mother role, then, is stripped of any political insight or analysis in order to serve as the vehicle for the assertion of liberal humanist values against the doctrines which are presented as the source of the divisions within the society. It is an idealisation that both occludes the realities of women's experiences of the conflict and suggests that they have little part to play in its political resolution.[10] Individual agency is detached from structural change. Seamus Deane (1987) provides a critique of O'Casey's characterisation of female figures in the Dublin trilogy which is apposite in drawing attention to how O'Casey uses female characters to express a humanist position which is never subjected to the political pressures to which male figures are subjected. The criticism is also taken up by Mustafa (2000). This idealisation of the female has been recurrent throughout the dramas of the Troubles.

In play after play, the concerns of mothers for their offspring and/or husband are matched by a struggle to maintain the semblance of domestic order in the face of external pressures which threaten it. Within the plays this is expressed frequently through an attachment to the decoration or ornamentation of their homes. The china cup stands in for the sense of domestic order for which all the women in Christina Reid's *Tea in a China Cup* struggle in the face of drunken and untrustworthy husbands, and the ravages of war at home and abroad. Ruth McCrea in McCartney's *Heritage* is exasperated by the lack of home-making skills in her daughter Sarah, and gets upset when Sarah breaks a jug which she had carried all the way from County Antrim to Canada. With it she has lost one of the last tangible ties with the place and people she has left behind. In Jones's *A Night in November*, Debrah's dedica-

tion to the materiality of their home is presented as part of the justification
for her husband Kenneth's disaffection with his Ulster Protestant identity.
Sandra in Mitchell's *As the Beast Sleeps* (1998) finds the means to have her
house redecorated despite her straitened circumstances. In *Somewhere Over
the Balcony*, Kate literally tries to keep her home together as the walls of her
flat crumble with damp, the reverberations of the helicopter patrols and the
controlled explosion which eventually causes one wall to collapse.

A type closely related to that of the mother in dramatic representations may
be added to Rolston's taxonomy: that of the female as waiting wife, the trope
of Penelope. These women figures remain behind loyally awaiting the return
of their absent husbands, essentially passive victims, brides awaiting fulfilment through the love of the right man.[11] The type appears in the figure of
Norah in O'Casey's *The Plough and the Stars*. Such figures largely exist in
relation to their men and their lives are bound within the domestic locale.
Marie in *Bold Girls* continues her loyalty to her dead husband Michael, despite
her awareness of his countless infidelities. Greenhalgh suggests that the
women characters in Devlin's *Ourselves Alone* 'spend their lives "waiting on
men" who are either in prison, committed to other women, or on the wrong
political side' (1990: 167). In *Loyal Women*, Brenda's bitterness at Terry's
infidelity when he gets out of prison is fuelled since she has remained faithful
to him for the sixteen years of his prison sentence.

Against the powerful norms of the mother/wife are set two anti-types.
Rather than standing against violence, the first anti-type, 'unmotherly
mothers', operate as seductive influences drawing others into the violence:
'They are often older women, often grandmothers. Deprived now of what is
supposedly their only real reason for existence they become cranky. Aged,
asexual, unfeminine, they can become purveyors of violence against their
previous natural instincts' (Rolston 1996: 409). This type is drawn historically in the figure of the Shan Van Vocht, and is recognisable too in figures
such as Emer Donaghue in McCartney's *Heritage*. Long-steeped in traditions
of Irish republicanism which she has brought with her to Saskatchewan, Emer
insists that her grandson, Michael, learn this history, which Michael's own
father, Peter, seeks to leave behind in order to build a new life in a new country.
When the teenage Michael gets involved in local sectarian struggles, Peter
turns to blame Emer: 'I know the fault lies with me: leaving him to you for all
these years to go filling his head with romantic nonsense about the Old
Country and coffin ships and martyred rebels' (McCartney 2001: 112).
Michael is eventually killed whilst setting a barn-fire on his Protestant neighbour's farm. In Gary Mitchell's *Trust*, Margaret's desire to protect her son
Jake becomes distorted when she not only enlists Trevor to beat up the lads
who have been bullying him, but insists that Jake is involved too so that he
will gain respect. In *As the Beast Sleeps* (see Chapter 8), Sandra abnegates her
maternal role by sending her son to stay with her mother, while she tries to

convince her husband Kyle to resist attempts to pacify him and his UDA gang. She is the one who spurs Freddie into the action of robbing the loyalist club which results in his horrific beating.

In acting as Freddie's accomplice in robbing the club, Sandra's role merges into that of the second anti-type: the violent woman or 'woman as villain': these are women who reject the role of motherhood for an engagement with violence expressed as an emotional force. However, 'having abandoned their natural vocation of motherhood, they can never be real "terrorists" like men'. (Rolston 1996: 411–12): it is Freddie who enacts the violence in the robbery, not Sandra. The accounts by Fairweather (Fairweather et al. 1984) and Dowler (1998) suggest that the attitude of communities to actual women terrorists is at least as ambivalent as the literary figurations. Women involved in paramilitary activities are treated differently from their male counterparts, becoming in some way tainted by their active public role in the violence. It is notable that few stage representations draw attention to the role of women as direct participants in the violence. Exceptionally, Anne Devlin has created two notable female terrorist dramatic roles. Based on her own short story, her radio and then television play *Naming the Names* explores how Finn McQuillen lures the son of a Protestant judge to an IRA ambush and how she is subsequently interrogated by the security forces. In Devlin's *Ourselves Alone*, Josie is an active member of the IRA. However, despite her trusted position, she has only been involved once on active service, planting a car-bomb on her own initiative outside the law courts. The bomb did not explode. Now, she lacks 'the killing instinct' (Devlin 1999: 56). Rolston notes that the female terrorist is fickle and switches emotional loyalty, demonstrating a fundamental instability. Thus, Josie is victim to her emotions, following help-lessly after the married Cathal O'Donnell and then, abandoned by him, falling for the suspected English agent Joe Conran. Pregnant by Conran, Josie is finally rehabilitated as her father's daughter returning home, having been passed from one male to the next.

In Mitchell's *Loyal Women*, the decision to portray the workings of a Women's UDA company allows for a developed figuration of female para-militaries. Brenda had been one of the hardest women in her youth and has committed the murder of a young Catholic woman suspected of being a member of the IRA. Now, with a teenage daughter of her own and a baby granddaughter, Brenda attempts to put her past behind her and is looking for a way out of the organisation and a means of keeping her family from its reaches. Maureen is seeking to step down as the company leader since her role has taken its toll on her personal relationships. Only Gail and Heather are enthusiastic and ambitious members of the organisation, although Brenda's daughter Jenny sees Gail as a role model. Mitchell juxtaposes Brenda's role as the dutiful wife and mother who cares for and seeks to protect her family with how she was as a teenager and with the roles of Heather and

Jenny in particular. Committed to the cause, as a teenager Brenda was a 'real head-banger', someone of whom everyone else is still afraid because of her capacity for unrestrained violence. Yet her mature approach to problems demonstrates a maternal willingness to listen to people and to empathise with them. Heather is a bully who thrives on violence and, unlike Brenda, is sexually promiscuous. She represents a threat to the family since she has slept with Brenda's husband Terry and seeks to lure Jenny away from her mother's influence. Jenny, as a teenage mother herself, is incapable of taking responsibility for her daughter and reluctant to assist at all in caring for her invalid grandmother. Her desire to join the Women's UDA stands in sharp contrast, a mark of her irresponsibility. Throughout the play, the rough behaviour and capacity for violence of the women is barely repressed by the routines and disciplines imposed by the organisation's codes and the feminine ideal of the dutiful and religious woman they promote. However, Mitchell establishes a distinction between the violence perpetrated by Brenda in defence of her family (justified maternal violence) and the violence of Heather when she attacks Adele (unwomanly violence), whom they are threatening to punish for her relationship with a Catholic boy. Heather demonstrates the fundamental instability of the female terrorist, unable to control her emotions and ultimately turning on Brenda. By contrast, Brenda's violent acts are to preserve her family and are determined by a cold and rational assessment of what needs to happen in this situation. Loyalty to family ultimately trumps loyalty to the movement. Thus, while Mitchell's depiction of women paramilitaries resists the stereotypes of the passive female victim, it conforms in a number of respects to the limited types already prevalent in the culture.

While these limited types have recurred in many of the characterisations of women on the stage, there has been resistance to them. In some instances this has come in the form of parody. In Frank McGuinness's *Carthaginians*, Dido's play-within-the-play, *The Burning Balaclava*, satirises the range of mother roles through the figure of Doreen O'Docherty (played by Dido) which mutates from the classic mother role to woman as villain. Her character description states that she is 'driven to distraction by the troubles but as she is one of life's martyrs who never complains she is very kind to animals and goes nowhere without her pet dog, Charlie, on a lead' (McGuinness 1988: 36). She is dedicated equally to her dog and her devotion to the Sacred Heart and she experiences a conflict between the two when a soldier kills the dog and she seeks vengeance. In the climactic scene, she shoots an RUC officer following her son's death. However her motivation is revealed as cold-blooded and cynical: she has a monopoly on the supply of balaclavas and like Mother Courage depends on the killing for her trade. The mothers within the main play are figured in a more complex way and it is against this complexity that the type is found wanting most obviously.[12]

A significant resistance to the containment of women onstage and off was

Figure 6. Carthaginians by Frank McGuinness, Lyric Theatre, Belfast.
Photographer: Jill Jennings

the work of Charabanc, and, in relation to representations of women in the Troubles, the play *Somewhere Over the Balcony*. While the history of the company extended from its foundation in 1983 through to 1995, it is most renowned for the style of working which was developed in its first three productions, *Lay Up Your Ends* (1983), *Oul' Delf and False Teeth* (1984) and *Now You're Talkin'* (1985) all directed by Pam Brighton. As mentioned already, the inspiration for the company was to provide work for five out-of-work actresses,[13] Eleanor Methven, Carol Scanlon, Marie (Sarah) Jones, Brenda Winter and Maureen Macauley who had come together initially for one production (Coyle 1989a: 42). The company was never exclusively female; indeed the cross-casting of women in male roles was more a matter of necessity than policy. When they approached Martin Lynch to write something for them, he in turn suggested that they should write their own material. This suggestion led the company into ways of working that distinguished it from a mainstream of Irish theatre still concerned primarily with the production of dramatic literature by individual playwrights. Marked by processes of collaboration, the devising of these initial productions gave the actors the authority to develop or decide upon their material, appoint the director and designer and identify audiences beyond conventional middle-class theatre venues. These early productions were developed from interviews with people across Northern Ireland whereby the company extended the right to be heard to working-class women and men. These interviews engaged with popular oral history in their focus on the Linen Mill Workers' Strike of 1911 for *Lay Up Your Ends* (1983) and the experiences of Belfast's market traders in 1949 in *Oul' Delf and False Teeth*. The final play in the trilogy, *Now You're Talkin'* (1985), looked to contemporary concerns in dealing with the experiences of women from across the sectarian divide coming together in a 'reconciliation centre'. The wealth of material generated through the research processes for the first three plays also allowed the company to devise *Gold in the Streets* (1986), dealing with Irish migration to England in three one-act pieces.

While the plays used the stories and characters related in the interviews, there was a concern to avoid straight biography and to meet the demands of theatrical representation. The material was reviewed and pieced together by the company members at the Tyrone Guthrie Centre (Martin 1987: 92–3). The outcome of this initial process would then be subject to change through the process of rehearsal with a director and subsequently on reflection as the production played before actual audiences, and often in the light of feedback from audience members. Such a process did not always provide the most effective dramaturgical decisions, however. For example, the company commented that, 'Although we have lots of ideas, one which appeals very strongly is a reworking of *Oul' Delf and False Teeth*, the play which was our second production. We were never happy with the structure but the content was very strong—the demise of non-sectarian politics in Northern Ireland,

told from a Protestant viewpoint' (Coyle 1989: 42). Irrespective of this reser-
vation, the company's first three productions attracted widespread acclaim
from reviewers and, more importantly, local working-class audiences across
Northern Ireland.

The productions were characterised by flexible performance modes,
recognisable to anyone familiar with the 1970s British alternative touring
theatre, influenced partly by the direction of Pam Brighton whose background
had been with Monstrous Regiment, but primarily by the financial restrictions on a new company. Sets were minimalist and could represent any
number of locales; actors doubled roles and were cross-cast, again as a means
of working within a limited budget. Music and songs were a key component,
combining with direct address and presentational acting to allow actors to
acknowledge the presence of their audience. Thus, characteristics which
might in other contexts be associated with politicised theatre practices (both
popular and feminist) were developed by the company in response to the
exigencies of their specific situation. Performances eschewed realism as the
basis of their authenticity, which instead came through the audience's recognition of the situations presented and, in some instances, actual dialogue or
narrative elements (Martin 1987; Coyle 1989).

Somewhere Over the Balcony was a departure for Charabanc at that time
since it was single-authored by Marie Jones. The production was directed by
Peter Sheridan with the roles of Rose, Ceely and Kate played by Eleanor
Methven, Marie Jones and Carol Scanlan respectively. It opened in London's
Drill Hall on 9 September 1987, transferring in November to the Arts Theatre
as part of the Belfast Festival and later to the Peacock in Dublin. It toured
successfully to the Unites States in 1988. Although well received by reviewers
in London and in Belfast, the run at the Arts was overshadowed by the events
of the Remembrance Day Bombing in Enniskillen, and it opened to a half
empty house. The *Irish Times* reviewer suggested that 'Perhaps recent events
in Northern Ireland made people less open to a wild loving piece of anarchic
comedy celebrating those who survive in the Divis Flats and identify it at some
level with the "nationalist" ethic' (Hunter 1987: 12). Set in the Divis Flats in
nationalist West Belfast, the play is a mixture of fantasy and farce revealing
the strategies by which the women endure the daily hardships of the squalor
of their environment and the violence around them. On the anniversary of
internment, three women observe the surrounding territory from the balcony
of their soon-to-be-demolished high-rise flats, providing a running commentary on the activities of their offspring, husbands and the British soldiers who
keep them under constant surveillance. The wedding of a neighbour's
daughter turns into a siege of the local church when troops attempt to capture
some on-the-run republicans. The siege is ended only by a fantastical rescue
by one of the women's father-in-law, flying a stolen army helicopter to rescue
the wedding party from the tower of the church.

With a number of songs and a presentational style of performance encouraged by both the frontal acting of a number of scenes and occasional direct audience address, the performance resembled the theatrical style of much left-wing British theatre of the 1970s. The variety of material, different modes of performance and significantly, the acknowledgement of the presence of the audience, exemplified the same approach to performance as John McGrath had articulated in his description of the work of 7:84 in *A Good Night Out* (1981).[14] Curiously for a company which strained to remain detached from an exclusive association with any one community or political perspective, *Somewhere Over the Balcony* is written entirely from the perspective of the female nationalist population of Divis. It assumes their perspective and values which challenge both bourgeois and patriarchal orthodoxy.

Rona Munro's *Bold Girls* shares the setting of nationalist West Belfast and the concern with the lives of ordinary women who are trapped within their society. The play was commissioned by 7:84 (Scotland) for whom she had already contributed *Saturday Night at the Commodore* as part of the company's collection of plays *Long Story Short: Voices of Today's Scotland* in 1989. *Bold Girls* premiered at Cumbernauld Theatre on 27 September 1990, before touring Scotland and Northern Ireland, playing in Belfast as part of the Belfast Festival at Queens. It transferred to London's Hampstead Theatre in the following year and was awarded the Susan Smith Blackburn Award for the best play by a woman in the English-speaking world. The production also saw Munro recognised with awards as Most Promising Playwright by the Critics Circle, *Plays and Players* and as part of the *Evening Standard* Theatre Awards. It has subsequently been performed in the United States, Canada and Australia and is a set text on the Scottish schools syllabus.

Munro was born in Aberdeen in 1959 where she grew up. Alongside her studies in Scottish history at Edinburgh University, she was active in the student theatre group, learning her craft by staging productions. On graduation, she worked as a cleaner and a receptionist while developing her writing with Edinburgh Playwrights Workshop. In 1981 she received her first stage commission from the Traverse Theatre in Edinburgh for *Fugue* and from 1985 she was writer-in-residence with Paines Plough Theatre Company. She has written for stage, television, film and radio. She has also performed as part of a comedy double act the MsFits. Her work has been strongly characterised by a concern to express women's voices, particularly in situations of conflict and stress. In that respect, then, the decision to accept 7:84's commission was hardly surprising. Munro herself had a long-term connection with Belfast where 'she'd worked and visited on and off for five years'.[15] It was, however, something of a departure for the company. 7:84 (Scotland) was launched in 1973 and under McGrath's artistic directorship, the company was at the forefront of left-wing political theatre in Britain through the 1970s and 1980s. In 1989, under sustained pressure from the Scottish Arts Council,

McGrathSaturday resigned from the company. Striving to find a renewed identity for the company, the team which replaced him mounted adaptations of existing contemporary plays while engaging on a policy to develop new writing. Without McGrath's ideological positioning, the company's work dealt nonetheless with working-class experiences and social issues and it was under this remit that the decision was taken to commission a play about Northern Ireland.

The play explores the conditions in which the three main characters live. Marie Donnelly is the widow of an IRA man, Michael, striving to bring up their young sons Mickey and Brendan. She is supported by her neighbour Nora Ryan who is widowed too. Living with Nora is her daughter Cassie. She is Marie's good friend and like her is bringing up her two children without her husband, Joe. He is a republican prisoner, due shortly for release. Nora is focused on making the most of her home, Cassie on leaving as soon as she has enough money saved. When a strange teenage girl, Deirdre, is taken in off the street during a gun battle, she ruptures the routine domesticity of the other women. It is revealed that Marie's husband Michael had cheated on her, fathering Deirdre and having an affair with Cassie. The play's title points up the key issue facing each of the women: how to be a good woman in these conditions through which they endure. Each female figure represents a different attitude to their shared circumstances and, through each, the play juxtaposes the strategies which they use to cope.

In capturing the minutiae of the conditions in which real women live, each production faced the danger that they might merely repeat, and thereby endorse, the circumstances which were depicted onstage. In both productions, for example, the women are left to look after their families, functioning in the traditional mother roles, while the men escape domestic responsibility by leaving to work, drinking or going on the run. In *Bold Girls*, it is sexual infidelity and ultimately death which allow Michael Donnelly to escape his responsibilities. In *Somewhere Over the Balcony*, Ceely's husband, Big Tucker, likewise achieves the ultimate escape through his death. The economics of their circumstances and the conditions under which they live, however, distort the capacity of the women to fulfil their nurturing role. Rose keeps the twins locked away in fear for their safety; Ceely's son is a joy rider; Kate's daughter is dead and only her son Dustin appears to have any prospects for the future. Likewise in *Bold Girls*, Marie and Nora struggle to care for their families. Marie has to wash clothes in Nora's unreliable washing machine; they cannot afford to heat their houses adequately; and the décor peels off with damp. In performance, much of the stage business within the house is given over to the domestic activities of the women as they mop and iron and prepare and serve meals and tea. It is this focus on the materiality of their existence which dominates the lives of the female characters.

In keeping with social norms, the women are confined by their domestic responsibilities in each production. Kate is cowed by her religious devotion and years of being psychologically undermined by her ex-husband Frank, her sole focus being the maintenance of the remains of her miserable flat. She clings to the ritual of emptying her metal bin herself despite the effort of having to lug it down the stairs of the tower block on her own. In confining her two twin sons to the interior of the flat, Rose chains herself too. Ceely likewise is confined by a male presence in the shape of Granda Tucker, her father-in-law, for whom she has been caring for twelve years. Granda Tucker achieves his position of dominance due to having been a former IRA commander and an internee, underlining the connection between patriarchy and aspects of republican values. All three women are mothers, and their male offspring enjoy a freedom which they can envy but never emulate. Like a Greek chorus, the women can narrate and pass comment on the actions of others, but they are never actors themselves. This reliance on narration to relay the events outwith the domestic space of the women is a long-standing tradition within Troubles dramas. Cleary notes that 'what goes on in that sinister and nightmarish space "outside" the home exists for the audience as something that cannot be directly apprehended but only imperfectly imagined' (1999: 519). Their lives and specifically the events over the course of the play are determined by the actions of the men around them: the 'on-the-run' republicans whom the army attempt to arrest; the army who carry out the controlled explosion; the boys who steal the armoured car; and Granda Tucker and Big Tucker who stage the dramatic rescue from the church.

This confinement is repeated for the women in *Bold Girls*. As in *Somewhere Over the Balcony*, the women never enjoy the freedom which their male offspring enjoy, playing outside on the street. While Cassie's brother Danny works outside the area, the women can only get as far as the club in escaping their homes, blocked in by poverty, the barricades of the rioters and the road blocks of the army. They are licensed to visit the prison where the men are incarcerated but this is only an extension of their domestic responsibilities. Nora puts her energies into the materiality of her home, battling against the interventions of the army which have ruined her suite and her garden, the damp which has destroyed her decoration and the struggle she has with poverty to buy the fabric to recover her latest suite. Marie, similarly, seems reconciled to a life in which she takes care of her children and maintains a home as the limits of her existence. Both women accept the limitations imposed by being a 'good girl' who conforms to social expectations.

Thus, each play might well have been merely a reproduction of the conditions of women's lives. However, the critique of these conditions is achieved in the shaping of the narrative and in the creation of perspectives on it. Each narrative includes a specific character who expresses the desire for something else, offering a rebuke to the narrowness of the community's expectations of them. In *Somewhere Over the Balcony*, it is Ceely who explicitly rejects the role to which she has been assigned by setting up her pirate radio station. She dreams of an affair with a soldier and escaping to become a bingo caller, or running her own pirate radio station across the border. Even if she does not achieve these dreams, however, her refusal to accept silently what is happening to her (and her community) resists the convention of enduring in silence. In *Bold Girls*, Cassie finds the confinement of her life suffocating, and has accepted that she is a 'bold girl' in being unable to reconcile herself to her circumstances. Married to a man whom she loathes, she has sought escape through sexual adventure with Michael and dreams now of emigrating with the limited savings she has scraped together. While both Marie and Nora are sceptical that she will ever achieve this long-term aim, Cassie resists the pressure to conform to the role of the prisoner's wife in her dress and behaviour in the club.

Each drama rejects also straightforward conventions of representation in its structure. The focus of each is split in a number of ways inhibiting identification with any one character and encouraging the audience to engage with the totality of the situation presented. In each, there is a split between the dramatic world which is known to the audience only through the narration or dialogue of the women and the audience's direct experience of the women themselves. In *Somewhere Over the Balcony*, the speeches granted to the women are articulate and endlessly engaging and allow a diversity of voices to emerge. In the world beyond the flats, however, the men are silenced and can only be known as objects of the women's speeches. A similar pattern is developed in *Bold Girls*, where the world of the women is created through their dialogue. It is a world which the audience comes to know from how it is talked about. The women's talk provides an ongoing process of exposition by which the relationships of Deirdre, Cassie and Marie to Michael and to each other become revealed to them and to the audience.[16]

The use of dialogue to create the external world which the women inhabit is supplemented by monologues through which the audience's engagement with the figures of the women is developed. This takes the form of uninterrupted narration within the dramatic scene, as well as conversations in which the other participant is implied by the uninterrupted speech of the onstage character (Castagno 1993). The latter is a recurrent device in *Somewhere Over the Balcony* which is given an added dimension through Ceely's announcements through her radio broadcasts. Each play also allows moments for individual figures to address the audience directly. This fulfils the function of exposition in Kate Tidy's opening speech in *Somewhere Over the Balcony*. Similarly, Deirdre's monologues in Scene 1 of *Bold Girls* describe directly to the audience the setting of the play while simultaneously creating a narrative suspense as to her relationship to the events in the house. More powerfully, however, monologue is used to chart the internalised psychological landscapes of the lives of the women in each play as they reveal their own hopes and fears in a series of soliloquies. Characteristically, in *Somewhere Over the Balcony*, the interior lives of the women are dominated by the minutiae of their daily concerns and the soliloquies spill out as if expressing directly the women's immediate experience. By contrast, in *Bold Girls*, the monologues are more reflective, a distillation of the women's thinking on the lives they are leading. Marie's monologues reveal the feelings for Michael which she continues to guard even in the face of the revelations which are made. Cassie's monologues juxtapose her feelings for her father with her realisation of the differential relationship which girls and boys have to their fathers and mothers in keeping with social norms. It is only through the use of song that such reflective analysis is achieved in *Somewhere Over the Balcony*. The songs, therefore, perform a key function in demonstrating the stifled possibilities of these women's lives. The use of monologue in these two productions repre-sented a shift in the concern of dramatists from a representation of how the social world might be registered objectively to a depiction of the subjective experience of individuals, the same shift from *histoire* to *discours* discussed in relation to *Bin Lids* (see Chapter 3). Thus, these plays celebrate the subjec-tivity of the women, validating their experiences and their authority.

Particular production choices shaped further the audience's perspective on the resistant potential offered. Each production demonstrated clearly the ways in which the women are trapped by economics, patriarchy and the presence of troops. The use of costume was one key indicator of the inscription of their situation on the bodies of the women. In *Somewhere Over the Balcony*, Ceely remains in her nightclothes throughout the play. She has no need to dress since her engagement with public space is limited to her presence on the balcony and her radio broadcasts. When Rose dons a riot helmet, police baton and bin lid shield, it is an hilarious moment: it is also a marker of how distorted the women's sense of reality has become in the situation in which they find themselves. In *Bold Girls*, the women's concern with the materiality of their world is demonstrated through the pile of ironing at the opening of the play, and Marie's worry that Mickey will stain his shirt with raspberry drink. Cassie's choice of a revealing dress for the night out at The Club provokes an argument between Nora and Cassie over the appropriate role for a pris-oner's wife in a public space. Deirdre's threat to Marie's domestic order is embodied in the theft of her clothes at the end of Scene 1. Their ultimate reconciliation is embodied after Deirdre has stripped off the stolen clothes, when Marie drapes a blanket around her in the final scene. In each instance, the costume serves as a form of *gestus* marking out the external circumstances in which the women live.

The *mise-en-scène* in each performance delimited the narrow dimensions of the physical spaces which the women inhabit. As in earlier Charabanc shows, the set for *Somewhere Over the Balcony*, designed by Blaithin Sheerin and Brian Power, was resolutely minimalist: scaffolding and three high stools.

The women are confined to the balcony or the interior of their flats, indeed a number of their speeches are delivered from the stools, demonstrating the limits of their space and their isolation from each other. In *Bold Girls*, the play is set within Marie's small rented house and The Club. The interior of the house is a room which 'is never deserted; it's too stuffed with human bits and pieces, all the clutter of housework and life' (Munro 1993: 1). While the women come in and out of this room, they get no further than the kitchen, the children's bedrooms or the Ryans' house across the road. While The Club is a much larger environment, the scene is established with the presence of a wall; the table at which the women sit; and a lectern from which Marie plays 'The Price is Right'. The rest of the space is implied. When Cassie takes to the dance floor on her own, this is an act of transgression, a challenge to the proper role for a prisoner's wife. Joined by Marie, however, they realise that the men in the room are enjoying their presence as a display of sexual avail-ability. The contrast between Marie's attitude to occupying space and Cassie's highlights the social norms governing their behaviour in public. The deployment of space within each play follows what Cleary has argued are the gendered aspects of specific dramatic genres: masculine forms are action-orientated and 'assume "open" spaces and dynamic heroes who can use violence legitimately'; while feminine forms (family tragedy and domestic tragedy) 'operate within a more enclosed and immobilized environment where the characters tend to be acted upon and violence is directed inward' (Cleary 1999: 521).

The argument that each play was an act of resistance to dominant repre-sentations of the Troubles in the depiction of the female figures seems to be borne out by this discussion. A further dimension which remains to be explored, however, is the context of their staging, a factor which complicates further the relationship between the resistance offered by these plays and wider discourses. Each play was first performed outside of Northern Ireland and neither was ever specifically staged for the community within which it is set. Two issues arise. The first is the extent to which the plays provided their audiences with the pleasures of bourgeois voyeurism (Hill 1986). The second is the extent to which this voyeurism might also have had a colonial dimen-sion for audiences in Scotland and England. This is a charge which has had a long history in Irish theatre criticism since it has been levelled at both Yeats and O'Casey (Mustafa 2000: 96). Whilst both plays articulate the oppressive presence of the British Army as a dominating feature of the women's lives, their critiques of the republican men might be seen to confirm the stereotypes of the terrorist dominant in representations of the Troubles (see Chapter 2). The issue is a perennial one for feminists who are also republicans:

> [T]hose feminists who strongly identify with Republicanism are some-
> times reluctant to discuss the oppression of Irish women by the church

and by men. They believe that it is essential to publicize women's experiences under the military war but dangerous to publicize their sufferings as women. Knowing the extent of anti-Irish prejudice, they fear providing ammunition for those who, far from identifying with women on feminist grounds, simply enjoy smug titters about 'thick, brutal, priest-ridden Paddies'.

(Fairweather et al. 1984: 111)

The inability of the republican community to acknowledge externally its shortcomings in accepting particular forms of patriarchy cannot be divorced, therefore, from the needs of that community to retain a show of strength and solidarity in the face of external threat (see Baron Cohen and King 1997). This need not mean, however, that internal debate and dialogue about the role of women and the development of the struggle more generally could not and did not happen, as the example of Derry Frontline in the next chapter will show. What it does suggest, however, is that the capacity of productions such as *Somewhere Over the Balcony* and *Bold Girls* (and Devlin's *Ourselves Alone*) to contribute to the liberation of women within these communities might depend on their engagement with them directly, not just their internal formal characteristics. Otherwise, the critique of patriarchy within republican communities can serve as a further fillip to colonial discourses, suggesting that Northern Irish women can only be liberated under the modernising influence of British rule.

7

Let the People Speak

Community and Theatre

MARIE: We might as well give up now if we're going to keep chucking our minds in the bin. The mind's a tool. It shouldn't have to be a bin lid or a barricade. God knows we all need the barricades. But we've got to take them down as soon as we're strong enough. Otherwise all we see of the world is the barricades. And ourselves crouching behind them. You know the worst about it, Diane. You can become the barricade yourself and not even know it.

(Dan Baron Cohen, 2001, *Threshold*, 236)

In studies of the conflict in Northern Ireland, and in widespread media reporting, its causes are presented frequently as internal with stress placed on the origin of the conflict in the breakdown in relations between 'the two communities'. Such accounts rarely draw attention to the difficulties in the conceptions of community underpinning them and therefore the limitations of their own analysis. Consequently, in the implementation of policies which have responded to this two-communities model, the state has camouflaged its own partial role and directed attention away from the necessary reform of its own structure. Within the post-1994 peace processes, it has been precisely these state structures which have been reformed. These policies were often directed through non-elected bodies, such as the Community Relations Council, and initiatives such as the Education for Mutual Understanding programme and the peace and reconciliation funding initiatives of the European Union (Rolston 1998b), seeking to reward 'cross-community' efforts rather than community development for existing communities. In this chapter, I want to examine how theatre projects have been implemented in relation to this model, to understand how the goals of community theatre practice may fit with or contradict the state's objectives for community development.

It is important, as a preliminary, to identify the sense in which community is to be used in this discussion. A community is a social group, membership of which might be based on identity, interest or location. A community of identity is a group marked out by a shared identity, such as ethnic or racial origins. Communities of interest are 'formed through networks of association that are predominantly characterised by their commitment to a common interest'.[1] The third category, communities of location, 'are created through networks of relationships formed by face-to-face interaction within a geographically bounded area' (Kershaw 1996: 30–1). In theatrical terms, perhaps the best-known community in which identity, interest and location are interconnected is Friel's Ballybeg or Baile Beag, described by Seamus Deane as a standard setting which 'has fused within it the socially depressed and politically dislocated world of Derry and the haunting attraction of the lonely landscapes and traditional mores of rural Donegal' (1984: 12). Ironically, although Ballybeg is placed somewhere in Donegal, the portrait of its community there tells us much about the nature of communities in Northern Ireland too, such that the factions which divide the actual state are delineated in the divisions within the fictional locale (Lojek 2004).

Much work has been undertaken within Northern Ireland to chart the inter-relationship between communities of identity and location, by examining how ethno-religious communities of identity are segregated from each other along clearly demarcated territorial boundaries (Boal 1987; Murtagh 1998).[2] Such segregation has benefits for communities to the extent to which it supports community cohesion and strengthens internal social networks. In *Translations*, Friel demonstrates that the integrity of the linguistic community of Baile Beag has been preserved by a social isolation which can no longer be sustained in the face of political, social and economic pressures. By contrast it is precisely this same sense of political isolation which has fostered the development of new Irish language communities within Northern Ireland's nationalist communities. In Northern Ireland, segregation has also provided for a degree of security and protection from external threats, such as in the declaration of 'Free Derry' as the focal point of resistance to police violence against nationalists in 1969.

One prominent feature of the inter-relationship of identity and location which must not be forgotten is the extent to which the creation of the state of Northern Ireland and the subsequent exercise of unionist hegemony within it was a means to assure the preservation of the majority's sense of itself as Ulster, Protestant and unionist. Rolston describes this official culture as 'rarely vibrant, but usually predictable, formal, conservative—restrictive rather than expansive' (1998a: 27). The influence of the hegemony exercised by this culture stretched well into the 1980s as a feature of internal politics, and a shaping force on Westminster (British) policy through which the preservation of the state served as the expression of the continuity of the Ulster Protestant community. Rolston argues, however, that 'loyalists did not see all their needs and aspirations mirrored in the official culture and institutions of the unionist state because the state and its institutions were middle class' (ibid.: 28). He suggests that the 'main effect of this was often political and cultural passivity' (ibid.: 29). By contrast, nationalists have generated a culture of resistance which has been both resistant to oppression and visionary in proposing political alternatives. One result of this is that 'there has been a stronger tradition of a community-based oppositional politics among the Catholic/nationalist population in Northern Ireland, because of its alienated relationship to the state' (McCoy 2000: 13). However, Rolston does not explore the sense in which he is using culture in this context. Certainly in terms of artistic practices reflecting communal identity, nationalism can harness itself to the artistic production of the island, although Rolston's own work on loyalist wall murals (1991) and songs (1999) suggests an invention and creativity which he critiques on the basis of its ideological underpinning rather than as evidence of the passivity he suggests. Loyalist culture in a wider sense, what Williams has described as a constitutive social process or whole way of life (1977b), has been widely celebrated by a number of dramatists. In Christina Reid's *Tea in a China Cup*, the ritual of the laying out of the dead is an opportunity for humour, while in Marie Jones's *Weddin's, Wee'ins and Wakes*, it is represented as part of the fabric of women's lives in the closely knit loyalist communities of Belfast. The paucity of the lives represented by Gary Mitchell's loyalist characters stands in contrast to these representations of older loyalist communities. The setting of Rathcoole suggests that the traditional values of loyalist communities in inner city areas has been broken down by their dispersal into such peripheral housing schemes and the difficulty in building substantive community networks outwith the paramilitary organisations.

In clarifying the use of the term 'community' it is important also to distinguish between the use of the term 'community' as a descriptive label and a sense of community which might be felt and experienced between people. Kelly argues, for example, that

> For a group of people to be defined as this kind of living community it is not sufficient that they live, work and play in geographical proximity; nor that to an observer they have habits, goals and achievements in common. These are necessary conditions, perhaps, but they are not on their own sufficient, for it also necessary that the members of the community acknowledge their membership, and that this acknowledgement plays a recognised part in shaping their actions.
>
> (1984: 49)

Whilst acknowledging the importance of the point Kelly makes, the distinction which is made between community membership which is declared and that which is ascribed by others has a particular (though not unique) dimension in Northern Ireland. Declared participation by an individual allows for the active and intentional engagement in the preservation and/or development of the community which Kelly describes. By contrast, ascribed membership rests on the assumption by others (both within the community and outside it) of equivalence between certain characteristics of an individual and a fixed range of values and beliefs associated with community membership. Within communities, paramilitaries have enforced this equivalence of location, ethnicity and politics, for example, using the threat of violence to discourage anyone who might seek to assert any alternatives. Thus, both tarring and feathering of women fraternising with the 'wrong sort' of men and punishment beatings, particularly of teenagers charged with anti-social behaviour, have been used to ensure strict conformity to a limited vision of community membership (Fairweather et al. 1984). Gary Mitchell's *Loyal Women* addresses the first circumstances in the loyalist Rathcoole estate; Macdara Vallely's *Peacefire* (2004) and Seamas Keenan's *Flight* (2004) explore the second in the context of nationalist communities. The way in which community membership can be ascribed has also motivated otherwise unjustified attacks on people assumed to be from the 'other' community. This has prompted, for example, attacks on GAA members by loyalists and the security forces on the basis of their assumed support for the IRA (Bairner 1996); and the murder of Protestants deemed to be supporters of the security forces on the basis of their religious affiliation.

Any application of the term 'community' to a group of individuals is potentially reductive of the differences which might exist between them or between sub-groups which exist within this larger category (Hyndman 1996). As discussed in the previous chapter, gender might function as an important differential in engaging with community. Class too might be considered as an important distinction. Those whose affluence provides them with access to goods and services have been able to insulate themselves against the worst excesses of the violence visited upon the most deprived peoples of Northern Ireland, where rates of unemployment have been historically the worst in the United Kingdom (Coulter 1999). Geographical location serves as a further difference, most obviously in the distinction between the rural and the urban experiences of the conflict (Poulter 1997; Murtagh 1998). Moreover, the relationship of any given locale to other locales has served to differentiate the experiences of individuals and sub-groups within particular communities of identity. Thus, for example, living as a working-class loyalist within the large Rathcoole housing estate on the outskirts of North Belfast, which is bordered by largely loyalist areas, will be different to living in the Fountain estate in Derry, the last loyalist enclave within the nationalist city-side. Generational distinctions will also provide different experiences, and it is notable that youth sub-cultures such as punk rock in the late 1970s and early 1980s and the clubbing scene in the 1990s (the subject of Maria Connolly's *Massive* in 2002) have provided examples of the kind of 'cross-community' activities which the state has tried unsuccessfully to initiate. Likewise, homosexuality has provided a largely underground sub-culture which has provided an alternative reference group to those of the dominant political identities, notably in plays by Frank McGuinness such as *Observe the Sons of Ulster Marching Towards the Somme* and *Carthaginians* and also in Joseph Crilly's *On McQuillan's Hill*. Thus, a community which is the result of active participation by a possibly diverse constituency, will include in its membership individuals who belong to a range of other communities, affiliation to which disrupts any view of a community as a static and homogeneous entity in which shared characteristics are always pre-eminent.

A final dimension to the definition of community is the way in which a community, once established, operates and develops. Communities rely on public symbols and expressions of identity through which the norms and conventions of communal membership can be demonstrated, tested and developed. The arts, therefore, have long been seen as a key means in the articulation of communal identity. In a number of discussions, a central debate has been around the issue of community participation in the development of theatre works. Kershaw, for example, makes the careful distinction that: 'certain approaches to making theatre and performance do not simply "model" ideologies or "reflect" the politics of their context; but, rather, they are actively engaged in widening the bounds of political processes, in opening up new domains of political action' (1996: 150). The extent to which such approaches to making theatre were possible within Northern Ireland will be discussed in relation to two different projects: the Stone Chair Project in Belfast and the work of Derry Frontline. The former, whilst having a long-term process, was geared towards the staging of a community play. The latter was the result of a process of workshops, training and discussion from which a production was only one of a number of results. Each project shared the assumption of the traditions of the workers' theatre movements which 'saw the working class and its organizations as the main historical force for bringing about a radical social change. For this reason they chose to perform mainly for working people on their own ground and focused in their plays on the problems of their audiences in the light of the struggle for change' (Stourac and McCreery 1986: xiv).

Thus, although they shared some elements, the differences in their emphasis represent contrasting approaches to enabling communities to speak for themselves, in Northern Ireland and across the world.

The Productions in Context

As described in Chapter 2, Martin Lynch's origins as a playwright were with the Socialist Fellowship Community Theatre in Turf Lodge and even after his success as a professional playwright, Lynch has remained close to his roots in community theatre, particularly through his work with Belfast's Community Arts Forum. In 1989, he undertook one of the largest community theatre projects ever mounted in Northern Ireland which culminated with a production of *The Stone Chair* in Belfast's Grand Opera House on 15 June 1989. In Lynch's own estimation *The Stone Chair* was 'the closest he's come to his personal concept of a perfect formula for theatre' (Wright 1989: 27). The production took its name from the ancient stone chair at which Conn O'Neill was anointed as successor to the Clandeboye dynasty in 1601, the last Gaelic chieftain of Ulster.[3] The play juxtaposes the memories of the people of the Short Strand area of Belfast of the Blitz in 1941 with a play-within-a-play about O'Neill's situation. Short Strand is a predominantly nationalist enclave within loyalist East Belfast. With a population of between three and four thousand, the nationalist community is isolated within the larger loyalist population of some 90,000 and the area was one of the first to be segregated by a physical barrier, a so-called 'peace-line', in 1969. This enclosure has consolidated both the community's sense of self and the connection between itself and its locale as territory.[4] Alongside other interface areas, Short Strand is marked by high levels of unemployment; restricted access to amenities; lower levels of educational achievement; and, poorer standards of health.[5] This physical containment has been matched by a sense of voicelessness within the community. This lack of a voice was emphasised when the BBC commissioned Erich Durschmeid to make a film, *A Street in Belfast*, about the lives of three families in the Short Strand. Although shot in 1975, the film was never released (Curtis 1984: 198).

For Lynch the attraction of working in this particular area was that it had retained the shared culture and energy which he associated with his family's background in the docks area, aspects lost in the move to Turf Lodge as a new peripheral housing scheme with little community infrastructure.[6] He also suggests that his experience of professional (often middle-class) actors playing working-class characters was that they had difficulty in understanding some of the dimensions of what was being portrayed; whereas non-professional working-class actors were not only alive to these dimensions but passionately committed to the work itself.[7] However, while Lynch was keen to engage with this sensibility, he was reluctant to return to the limitless personal demands placed on him when he was working with the amateur set-up of the Socialist Fellowship in Turf Lodge. Armed now with a substantial experience of the professional process of making theatre, Lynch decided to initiate a project which would bring both aspects of his theatre work together: a community play in Short Strand in which he would try to give voice to a community. This was a significant project of empowerment for a community which had been silenced by its isolation from its surrounding environment.

Lynch gathered around him a small group of professionals who would act as a 'scaffolding' around the involvement of the community, giving it shape and structure. This conforms to the model of community plays advanced by Ann Jellicoe (1987) which is summarised by Kershaw: 'The complex business of steering the project is undertaken by a "core group" of professional theatre workers which normally includes a director, a writer, a stage manager, a designer, a musical director' (1992: 193). With Lynch acting as producer and scripting the piece, John Haswell was appointed to take on the direction of the project. Haswell had worked under John McGrath at 7:84 (Scotland), directing Donald Campbell's *Victorian Values* as a community project in Edinburgh. Haswell was to be assisted by Lenny Mullan whom Lynch had met during his term as writer-in-residence at the University of Ulster in Coleraine, while Mullan was taking a Theatre Studies degree there. Mullan also brought experience in community theatre in Belfast through a variety of projects and organisations, most notably Neighbourhood Open Workshops. Lynch recruited four professional actors who he considered would be willing to work creatively within the community context. Of these, Sean Kearns and Birdie Sweeney were to earn particular plaudits from reviewers. Lynch had garnered funds from the Arts Council by appealing directly to then director, Michael Longley, having been refused a grant from the Combined Arts officer. £5,000 was provided. Lynch then approached an economic regeneration initiative, Making Belfast Work, which although it had not had any experience of using the arts, provided £14,000.[8] After lobbying, a further £5,000 was provided by Belfast City Council, despite the objections of DUP councillor, Sammy Wilson, since the project was only focused on the nationalist community. Further money was raised from the Northern Ireland Voluntary Trust, the Carnegie UK Trust, Children in Need and through events in the area (Wright 1989: 27).

   One of the first tasks facing the group was to become established within the area. This was to be no small task. Short Strand, although ostensibly a homogeneous nationalist community, was also riven by factions, both personal and political. Of the latter, the most prominent was the legacy of the split between the Provisional and Official republicans in 1969 (and the subsequent Official IRA cease-fire in 1972), which gave rise to Sinn Féin and the Workers' Party respectively. Such factions were mutually suspicious of each other and wary of any project which might be used by another faction to its own advantage. This cut two ways since some Workers' Party representatives wanted a more political intervention than it was possible for Lynch to make, while Sinn Féin regarded Lynch with suspicion because of his association with the Official movement and the Workers' Party of which he was still a member at that time. Without a tradition of performance in the area, there was resistance too to the idea of using theatre as a medium, particularly amongst males. Lynch and the team addressed this by talking initially to already constituted community organisations, such as a local mothers and toddlers group, and then running workshops to enable people to feel comfortable in acting out of their own experience in improvisations. Lynch's own background allowed him to connect with men whom he knew from the docks and to engage with the male culture of the area, drinking in local clubs and playing snooker to try to attract men to the project. This slow process of becoming part of the community lasted over a year.

Residents took part in the production processes and the performance alongside the professionals in key roles. The script itself was an amalgamation of reminiscences collected from over fifty local interviewees and original writing by Lynch. Sean McGuigan, Kevin McNally and Karen Carlisle along with Lynch carried out a series of interviews with local residents. These were to provide the raw material from which Lynch would script the final piece. This approach to composition echoes the process which Charabanc had employed in their early work (see Chapter 6), on which Lynch had collaborated, and has a long history in community theatre across the world (see Filewod 1987, for example). It has also been adopted by a number of other theatre projects in Northern Ireland such as *Binlids* (discussed earlier in Chapter 3).

Having reviewed the collected interviews, Lynch presented an initial outline to an advisory board, constituted by representatives of local community organisations. The importance of this approach is recognised by Brady, who suggests that 'the community theatre must find ways to involve community workers and other interested parties in its work, and to provide a model of accountability' (1994: 13). Lynch proposed that the piece would focus on the experiences of people in the area during the Blitz. The choice of setting was prompted by a number of considerations. The period was prominent in the stories provided by the interviewees, many of whom were pensioners with vivid memories of the war. The process of staging such personal anecdotes created social memories from personal recollection, creating or expanding the community's sense of itself and its history. Thus, the community was enabled to create a form of what Taylor (2001) has called 'embodied memory'.

Lynch himself welcomed the chance to work outside the immediate experience of the conflict, since this had been the focus in so much of his own writing up to this point. Moreover, the divisions within the area meant that any more recent time setting would have disrupted the sense of unity which the project was trying to celebrate and engender. The emphasis on consensus (by avoiding politics) is a key goal in Jellicoe's model of community plays: 'Politics are divisive. We strongly feel that the humanising effect of our work is far more productive than stirring up political confrontation' (1987: 122). Additionally, the World War Two setting allowed for the establishment of an external threat in the form of the German bombing of the city in accordance with Jellicoe's advice that outside villains provide people against whom the community can comfortably unite (ibid., 125). Woodruff critiques Jellicoe's desire for a depoliticised consensus, by arguing that 'Ann Jellicoe appears to think that this formulation of community plays avoids politics. Of course, it does nothing of the kind. It reinforces an idealized notion of community as an unchanging entity' (1989: 371). However, in the context of a history of violent factional feuding within the community, it was considered crucial to avoid anything too contentious, even at the risk of creating a roseate view of life in the past or present. Kershaw notes also that participation in community play projects and the celebratory atmosphere which the performance creates itself helps to build community cohesiveness (1992: 1990). This is important since the community play is not just proposing an idealised version of the community, but by its process is enabling such a community to be experienced.

With the outline agreed, Lynch took all the collected material away to compose the script. He blended documented history with the anecdotes, memories and apocryphal stories of the interviewees without drawing distinctions between them. His process was guided both by the opportunities for developing characterisation and the distillation of the most theatrical anecdotes. He had to be mindful too of the need to provide roles for all of the cast who were attending the workshops. He created a central linking device in the form of a young couple with a young baby and around them structured a series of vignettes, with set piece moments and musical interludes, including big band dance tunes, popular songs from the time and children's street songs. In some instances, individual characters or moments were tailored directly for individuals to ensure that their particular talent would be displayed. The *Newsletter* reviewer commented that the effect was to create 'a pageant rather than a play' (Fitzgerald 1989: 9). Once an initial script was completed this was passed for feedback to the advisory board and the director. A subsequent draft was provided for the first cast readthrough and from that point on redrafts and rewrites were being made in both the rehearsal room and by Lynch as the project evolved.

The decision to use the Grand Opera House as the venue was pragmatic. Although the initial intention was to stage the performance in a local parochial hall, the scale of the project and a plan to refurbish that building made this impractical. The Grand Opera House had the only stage large enough to accommodate the cast (the programme lists over sixty cast members) and the scale of the production. Such a foray into community theatre was a departure for a venue whose programme was more routinely filled by established commercial productions or large-scale high art performances such as ballet. James Helps's design established the dominating gantries of the shipyard[9] and the red-brick gable ends of the terraced houses of the area and was an important feature in providing the context and structure of the performance as a whole. The project represented a repetition for Lynch of his earlier successes in opening up theatre venues to working-class audiences (as he had done at the Group and the Lyric) as an act of 'strategic penetration'. However, the internal structure of the auditorium effected a separation out of the audience from the performance and created divisions within the audience itself, embodying the bourgeois conventions of spatial arrangement of the building's original design. The production ran for ten nights with an average audience of 60% capacity for the run. The budget for the production relied on box-office takings of £16,000, a figure exceeded (just) by the final returns of £19,000. The success of the project was not to be marked by its box office take; rather it was in achieving Lynch's ambition 'to bring the "ordinary" people into the theatre' and as Ian Hill's (1989) review for the *Guardian* noted 'now he has succeeded doubly by having them on both sides of the footlights' (cited Byrne 2001b: 99).

The ambition of Derry Frontline was less widely focused but perhaps deeper by contrast. The group was inspired by a visit to Derry by Manchester's Frontline: Culture and Education in 1988, forming initially through a series of drama workshops in the Bogside and Creggan areas of the city.[10] For the next four years Derry Frontline was involved in radical arts interventions based on a range of models from Paolo Freire, Augusto Boal, Theatre for Development and the work of Edward Bond. The group focused on unemployed young people in a series of workshops across drama, music, creative writing and visual arts. These cultural education projects shared four main objectives:

> To enable young people to articulate and critically celebrate their history and experience.
> To enable young people to understand the democratic principles of self-determination.
> To pass on skills in communication, organization, cooperation, and conflict resolution.
> To launch independent community initiatives which further the development of cultural education.
>
> (Baron Cohen and Pilkington 1994: 24)

Baron Cohen explains the principles that underpinned the workshops:

> [T]o prioritize the life-experience, the living needs and the knowledges of every workshop participant; to structure every workshop in a dialogue between the needs of its participants and the agreed cultural aims of its co-ordinator(s); to build a workshop culture of intimacy, friendship, democratic participation, supported risk, experimentation, questioning and affirmation; and to recognize all resistance as knowledge—particularly as expressed through the right to question and the right to say 'no'.
>
> (2001: 14)

The dangers, identified by Brady for example, that these principles might produce work which 'wanders at times into a kind of individual and group therapy' (1994: 10) were guarded against by the different phases of the workshops. From an initial story-telling phase in which participants were able to share their stories and concerns, a central workshop theme would be identified. The participants would then move on to a phase of 'experimentation and critical questioning—in search of realistic, democratic and just solutions to collectively identified relevant problems or contradictions' (Baron Cohen 2001: 15). The insistence within this phase of choosing dilemmas which would most clearly pose a question suggests a link through to the forum form of the Theatre of the Oppressed. According to Baron Cohen 'the overriding concern within this phase was to judge when to respect and when to coax open the silences individuals and communities used for self-protection, and to understand the complex and shifting boundaries between educational theatre or theatre-for-development and drama-therapy' (ibid.). A third phase, narrative construction, was based on a series of recorded improvisations around the central theme which were then worked into a final script by a single writer. The final production phase saw the material being prepared for public presentation to the defined community or communities.

Three plays were to emerge from the group over its four-year existence: *Inside Out* (1988), *Time Will Tell* (1989) and *Threshold* (1992). Of these *Inside Out* and *Threshold* were created within the republican community, while *Time Will Tell* was a long-term collaboration with Frontline in Manchester, playing on a tour of Greater Manchester, Salford, Sheffield and Liverpool. They were produced by a group of people who were 'highly politicised republicans and young community activists' (Baron Cohen and Pilkington 1994: 20), and shared an antipathy to those forces identified as oppressing the working classes: the colonial British presence in Ireland, the hierarchy of the Catholic Church, and globalised capitalism. Links to the Republican movement made the group's members a target for attacks by loyalist paramilitaries and the work of the group was disrupted by raids by the RUC and army (Baron Cohen and Pilkington 1994; Baron Cohen 2001).

All three performance pieces demonstrate a clear awareness of issues of gender as a fissure within the community. *Time Will Tell* examines issues of domestic violence, gay sexuality and the Ulster Protestant experience. *Threshold* links issues of the community's silence on rape and abortion with silence over the complicity of church and state in the exploitation of the community by globalised capitalism in the name of urban regeneration. Notably the production, as with *The Stone Chair*, was the culmination of a two-year project, based on fifty interviews, 'various visual arts projects. . . and projects arising from Augusto Boal's techniques of "forum" and "invisible theatre" ' (Baron Cohen and Pilkington 1994: 17). It is *Inside Out* which treats gender and the conflict most directly. It was first staged in July 1988 at the Corn Beef Tin and Pilot's Row, Derry and at the Conway Mill, Belfast. While each of the eight scenes was largely naturalistic in its presentational style, the acting area eschewed the kind of set associated with realism. While the stage directions provide for an indicative setting for each of the interior domestic scenes these were augmented by the presence of stage sculptures produced by the Bogside Sculptors' Group. The sculptures functioned to disrupt the realism of the performance conventions offering a form of social *gest*, a clear delineation of the social relations at work within the scene (Reinelt 1996). One of these is 'a sculpture of a cooker embedded in the roof of a landrover' (Baron Cohen 2001: 24) on which the performance opens. The other is a three-sided sculpture with a separate image painted on each face: a labourer behind bars; a mother and child; and a petrol bomber. The central narrative focuses on the pregnancy of the fifteen-year-old Ann Deehan and the pressures on her to keep or abort the foetus from those around her, particularly under the influence of the Catholic Church. Ann's boyfriend, Sean Doherty, has few prospects for work and the play turns on his conversion from opposing an abortion to supporting Ann's right to choose. What might appear to be a personal or domestic conflict, however, is raised to the level of a public issue by the linkage made between Ann's right to determine her future and the republican armed conflict: she is as right to take a life to preserve her freedom as the men in Long Kesh are to wage a campaign of violence to free Ireland. The church's support of the state's security forces is connected by Ann to its role in opposing a woman's right to choose.

While there is a chronological narrative development within the scenes, their function is clearly linked to establishing the nature of the problem which Ann faces. In Scene 1, a priest delivers a letter from the bishop calling for the congregation to support the security forces. Scene 2 in the Doherty home demonstrates the difficulties ordinary women face in struggling to maintain a household without an income, as Mrs Doherty struggles to provide a Sunday lunch on an unreliable cooker. In Scene 3, Gerry Deehan, Ann's father, leaves the house on the run from the security forces. In Scene 4, Ann reveals to her friend Cathy and Sean that she is pregnant. Despite his ideas about supporting Ann materially, Sean is incapable of providing the emotional support she wants from him, further constrained by his awareness of social taboos. When Ann and Cathy are joined by another friend Tara, the central debate over the future of the pregnancy is staged. Scene 5 takes place in the house of Sean's aunt and uncle where his cousin Joe has announced that he wants to join the police to play a part in changing his society. The church's support for the police is introduced and debated when both the parish priest and Sean enter. In the next scene Sean and Ann argue over the prospect of Ann terminating the pregnancy. Back at his own house in the next scene, Sean breaks the news to his mother and father, already reconciled himself to Ann's right to choose. He sees in his mother's circumstances the future facing Ann if she goes ahead with the pregnancy. When it is suggested that the matter be referred to the priest, Sean seizes the broken cooker and staggers out. The final scene of the play is a direct statement by Ann to the audience in Irish and then English: 'Last night, as the news passed from home to home of the death of the priest, the town came to a standstill. It rained all night. This morning cookers could be seen outside the flats on Rossville Street. The RUC want names' (Baron Cohen 2001: 79).

The closure of classic narrative is refused and the audience is confronted with a situation with which they must come to terms for themselves. The performance, then, carries out an agitational function in juxtaposing one set of accepted social values (the sanctity of life) against another (the justice of the armed struggle) without resolving the contradictions between them. Indeed to the extent that the production validates the armed struggle, it accentuates the contradictions around the right to choose. This validation takes place through a series of songs which link the struggle in Northern Ireland with that against apartheid in South Africa, against the Taliban in Afghanistan and for democracy in Nicaragua. The play ends on a repeated lyric sung by the whole company emphasising the sacrifice and bloodshed which have characterised liberation struggles across the world. The endorsement of Republican violence and resistance to the authority of the church over a woman's fertility produces the kind of effect which Kershaw (1992) suggests is fundamental to the ideological efficacy of performance. This effect is the creation of a crisis within the performance which is recognised as critical also to the audience's own fundamental beliefs and values: where 'the necessary duality of conventions. . . allows performance to "play" with the audience's fundamental beliefs, and to provoke a potential crisis in those beliefs, without producing immediate rejection' (1992: 28). Even if the audience does not accept the linkage between a woman's right to choose and national wars of self-determination, thinking through the arguments for oneself may provide the kind of personal liberation that the production was seeking.

In *Inside Out*, the very form of the play in its mix of monologue and dialogue constitutes the drama at its heart. The play begins with a priest reading out a letter from the bishop. This opening follows a conventional monologue form in which the speech is delivered without any acknowledgement of the exact constitution of its audience or in any expectation that it will (or should) be met with a response. Castagno argues that 'the authority of monologue is related to its inherent resistance to interruption or disruption' (1993: 134). This monologue is a closed and static dramaturgical element in its form, in what it states and in how it is delivered. It is against this definitive closure that the rest of the play reacts to develop a dialogical engagement. This engagement is created through the intermixing of dialogic scenes and further monologic elements throughout the rest of the play. These monologues, however, do not serve to clarify the internal aspects of character. Instead they act as a means to relate the private discussions and debates of individual characters within a wider set of social contexts. Thus, at the end of Scene 2 of the first act, Sean's direct address to the audience is a poetic explanation of the structures which inhibit free thinking. It is used to develop a metaphorical link between his work as a builder and the barriers which confine the people around him.

Discussion: Protection and Expansion

There are clear differences then in the approaches which each project adopted. These differences did not reside in the distinction between a participatory and an exclusive process, since each project involved members of its intended constituency. Thus, distinctions between plays *by* a community and plays *for* a community which have been widely discussed elsewhere (Woodruff 1989; Kershaw 1992) do not apply. Each project had at its heart processes of cultural democracy in one form or another (Kelly 1984). There is a clear distinction between the nature of the participation in each project, however. The controlling presence of the core group within the Stone Chair Project stands in contrast to the democratic participation in the development of *Inside Out*. Frontline's emphasis on the responsiveness of workshops to the needs of individuals and of the group would not have sat easily with the demands of mounting a production which was the primary driver of the process as Baron Cohen acknowledged in discussing the later *Threshold* project: 'I think the necessary emphasis on production deadlines contradicted our declared methods, for it allowed little time for experimentation, error, or radical personal development and support' (Baron Cohen and Pilkington 1994: 25). The Stone Chair Project was always conceived of as a process leading to a public production, however. While acknowledging that the involvement of professionals might allow for 'mystification and manipulation', Kershaw borrows Barba's idea of 'barter' to suggest the possibility of a more egalitarian process: 'the skills of the professionals are exchanged for performances (and other types of work) by local people, not as equals but as a way of achieving equality' (1992: 193).

Nonetheless, it is tempting to suggest that one process was preferable to the other on some ideological basis, a debate which has been a recurrent feature of discussions of radical theatre practice. Woodruff (1989) emphasises the element of control in castigating Jellicoe's model, for example. His position is that only by enabling working-class participants the control to express their concerns and material struggles can community plays fulfil their radical potential. His example of the *No More Cream Buns* theatre workshop in Telford draws attention to the ways in which professional practitioners were involved but 'worked as part of the group and to the instructions of the group' (1989: 372). *Inside Out* would undoubtedly win his approbation based on this. Kershaw argues that the criterion for assessing the efficacy of community plays should be based on a relationship between celebration and criticism:

> The crucial dynamic for the efficacy of community plays is that the community is being confronted by the community, in large part through the dialectical interaction of celebration and criticism. If and when this occurs, the plays are not simply giving the community a voice—they may be contributing to its ideological development by prompting a crisis in its identity which may not be resolved in its 'real' relations in the socio-political present.
>
> (1992: 203)

Kershaw's argument points up that judgements of such works need not be on the basis of the constituency of those involved in the making, or even the process by which they are made. Rather, it may be better to question the extent to which the process and the performance contribute to the specific constituency which they seek to address. This too is subject to qualification since such contributions may vary strategically or tactically at any given point in time by interventions which may be either protective or expansive. According to Kelly, 'Protective acts will aim to protect, nourish and maintain those minimum social meanings and resources without which community would be impossible. . . Protective action is concerned with ensuring that members of the community receive the benefits and provisions to which they are entitled, and that these are both sufficient and satisfactory' (1984: 51). This definition is extended here to a specifically cultural role through which the community as it is already known is consolidated, conserved and/or celebrated. Fintan Brady criticises this as work which is 'typified by a conservative desire to repeat only what everyone is already familiar with' (1994: 10). However, at specific moments when communities come under particular stresses or in response to long-term and chronic pressures such protective acts may form a vital role in the maintenance of a community under threat.

The importance of a community theatre project as a protective act can be identified once it is recognised that community formation is not a one-off moment, but a process of continual renewal. The necessity for such renewal derives from the tensions between individual desires and membership of the community, itself regarded as the source of the Aristotelian tradition of drama, and exacerbated by pressures of a violent conflict. Baron Cohen explained that the reality of war required a coercive unity, where 'the conflict between personal desire and community solidarity is all but unspeakable within the culture of self-sacrifice, where self-development is defined as a *betrayal of your own*' (Baron Cohen and King 1997: 274). Within Northern

Ireland, in addition to economic deprivation and its related manifestations in poorer health and access to goods and services, working-class communities have come under particular pressures from within as a result of internal political and social divisions between, for example, paramilitary groups. They have also come under external threat from paramilitaries from the other side and, in the case of nationalist communities, threats from the British army and the police (Coulter 1999: 89). These are not the manufactured enemies which Jellicoe (1987) suggests should be identified in the community play, but sources of everyday danger to many individuals and communities. Providing a united front against such external threats is one important protective act to which community theatre might contribute.

The Stone Chair, then, might be seen as an example of such a protective act. Its processes and production can be seen to have contributed to greater social cohesion within the community of the Short Strand, confirming rather than subverting the social meanings of the community (Brady 1994: 10). In so doing, it provided for a particular kind of pleasure for its audience in performance, what Terry Lovell has termed 'pleasures of resistance' which are described as: 'pleasures of common experiences identified and celebrated in art, and through this celebration given recognition and validation; pleasures of solidarity to which this sharing may give rise; pleasure in shared and socially defined aspirations and hopes; in a sense of identity and community' (Lovell 1981: 95). Such pleasures need not inevitably be seen as exclusive. Lynch certainly believes that much of the work which he did with community groups spoke too to other members of the working class who were hungry to see lives like theirs represented on the stage. Brady argues that, 'in allowing space for an active reflection on the social facts of life, the community theatre works *between* communities as well as *within* communities' (1994: 12). Thus, perhaps one of the most important effects of the choice of the Grand Opera House as a venue for the performance was to make it accessible to people from outside Short Strand. In using the experience of the Blitz as the milieu for the performance, the production was able to open itself to loyalist and unionist audiences where the shared experience pre-dated the contemporary conflict. Thus, even though the myth of republican collusion with the Luftwaffe by guiding German bombers to the Belfast shipyards has had a wide circulation, the production's emphasis was on the shared experience of a common external enemy who made no distinction between ethnicity or politics in bombing the city. In a review of the production for BBC Radio Ulster, McAughtry commented that

> on the night that I was there a proportion of the audience was Protestant working class, watching closely as for the first time in their lives some of them saw right inside a Catholic city village and saw that the people they were watching were themselves. . . not just a smashing night out, it's a

powerful contribution to community relations in this place where it's so
badly needed.

(cited Byrne 2001b: 99)

Further, the production allowed other people to appreciate the talents and
resources of the people within the area (and of working-class people more
generally), something frequently missed by decision-makers in a society
where class segregation is deeply embedded (Coulter 1999).

An awareness of the importance of context in determining the strategic or
tactical contribution which a community theatre project might make as a
protective act provides an important qualification of Kershaw's emphasis on
criticism as well as celebration. The development of cultural interventions
which can challenge a community's sense of itself may need particular conditions to support them. Kelly terms such interventions 'expansive acts'. He
suggests that expansive acts

> will aim to encourage and expand social meanings wherever they are
> strong. They will move beyond the determinist fallacy of seeing people
> solely as the products of a given, and pre-existing, culture, and take into
> account their roles as co-authors of that culture. People are constrained
> within limitations, but they are capable of changing and expanding those
> limitations, of pushing against then and making them move.

(1984: 51)

Expansive acts then can involve critical questioning of the values of the
community and externalising those norms, beliefs and habitual responses
which have become internalised in response to particular social conditions or
contradictions. Expansive acts tend to be regarded as the proper role for the
arts as political interventions. For example, in Chapter 5 the distinction made
by Kearney between ideological and utopian myths is discussed. This distinction leads him to postulate a further distinction between authentic and inau-
thentic uses of myth:

> At best, myth invited us to reimagine our past in a way which challenges
> the present status quo and opens up alternative possibilities of thinking.
> At worst, it provides a community with a strait-jacket of fixed identity,
> drawing a *cordon-sanitaire* around this identity which excludes dialogue
> with all that is other than itself.

(Kearney 1997: 121)

Kearney's preference is clearly for art as an expansive intervention. However,
his denigration of what might be regarded as protective acts does not acknowledge that the capacity of the community to engage with such expansive acts

may well be circumscribed by the specific conditions with which it is faced at any given point in time. In discussion of the work of Derry Frontline, for example, much is made of the ways in which the community was engaged in a culture of resistance, making what Baron Cohen refers to as 'barricade theatre' (Baron Cohen and King 1997: 272). He recounts that in the group's workshops,

> In conditions of armed conflict, the most we could do was expose the barricades (particularly cynicism) which are often used to rationalise or conceal the fears that keep contradictions and suffering in place. We never attempted to dismantle emotional or psychological structures; at best, we'd get the barricades to speak, most profoundly through the anonymity of fiction in the playwriting stage of the project.
>
> (Baron Cohen and King 1997: 275)

This sense of the necessary security of psychological barricades was mirrored in the decision of the group to work primarily within the Bogside, providing physical security and easy access for the community. Crucially, however, the processes undertaken by the members of Frontline did produce work which was critical of the community in a movement away from resistance to liberation. The earlier description of *Inside Out* demonstrates the way in which a community can be scrutinised from within and confronted with the contradictions between its own values without representing a threat to the community. According to Baron Cohen, 'the primary reason for their community coming to see that play is to see and hear their own people in control of their own medium, talking about their lives and talking about their future' (Baron Cohen and Pilkington 1994: 26). In challenging the operation of patriarchy, inculcated by the church and lived out in social structures and personal relationships, *Inside Out* was a deliberately expansive act for its community. Baron Cohen suggests that 'our productions (both rehearsed improvisations and scripted performances) were designed to expose central ideological contradictions and to encourage radical questioning' (Baron Cohen and Pilkington 1994: 25).

The conditions that allow for such radical questioning depended on the relationship between the community audience and the performance; and the community's own state of development. The relationship of the audience from the community to the performance is already established prior to the performance due to their relationships with the performers, their contribution to the script or research, contributions to the props or making of set and costumes. These are features of many community plays, of course, and do not distinguish *Inside Out* from *The Stone Chair*, for example. What does distinguish the projects is the state of development of the community itself at the time of each production. Cultural interventions were already a feature of community life by the time of *Inside Out*: by the Bogside Sculptors group, for example, and by a range of interventions by members of Frontline. The group had already been provided with a model in Manchester Frontline's initial visit and its members were also involved in a range of other highly politicised community networks. Thus, the performers are allowed a licence to take a critical stance as members of the community. By contrast, the impulse for *The Stone Chair* came from outside the community, initiated by Lynch and in a context in which the community's engagement with its own representation and self-determination were underdeveloped.

Community plays, then, have played a particular role in the staging of the conflict. Whilst the involvement of the community in the processes of composition and production allows for control over its representation and may itself be a means of community development, the function of performances as protective or expansive acts may depend as much on the existing stage of the community's development as on internal features of the performance or the nature of the process.

8

Theatre after the Cease-fires

BILL: I don't think it is a peace process for a start. I think it is a Nationalist
     process. I think it's playing into the hands of the enemies of Ulster.
     I don't believe David Trimble when he says that the Union is safer
     now than it ever was. I don't believe the Irish government when they
     lifted their territorial claim over Northern Ireland. But I do believe
     Gerry Adams when he says that this is a stepping stone to a United
     Ireland.

(Gary Mitchell, 2000, *The Force of Change*, 48)

On 31 August 1994, the Army Council of the PIRA announced a complete
cessation of military activities. In October, the Combined Loyalist Military
Command issued a statement on behalf of all loyalist paramilitary groups,
announcing that they would be on cease-fire from midnight on Thursday 13
October. The political manoeuvrings from which these statements emerged
involved protracted and secret negotiations between the British government
and republicans, and between the British and Irish governments. The issuing
of the Downing Street Declaration by Irish Taoiseach Albert Reynolds and
British Prime Minister John Major in December 1993 was the public acknowledgement that the future could be a matter of open discussion in which paramilitaries could play a part, provided peace could be assured. Although the
PIRA cease-fire was to break down, most notably with the bombing of
London's Canary Wharf in February 1996, the political process towards a
negotiated settlement was set in train and by mid-1997 a commitment by
mainstream republicanism to the pursuit of purely political means ushered in
the possibility of the all-party talks. On 10 April 1998 the principles and
processes agreed in these talks were announced in what was to become known
as the Good Friday Agreement. Just over a month later, in referenda on the
Agreement on each side of the border (though not within the rest of the United
Kingdom), there was overwhelming support for it: in Northern Ireland,
71.12% and in the Republic 94.4% of voters voted in favour. It appeared,
then, that playwrights and theatre-makers were overtaken by the imaginative
powers of the politicians in formulating a path out of the conflict: the role
claimed by Stewart Parker for the playwright had had to be ceded to the polit-

ical leaders who had brought the paramilitaries to the negotiating table.[1] What remained less clear was what the appropriate response of theatre makers might be, and what perspective they could bring on the unfolding processes. To suggest that peace could break out instantly would be a form of utopianism in which few shared once the euphoria around the Good Friday Agreement subsided; while criticism of the processes of moving towards peace might be considered either unhelpful or negative to the point of destabilising the process.

Since 1998, the provisions of the Agreement have run into continuous difficulty. The devolved assembly in which the parties would share power was suspended on four occasions, and has yet to be reconvened since the then Secretary of State, John Reid, announced the latest of these suspensions on 14 October 2002. Whilst the Agreement received support across the political spectrum, a significant rump of dissidents opposed to it remained: within unionism, led by the DUP; and within republicanism through the continued campaigns by the Real IRA and Continuity IRA and a variety of associated political groupings. However, whilst mainstream republicanism, and nationalists more generally, perceived that the Agreement was a major improvement in their position within the state, dissident unionism has attracted greater and greater support in its opposition to it, such that the DUP has overtaken the UUP as the largest unionist party.[2] Even before the signing of the Good Friday Agreement, James White McAuley noted 'a growing feeling among unionists that their whole social and political world is in danger and notions of "crisis" and "unionist alienation" have come to the fore' (1999: 73). Since the signing of the Agreement, issues such as the involvement of republicans in government; the reform of policing; restrictions on or the removal of British symbols from certain state institutions; the closure of British Army bases; and the creation of a commission to oversee the staging of parades (which disproportionately affects Orange marching given their predominance) have contributed to a feeling amongst unionists that the peace process has precipitated a 'hollowing out' of Ulster's Britishness (Murray 2000). The confidence and visibility of nationalist cultural expression (aided by the increasingly global appeal of Irish cultural products) by contrast has grown, no longer evacuated from the public spaces which had hitherto been reserved for expressions of unionist identity (Rolston 1998a). Since many measures implemented under the Agreement recognised Northern Ireland's dual position as both British and Irish, for unionists it appeared that a state once regarded as their preserve and with which they were strongly identified was fast becoming 'a cold house for Protestants'.[3] This alienation from the state is a key dynamic in the work of Gary Mitchell as the quotation from a speech by Bill Byrne in *The Force of Change* with which this chapter opened exemplifies. Within loyalist communities and organisations one reaction to the disillusionment expressed in this speech has been the splintering of unity:

between those committed to the peace process and those wedded to resisting it; between political parties seeking to be seen as sole representatives of 'the people' (Finlayson 1999); and within and between paramilitary organisations in a series of turf wars for control of loyalist areas.

By contrast, nationalist communities, already supported by infrastructures originally developed to compensate for state antipathy, were able to access the economic and social provisions of the Agreement to their benefit, although a number of commentators have expressed doubt about the abilities of the working class to benefit from the economic dividends of the peace (Neill 1995; Shirlow and Shuttleworth 1999). Republican influence has grown within political structures at all levels and Sinn Féin overtook the SDLP as the leading nationalist party in the assembly elections in 2003. The preparation of republicans for the peace process had been ongoing for some time in advance of the cease-fire declarations and the Good Friday Agreement. In cultural terms, contributions were made through Féile an Phobail and companies like DubbelJoint, JustUs (see Chapter 3) and Derry Frontline (see Chapter 6), providing opportunities for public articulation of and reflection on the strategic shifts within the movement.[4] Thus, with republican paramilitaries engaged in an uneasy cease-fire, a number of significant new works that attempted to stage the peace focused on the unionist/loyalist experience to explore what its reaction might or should be to the circumstances in which it now found itself. The issue that each faced was what it would take for loyalists to be accommodated within the new politics. Three productions in particular represent different approaches to staging the peace at different intervals since 1994. Marie Jones's *A Night in November* was staged around the period of the first PIRA cease-fire; Gary Mitchell's *As the Beast Sleeps* (1998) was mounted shortly after the signing of the Good Friday Agreement; and Tim Loane's *Caught Red Handed* addressed the crisis in unionism just as Northern Ireland's devolved legislative assembly was stumbling towards dissolution in 2002.

The Plays in Context

Although Marie Jones was raised within the staunchly loyalist working class of East Belfast, *A Night in November* was a public repudiation of the politics of her background. An experienced actress, Jones had developed as a writer as a member of Charabanc Theatre Company of which she was a co-founder (see Chapter 6). She resigned from her role as a co-artistic director with Charabanc in 1990 and established DubbelJoint Productions with Pam Brighton in 1991. While Charabanc's work was characterised by its commitment to touring across political and sectarian boundaries, DubbelJoint's work was soon to be primarily identified with the nationalist communities close to its home base in West Belfast. With the creation and growth of the West

Figure 7. *A Night in November* by Marie Jones, Dubbeljoint Productions,
Belfast Institute of Further & Higher Education. Photographer: Jill Jennings

Belfast Festival (later Féile an Phobail), DubbelJoint premiered its work as a
mainstay of the festival each August. For Jones, this close identification with
a working-class nationalist community would appear to be a remarkable
journey from her own roots. It is a journey mirrored in the play, a one-man
show, performed originally by Dan Gordon. Gordon himself contributed
much to the development of the script alongside Jones, along with the director
Pam Brighton.[5]

A Night in November opened on 8 August 1994 at the Belfast Institute
of Further and Higher Education on the Whiterock Road. It was Jones's
response to her experience of the sectarianism of the home fans at a soccer
match in the World Cup qualifying competition between Northern Ireland
and the Republic of Ireland at Windsor Park, Belfast. It is from this match in
November 1993 that the play gets its title. The match was played out in the
midst of vicious tit-for-tat attacks by paramilitaries. A month before the
match, a bomb attack on the UDA headquarters on Belfast's Shankill Road
led to the death of the PIRA bomber and nine passers-by. In return, the UDA
mounted a gun attack on a bar in Greysteel, County Derry, leaving seven
people dead. The situation was not improved with the issuing of the Downing
Street Declaration in December 1993 by the British Prime Minister John

Major and the Irish Taoiseach Albert Reynolds. It read: 'The British government agrees that it is for the people of the island of Ireland alone, by agreement between the two parts respectively, to exercise their right of
self-determination on the basis of consent, freely and concurrently given,
North and South, to bring about a united Ireland, if that is their wish'
(McKittrick and McVea 2001: 196). This represented a seismic shift in the
political terrain of Northern Ireland, marked by a further upsurge in the
violence.

At the time of the World Cup competition in June 1994 (on which the
second act of the play is centred), the UVF shot dead six Catholics watching
the opening match in a bar in Loughinisland, County Down, an event referred
to in the play. Despite a three-day PIRA cease-fire in July, the situation escalated. In August rumours were rife about the possibility of a second PIRA
cease-fire and the concessions which were to be made by the British government to achieve it. After their murder of Kathleen O'Hagan, a pregnant
mother of five, the UVF issued a statement declaring: 'We in the UVF will
show republicans how hard it is to listen to a diet of peace while they wage
the deadly deed of war. Brace yourselves for death because you are going to
see plenty of it' (*Newsletter* 8 August 1994: 1). Nationalist communities feared
a return of indiscriminate sectarian attacks. On the twenty-fifth anniversary
of the start of the Troubles, following the deaths of over three thousand
people, peace seemed as distant a prospect as ever.

The play follows a conventional conversion structure in charting the
journey of its central character, Kenneth McCallister, from the bourgeois
unionist values of his aspirant Protestant lower middle-class community. It
ends with him on the streets of New York, part of a throng of fans supporting
the Republic of Ireland at the World Cup Finals, proclaiming loudly, that he
is finally free: 'no-one can point the finger at Kenneth Norman McCalllister
and say, these people are part of you. . . tonight I absolve myself. . . I am free
of them Mick. . . I am free of it, I am a free man. . . I am a Protestant Man,
I'm an Irish Man.' (Jones 1995: 47). This journey is precipitated by an
epiphany when he takes his bigoted father-in-law Ernie to the match at
Windsor Park. He is appalled at the sectarian chants of the Northern Ireland
fans and is forced to confront his own sectarian behaviour in his role as a low-
level dole clerk. He re-evaluates his whole life, concluding that he and his class
have been complicit in the overt sectarianism of the bigots and the violence
of the paramilitaries. Joining the fans in New York is the only act he can make
to disavow this complicity and to liberate himself from the stultifying definition of identity into which his class has led him. Of course, this dramaturgical
manoeuvre switches the focus of the play from a concern with inequality and
injustice to a concern with personal identity, with two effects. The first is to
avoid the difficulties in proposing any resolution to the conflict more widely;
the second is to endorse versions of the conflict as a matter of identity.

Individual integrity substitutes for social justice and political equality.

In focusing on issues of identity, the play is trying to overturn dominant discourses, conjoining the two apparently antithetical ideas of Irish and Protestant. This antithesis was reified historically in two simultaneous processes activated by partition: a narrow equation of Irishness and Catholicism demonstrated in the pre-eminence awarded the Catholic Church within the Free State (and later embedded in the 1937 Constitution); and the identification of the British state of Northern Ireland with Protestantism in its very conception and soon after embedded within its constitutional and legal frameworks.[6] Such mutually exclusive and monolithic views of identity became operative in Northern Ireland (irrespective of contradictory evidence) producing a set of binary oppositions defining the Irish Catholic and the Ulster Protestant to justify the discriminatory treatment of Catholics. In this binary relationship Protestants are hard-working, loyal and trust-worthy, free-thinking and rational individualists, civilised and with a great care for propriety. By contrast Catholics are indolent, unreliable, priest-ridden and superstitious, wild, slovenly and without pride in themselves. Their lowly economic and social status was an effect of their own recalcitrant behaviour.

The representation of the events in the play from a single point of view, what Pfister calls the super-ordinate figure perspective (1988: 59), presents the audience with the experiences of Kenneth McCallister to confront the limitations of these stereotypical oppositions. McCallister recounts how he visited the home of his Catholic boss Jerry and contrasts it with the values underpinning his own home and upbringing: 'Bikes and scooters scattered over the lawn meant slovenliness, a pile of jumbled up books meant no pride or dignity in their lives, a wife who said cook your own tea meant low life at its lowest and all this meant second class, filth, scum and hatred. . . and I believed it' (Jones 1995: 25–6). The process which McCallister recounts, and of which his visit is part, is one which reverses the relative value ascribed to each side of this opposition without questioning its foundations. Thus, Irish Catholics are portrayed as liberated from the claustrophobic, petit bourgeois taboos of McCallister's Ulster Protestants. Now, they are spontaneous, garru-lous, welcoming of the stranger, emotionally articulate. McCallister accesses these characteristics by renouncing his Britishness. According to one reviewer, this dramaturgical strategy 'challenges traditional loyalist fears of being crushed and destroyed by the Awful Catholic South by placing Ken among hundreds of Ireland's World Cup fans who treat him as one of the lads' (Carlson 1994: 10).

The performance is in the form of a monodrama with a single actor taking on the role of Kenneth McCallister, within which he plays out the incidents leading up to and resulting from McCallister's attendance at the Northern Ireland–Republic of Ireland soccer match. Indeed, it was from the capacity of the actor to achieve the representation of complex dialogical interchanges within a narrative framework that much of the pleasure of the performance derived. It is through the complex performance of this script by the single actor that the audience is implicated in its action. There are three main and inter-related processes at work here: the ways in which the performance refers to the dramatic world; the ways in which the performance evaluates the events within that dramatic world; and the trust elicited from the audience by the performer by dint of his skill as performer.

The primary means by which the performance refers to the dramatic world which it seeks to create is in the manipulation of deixis by the performer. Deixis is a feature of both linguistic and gestural communication which defines 'the protagonist ("I"), the addressee ("you") and the context ("here") and thus [sets] up a communication situation' (Elam 1988: 72). Within dramatic action, it relates the speaker and his situation to the rest of the dramatic world. At its simplest, this situation of utterance can be readily established by narration. Through his words the speaker locates the 'here and now' in which he is speaking in relation to the 'there and then' moment in which the action described happened. Verbal indicators of deixis (verbal tense, markers of time, prepositions, adverbs) are contained also in dialogue, relating the speaker to other characters within the situation. An important distinction between drama and story-telling is in the direct representation of the situation through action which brings the 'there and then' of the narrative into the 'here and now' of the moment of performance. Embodying deixis involves a manipulation of the focus of the actor to represent the attention given by the character to other participants in the conversation or elements in the dramatic world.

Although such examples of deixis are present in all forms of drama (ibid.: 139ff.), in monodrama, deictic elements are used in two characteristic ways. The first of these is to establish the speaker and addressee within the dramatic world while only one can be physically represented at any one moment in the theatrical performance. The second is to establish the situational relationship between the performer and the audience as addressee, as I will discuss below. In the first instance, the actor in taking on the speaking role must interpellate the role of the absent addressee. At its simplest level this can be achieved through commentary such as 'And you are standing with crisp bags in your hand' (Jones 1995: 32). This is augmented physically as the actor focuses on where the addressee would be in relation to the speaking role. Thus, the actor can switch between roles without changing location on the stage if he can establish quickly where each of the participants in the dialogue is located in relation to each other. This allows rapid transitions between roles in a dialogue.[7]

This principle by which the onstage addressee is configured in relation to the onstage speaker is extended to the relationship between the narrating figure of McCallister and the audience. Through direct address the audience too are situated within the action by and in relation to McCallister through the same means: verbal deixis and the use of focus. This audience role is as a sympathetic confidant for McCallister. This sympathy is unstinting and the figuring of the audience in this role does not acknowledge the possibility that McCallister's experiences and decisions might be viewed in another light. For example, the impact of McCallister's changed attitudes and behaviour on his family is treated briefly in a scene where Debrah breaks down in tears. However, since McCallister never articulates the possibility that he has responsibility for such hurt, the audience is unable within the terms of the communication available to explore this responsibility or the consequences of his actions. Existing only as a voiceless addressee, the audience is entirely reliant on the performer to organise their perspective on the scenes enacted; to direct it to where it should attend. This reliance on the performer creates a selective perception of the dramatic world. Where the spectator watches two or more actors he can make judgements about scenes based on the simul-taneous engagement of all the participants. Where the audience or individual members of it do not subscribe fully to the role which is assigned them, they are coerced into either rejecting the play in its entirety or accepting an iden-tification with McCallister that runs counter to their own judgement. The latter produces a sense of masquerade a concept which McIlroy adopts from feminist theories of film spectatorship, using its sense of "fooling oneself but consciously" in relation to the positioning of the Irish Protestant spectator from the north by filmic depictions of the Troubles (1998: 19ff.).[8]

The interpellation of the audience as addressee is reinforced by processes of evaluation within the performance. Evaluation has a narrative dimension whereby McCallister comments directly on scenes which he has retold or re-enacted, and thereby directs the audience to a specific interpretation of them. Indeed much of the performance is taken up with such evaluation. In addi-tion to this narrative dimension, evaluation is a crucial process of drama since it is in the enacted impact of behaviours on participants that the spectator's attention is drawn to how these behaviours are to be viewed. In monodrama, such impact cannot be registered at the same time as a speech or action is played; instead the normal simultaneity of action and reaction or conversa-tional speaking and listening is interrupted to allow the solo performer to dwell on moments of reaction in sequence rather than simultaneously (in the same way as the camera might in film). Which moments are dwelt on and which omitted from such sequences are crucial in developing the perspective of the performance: it is almost always McCallister's reactions which determine how the other characters are represented. This occurs even where the reaction is not spoken. Physical embodiment in the role of McCallister of the reaction to a particular speech by another character can reinforce or undercut the effect of that speech. This is potent where the reaction is shared directly with the audience, inviting them to share the evaluation which McCallister makes.

The third element by which the audience is implicated in the performance is through the skill of the performer. Here, I draw on Bauman's anthropological discussion of verbal art as performance in which he argues that:

> It is part of the essence of performance that it offers to the participants a special enhancement of experience, bringing with it a heightened intensity of communicative interaction which binds the audience to the performer in a way that is specific to performance as a mode of communication. Through his performance, the performer elicits the participative attention and energy of is audience, and to the extent that they value his performance, they will allow themselves to be caught up in it. When this happens, the performer gains a measure of prestige and control over the audience—prestige because of the demonstrated competence he had displayed, control because the determination of the flow and interaction is in his hands. When the performer gains control in this way, the potential for transformation of the social structure may become available to him as well.
>
> (1975: 305)

A high degree of skill is demanded of any monodramatic performer. Dan Gordon's performance in the role of McCallister earned him substantial praise. Robin Greer described it as 'the greatest single performance I have ever seen on a Belfast stage' (1994: 13). Other reviews were in a similar vein: it was described as 'a powerful and convincing performance' (Clarke 1994); and 'a virtuoso performance' (McFadden 1994; cited Byrne 2001b: 111). This degree of skill can be regarded as one of the main factors contributing to the longevity of the play in both its initial run and subsequent revivals, particularly as the script has been regarded as unsatisfactory. It draws the audience to the performer, and encourages them to subscribe to the control which he exerts in the selection and representation of the dramatic world, placing their engagement and attention in his hands. This feature of monodramatic performance helps to overcome reservations which the spectator might have with regard to the scenes which they are witnessing, encouraging masquerade from otherwise resistant spectators. The enjoyment which the performance offers is as an entertainment in where all the difficulties of identity can be resolved in one decisive act. It is in sharing the triumphant feelings of McCallister that the audience can share in its utopianism (Dyer 1992).

Gary Mitchell's oeuvre has similarly questioned aspects of the loyalist and unionist experience, primarily within the working-class milieu of the Rathcoole housing estate on the outskirts of Belfast in which he was brought up and where he continues to live. Born in 1965, Mitchell left secondary school at fifteen. His first dramatic success came in 1991 when his radio drama *The World, the Flesh and the Devil* won a BBC Radio 4 Young Playwrights Festival Award. His second radio drama, *Independent Voice* (1994), received a Stewart Parker Award. Although both plays were originally conceived for the stage, his first stage productions were with *That Driving Ambition* (1995) and *Sinking* (1997), both for Belfast's Replay Theatre Company. It was in 1997 that he came to prominence in Britain and Ireland when his *In a Little World of Our Own* was staged by the Abbey both in Dublin and at the Lyric, Belfast for the Abbey's first production there. It was awarded the *Irish Times* Theatre Award for best new play and transferred to London's Donmar Warehouse in the same year. This is only one of many awards which Mitchell's work has received, and he was appointed writer-in-residence at the Royal National Theatre. His work has been staged in Dublin, London, Derry and Belfast, although venues have been reluctant to stage new work by him in his native city (Llewellyn-Jones 2002: 109). By his own estimation, this is partly due to the operation of a cultural bias against material dealing with the experience of Northern Ireland Protestants and a mistaken charge that he himself refuses to work with Catholics (Mitchell 2003a). He has also written several screenplays, including an adaptation of *As the Beast Sleeps* (BBC Northern Ireland, 2002) and a number of radio plays.

Throughout his work, Mitchell faces a dilemma in turning his experience before a public eye: how to remain faithful to that experience, while resisting pressures from outside to conform to particular perspectives on the community from within which he writes. His material is sometimes felt to be too critical by his peers; too parochial for audiences outside. This has prompted him to assert the relevance of his work to audiences outside of Northern Ireland on the basis of its universal themes and the extent to which its milieu is a matter of happenstance, rather than an explicit political strategy. He has written that 'Some of my neighbours have threatened me because I criticise the Protestant people. I can only offer that if I am being critical, then I am criticising the human experience and not the Protestant community of Northern Ireland alone' (2003a: online). Mitchell's own caveats notwithstanding, he has come to be seen as a vital representative of his community, exploring the effects of the peace on it and the strategies with which it has responded to the new dispensation. Whilst many of the topics of his plays could be set in other British cities, they are made specific to Northern Ireland by the governing presence of the paramilitaries and the violence which hovers at the edge of the personal relationships which are established. In particular, he has charted the dilemmas facing the paramilitaries within loyalist working-class communities in plays such as *In a Little World of Our Own* (1997), *As the Beast Sleeps* (1998) and *Trust*. He has explored the changing dimensions of policing in his radio series, *Dividing Force* (BBC Northern Ireland), and onstage in *The Force of Change* (2000), exploring the sense of both betrayal and of loss experienced by unionists in the reform of policing dictated by the

Agreement. He is also consistent in alluding to the close relationship between the police and elements within the loyalist paramilitaries.

As the Beast Sleeps is his most acute representation of the internal dynamics of the UDA as it has struggled to adjust to political change. In it, he confronts the concept of loyalty and what it might mean to individual activists who have been left behind in the shift of the conflict from violence to dialogue. The play opened on 10 June 1998 at the Peacock in Dublin, under the direction of Conall Morrison, himself a playwright, who had directed *In a Little World of Our Own* at the Peacock. Stuart Graham, Patrick O'Kane and Cathy White, actors who have appeared in a number of productions of Mitchell's work, played Kyle, Freddie and Sandra respectively.[9] *As the Beast Sleeps* was revived by the Lyric Theatre, Belfast in May 2001 and received its London premiere at the Tricycle Theatre as a co-production with the Lyric in September 2001. It was adapted for film for BBC Northern Ireland in 2001. In ten scenes, the play analyses the dilemma faced by Kyle, a former unit leader in the UDA, as the organisation attempts to lay aside its violent past. Kyle is trapped between loyalty to the organisation and its command structure and loyalty to his wife, Sandra, and to his best friend and fellow paramilitary, Freddie. Freddie and Sandra are disenchanted, feeling discarded now that the unit's role as defenders of their community has gone. Whilst Freddie is almost

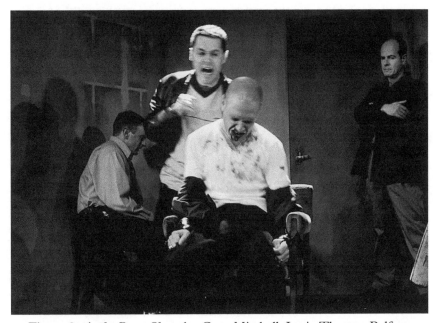

Figure 8. *As the Beast Sleeps* by Gary Mitchell, Lyric Theatre, Belfast.
Photographer: Jill Jennings

pathological in his hatred of Catholics, Kyle's position is made worse by his sensitivity to the nuances of all the pressures placed on him and his inability to resist them. Mitchell includes three figures from the higher strata of the loyalist hierarchy in addition to the central trio of foot soldiers: Jack who is responsible for a local loyalist club, and is ambitious to take on the role of the legitimate entrepreneur; Larry, the next up the chain of command, who has aspirations to a part in the new politics, but is too sullied by his connections with direct action to be included; and Alec, the public face of loyalist politics, a man who talks peace and negotiations while extorting money from Larry and issuing threats of violence which he will never have to implement personally.

Mitchell intertwines two main narrative strands and two settings: the redecoration of Sandra and Kyle's living room; and the running of the club which is still used as a front and a means of generating funds for the UDA. A back room in the club had once been the scene for the violent interrogation of prisoners by the UDA, and it too is being redecorated. Blaithin Sheerin's set design used a revolve to cope with the fluid interchanges between these settings. As in *Bold Girls* (see Chapter 6) the two locations, home and club, represent the extent of the lives inhabited by the characters, interrupted only by the occasional trip to the shops. The responsibility for wallpapering the house falls to Kyle who has enlisted Freddie's help. However, as the couple are strapped for cash, it is Sandra who has to borrow the money to pay for materials from her mother. Kyle cannot provide for his family because his role with the UDA (and the financial rewards associated with it) has diminished and he cannot do anything else. While Kyle's enthusiasm for wallpapering wanes, Freddie takes on the job of finishing the room. Kyle is powerless also to prevent the changes at the club which is remodelling itself as a legitimate and respectable establishment now that the UDA's public strategy has changed. Where he and the members of the gang had once been treated as heroes, they are now an embarrassment and a threat to its new image, particularly when Freddie takes a pool cue to its refurbished décor. Kyle has to bargain to acquire even access to the club for the gang, to the disgust of Freddie and Sandra. When the club is robbed and Freddie is identified as the prime suspect, Kyle takes control of the vicious interrogation of Freddie to recover the money and discover the identity of his accomplice. In a melodramatic turn, when Kyle returns home, Sandra reveals that she was the one who had helped Freddie. Kyle fails then as provider for his family and defender of his friends, usurped by his best friend and his wife, serving as an instrument of Larry, his commandant, to be used and discarded at will as Larry and Alec attempt to carve for themselves a stake in the new political dispensation.

It is possible to analyse the ways in which each of the two territories on which the action is played out serve as metaphors for loyalist Ulster. Kyle's domestic impotence suggests that it is only through the actions of Sandra and

Freddie that their vision of Ulster in which loyalists look after themselves against the external threats to their solidarity can be sustained. This vision, albeit infused with Freddie's naked sectarianism, is not specifically criticised by any figure with credibility. Larry's rebuke to Alec that he finds it difficult to change the minds of the foot soldiers because he may have been right in the analysis through which he recruited them hangs unchallenged at the end of Scene 7. Its emotional appeal is strongly articulated in the resentment that Larry and his team feel about now attacking former comrades, and in the warm relationship between Freddie and Sandra, in which they share an increasing closeness as Kyle becomes isolated from them. This developing closeness is endorsed visually since the mess in the living room of half-stripped walls and bags of shredded wallpaper on which the play opens is transformed by Sandra's resourcefulness and Freddie's efforts in getting the job completed. The kind of loyalist Ulster which the club represents is one in which the image of normality is being constructed (and in the case of Jack actively promoted), but in which dark rooms still remain where real power is exercised, through actual violence or violence by proxy in the threats exchanged, as individuals contend to move up the hierarchy of control. Although these settings and the kinds of Ulster which they represent appear distinct, the use of the revolve emphasises the ways in which the action in one setting serves as the converse of the other. In either dispensation, Kyle can only be included if he returns to violence. The option to relinquish all para-military involvement is largely unexplored, but it would entail a wrench from Kyle's known world of which he is not capable. So it is that the rebuttal of the position of Freddie and Sandra comes through the action in the club. Their view of a safely enclosed loyalist Ulster in which the community looks after its own, an extension of the living room, is predicated on the continued pres-ence of the punishment room through which the community is policed, not by itself, but by and on behalf of its self-serving leaders. Giving a make-over to the political position of the paramilitary leadership requires that Freddie too is removed. He is too potent a reminder of the old dispensation. A third space in performance, representing the main parts of the club, is used to play out the conflicts between the utopian vision which Sandra and Freddie have established and the reality in which they are now placed.

The third production under discussion here takes up this theme of meeting the new post-cease-fire reality head-on. *Caught Red Handed, or, How to Prune a Whin Bush* by Tim Loane was staged by Tinderbox, opening in a former bank building in Belfast on 9 February 2002, before touring across Northern Ireland.[10] Its reception was given an added dimension through discussion in the press and media of statistics from the most recent census which suggested that there would be inevitably a majority nationalist population within Northern Ireland within the foreseeable future. Such a demographic shift would have the potential to undercut fundamentally the unionist majoritarian claim to a continued link with Britain. The play explores what might happen if such a circumstance should come to pass. Tinderbox is one of a number of companies to have helped to alter radically the profile of Northern Irish theatre in the last fifteen years. It had a low-budget beginning at the Old Museum (now the Old Museum Arts Centre) in 1988 when two Belfast actors, Tim Loane and Lalor Roddy, were directed in a pair of Pinter plays by David Grant. Alongside their peers, the company members largely subsidised the work for much of the company's initial period of operation, working for other companies, paying themselves a minimal wage and keeping production costs at a minimum. Remarkably, despite both its inauspicious beginnings and the centrality of actors to its operation, the company has gone on to champion much of the new writing through which dramatic output from Northern Ireland has been reshaped.[11] Within its first three years, it commissioned a number of scripts as part of a series of new writing festivals: six in 1989, with four scripts being taken to full production for the Belfast Festival in 1990. Since then and irrespective of changes in its funding and personnel, it has championed writers like Joseph Crilly, Daragh Carville and Tim Loane, as well as seeking innovative venues for productions such as Rosemary Street Presbyterian Church for the co-produced 1998 revival of *Northern Star* (see Chapter 4); the former Crumlin Road Courthouse for the multi-scripted *Convictions*; and a former bank building in Belfast's Waring Street for *Caught Red Handed*.

The production considered what in the future might be the last move in the political endgame in Northern Ireland: a referendum on a united Ireland. The leader of the fictional Alternative Unionist Party (the Leader) condemns the referendum as a treacherous betrayal by the British government and mainstream unionism and calls for a mobilisation to stop the referendum by bringing the state to a standstill. Unfortunately, the Leader drops dead immediately after his announcement. Faced with two hundred thousand loyal supporters massed outside, his acolytes are left to deal with the consequences of the death: his son, Wayne played by Richard Clements; a clergyman, Reverend McIlroy, played by Peter Balance; Watson, a former paramilitary, played by Ian Beattie; and a spin doctor, Wylie, played by Alan McKee. Aside from Wayne, each wants to run the party but until they can find a way to choose a new leader, they decide to keep the Leader's death secret. An interim solution presents itself in the form of a Catholic farmer, living in isolation in the glens of Antrim, Pat MacStiofain. MacStiofain is physically identical to the Leader. His first test is to be accepted by the Leader's wife, Constance (played by Amanda Hurwitz). She is surprised by the changes Pat makes in personality and behaviour, but accepts this new version willingly, even when she discovers the truth. Pat takes on the role of the Leader with gusto, under the command of this inner circle. The ruse seems to have worked until Pat extemporises in his role as sectarian bigot on a live television programme, throwing the whole province into a spiral of violence. The plot twists further as Constance and Wayne connive with Pat to hatch a scheme of their own to wrest power for themselves away from the inner circle and pull the situation back from the brink of civil war. With plot complications and reversals multiplying, Wayne eventually becomes the new leader of the party, despite revealing that he is gay. He commits his efforts to an honest form of politics and backs the referendum as a means to a peaceful negotiation of the future. The play ends on the announcement of the referendum result: however, the figures are drowned out by closing music and the audience left to contemplate the repercussions of each of the possible permutations.

Although the setting of the production was 2005, much of it relied on a recognition of the strong echoes of the 1974 Ulster Workers' Council Strike against the then power-sharing assembly convened under the terms of the Sunningdale Convention.[12] One of the challenges which the production posed was to identify the ways in which the intervening period had changed the political landscape. It attempted to do so by directing itself specifically to the unionist majority, demonstrating that the old ways of thinking epitomised by the cleric, the paramilitary and the spin doctor cannot hold and that a new politics of Protestantism has to emerge. Within the play, this is articulated through the roles of Constance and Wayne. Faced with the escalation of the peaceful protest into violent conflict, they ally themselves with Pat to manipulate public opinion to change the course of events. However, these figures are endowed with a perspective outside of the discourses which have dominated unionism and which shifts the basis of their engagement from politics to identity, just as in *A Night in November*. Wayne makes a final public address on behalf of the party in which he declares:

> There is another way for us. There has to be. . . And if we lose the referendum—we deal with it. . . We might lose our flag. . . but no-one could crumple our true culture. And let no one tell you that Protestant culture is about how we fight or who we hate; it's about our reasoned voice of dissent, the strength of our character and the achievements of our minds and our bodies. . .
>
> (Loane 2002: 59)

Clearly then, this speech and these two figures exemplify a pragmatic approach to political conflict which resonates with the liberal humanism familiar from many Troubles plays and associated with female figures (see Chapter 6). The extension of this humanism to the subject position of the gay son was perhaps a radical manoeuvre in a society which is deeply homophobic. However, it follows the dramaturgical traditions of Troubles dramas in which women or outsiders are used to offer alternative perspectives, such as in Reid's *The Belle of Belfast City* (1989), in which Belle is a young, *black* and English woman. Moreover, the representation of both Wayne and Constance repeats the widely prevalent stereotypical depiction of women and homosexual men in Northern Irish society. Constance accepts Pat only because he is able to fulfil her sexually and her involvement in the political manoeuvrings are motivated by her desire to resurrect a happy family unit. Wayne is weak and passive, constantly swayed by the posturing and bullying of the stronger men around him. The change by which he comes to defy Watson, Wylie and McIlroy is weakly motivated within the action; he has always known what is the right thing to do, but fails constantly to do it until the final scenes of the play. Stereotypically, action only results from his ethical awareness when prompted by the urgings of his mother.

In performance, the production resembled the political farce of Dario Fo, in which the politics of the participants becomes manifest in their grotesque attempts to maintain and exercise power. Dan Gordon was cast in the role of the Leader; Pat MacStiofain; MacStiofain's brother who works as a steward in Stormont; and, on video-tape as a gay man who has had a fling with Wayne. In accordance with the stage directions, Gordon's performance constantly points up the theatrical device at work of having the same actor play all the characters. This is particularly apparent at those moments when two of them might have been expected to be present at once. Furthermore, as with Dario Fo's performances of his own work, the audience is keenly aware of Gordon's dual presence as celebrity actor and character (Quinn 1990). A further dimension to this was the recognisable relationship between the dogmatic political rhetoric and its delivery within the role and the leader of the DUP, Ian Paisley.

With the basic premises of the plot established within the opening four scenes of the performance, the production then increased in pace as the repercussions of the decision to use a stand-in for the Leader rebound on the conspirators: the second act contains thirteen of the twenty scenes in the play. The set provided for many of the opportunities for the complications and reversals through which the plot twists. Taking a cue from the neo-classical design of the Northern Bank building itself, David Craig provided a symmetrical configuration of three white walls angled on three sides. Within each wall was a door and overhanging them all was a crumbling white Georgian façade. Above the central door and cornice was a large projection screen on to which 'broadcast' elements are projected. The doors and walls were offset by the use of lush purple drapes, further contrasting with the white. The suggestion of the back rooms of Stormont was compelling, and with minor changes the set was changed into a variety of other locations, including the kitchen of the Leader's home, Pat MacStiofain's cottage, and a television studio in which the theatre audience becomes the audience of a political discussion programme.[13] Much of the play's visual humour is rooted in dramatic irony arising from the use of the doors to motivate near-miss entrances and exits between characters and from which confusion about identity develops.

This confusion of identity is at the heart of the play which strongly suggests that self-directed transformation is not only possible but desirable as a means to an honest political democracy. This manifested itself through the central transformation in the remodelling of Pat MacStiofain as the Leader. This was undertaken as an onstage makeover, with the Leader's henchmen 'shaving' and redressing Dan Gordon as he shifts from one role to the next, beneath the cover of a Union Flag to protect his modesty. Whilst this was a highly amusing extended visual gag, its more serious dimensions were pointed up by the soundtrack of Stiff Little Fingers' 'Alternative Ulster', one of the anthems to emerge from Belfast's punk scene in the late 1970s rejecting existing political divisions. The issue which is explored in the rest of the play is the extent to which such alternatives might be possible for the unionist body politic. Again, as with Fo, the emphasis is on situation, rather than character. MacStiofain acts out the role allotted to him until the point where the circumstances of his situation force him to change what he is doing.

Discussion: Representing Loyalists

In a review for *Tribune* of Mitchell's *Trust*, Aleks Sierz (1999) pointed out the dominant tropes governing the representation of loyalists:

> Our image of Belfast loyalism is dominated by pictures of Union Jacks, bowler-hatted fanatics and marching bands; the hard men of loyalist paramilitaries are seen as cold-blooded killers—even worse than the IRA. So the first victory scored by Gary Mitchell's *Trust* is to show how even the ethnic group you love to hate are human beings too.

Thus, despite the political advantages afforded the unionist population by the historical colonial relationship to Britain and its supremacy within the Northern Irish state, to many outside of Northern Ireland, and increasingly within it, the representation of unionists, and working-class loyalists in particular, has obscured any engagement with the politics of loyalism.[14] While an increasing international commodification of Irish culture has provided for a generalised sympathy for nationalism, loyalism has been found wanting in relation to the apparently rich and endlessly marketable resources of Irish nationalism, not least by some nationalists (see Bennett 1994). John Wilson Foster has suggested of *A Night in November* that the play demonstrates an Ulster Protestant self-distaste whose indirect expression 'might be the embrace of "Irish" culture at the expense of the lesser "Ulster" culture' (2001: 13).

Such a cultural perspective has a political dimension too. Loyalism has been regarded as a kind of false consciousness, whereby workers are fooled into giving allegiance to the British state or their own leadership, an allegiance which is exploited to their disadvantage. In *Caught Red Handed* the narrative and the figuration of the politicians within it argue that ordinary working-class loyalists have been misled by leaders who peddle lies and treat them as stupid. However, the ease with which this is achieved suggests simultaneously both a fickleness in the mob and that ordinary people would avoid violence if only they were treated honestly. One of the effects of attacking the ideological basis of loyalism as the product of false consciousness has been to de-legitimate the basis of loyalist violence, which is then presented as the product of pure sectarianism. This de-legitimation has been achieved in part by representations of loyalists in contemporary drama (Cornell 1999a). For example, in a number of films and television dramas from the 1990s, loyalists have been represented as 'monstrous' (Bell 2001) and 'psychos and sickos' (McLoone 2001).[15] Robin Greer's review of *A Night in November* was one of many which noted that 'There is an implication that hatred and intolerance is only by "ugly bloodthirsty barbarians" of the Protestant community' (1994: 13). In the domain of competitive victimhood such a view of loyalist politics hands the advantage to nationalists on every count.

This negative figuration on loyalism has a long tradition on the stage. Laura E. Lyons (2000) traces the emergence of the stage Orangeman in the productions of the Ulster Literary Theatre, specifically in the work of Gerald McNamara in his plays *Suzanne of the Sovereigns: an Extravaganza* (1907), *Thompson in Tir-na-nOg* (1912) and *No Surrender* (1926). McNamara's figure of the bigoted Andy Thompson, who insists on one flag, one crown, one constitution and one faith, is used to lampoon the traditions and beliefs of Orangeism and to suggest that the Orange identity has little historical basis. Each of the three productions discussed here might be seen as invoking and repeating McNamara's negative figurations of loyalism. *A Night in November* has been attacked by a number of commentators for its representation of the constituency which McCallister rejects. Suzanne Breen's *Irish Times* review accused the production of representing crude stereotypes of Protestants, suggesting that 'DubbelJoint played to the lowest common denominator. If the Catholic community had been subject to such base jibes, the audience would have been screaming "sectarianism" ' (1994: 8). It might be argued that the play confirms loyalist fears of republican aspirations for an all-Ireland state, since it is only by erasing all physical markers and symbols of his identity that McCallister achieves his apparent liberation.

While the binary oppositions upon which the play relies may have been operative within the state of Northern Ireland historically, the play's engagement with the stereotypes at work in society is only partial. Likewise *Caught Red Handed* happily sends up Protestant stereotypes of Catholics whilst, as I argue in the following section, relying on stereotypical representations of loyalists. The revulsion expressed by McCallister at the sectarian chanting of the Northern Ireland fans can be seen as part of a discourse which demonises the loyalist working class in the same terms which have been reserved hitherto for republicans, on the basis of the same threat to 'Unionist identity, system and order' (Bell 2001: 5). Embodied in the figure of Ernie, the working-class loyalist is a sectarian and racist bigot, stupid, irrational, idle and dependent on the state. He is an affront to both nationalists and to the newly acquired liberal values to which McCallister now adheres.

Mitchell's Freddie is a more extreme version of Ernie: younger and active, though no less volatile. He is belligerently stupid and temperamental, and on a number of occasions he is referred to as being mad and stupid. He understands only violence as a means of solving disputes and forcing his will on others, enjoying the macho power plays he engages in with every other male character at some point. Even when he is tied to a chair and beaten he deploys a range of sexual taunts to his captors, out-facing them since he cannot fight them, until he is finally silenced. He is the epitome of the 'psycho' stereotype. While Kyle is shown as torn between competing loyalties and more emotionally complex than Freddie, he falls back on the same strategies when cornered: threatening to fight anyone who disagrees with him, exchanging insults in repeated bouts of verbal violence, and ultimately, meting out violence to anyone who stands in his way. That it is Freddie who suffers this fate is a cruel fact of political reality, at which Kyle can only laugh ironically once he realises that Freddie's refusal to name names was protecting Sandra. Sandra shares much of the characterisation of her male counterparts. She is aggressive and foul-mouthed, her behaviour aping theirs. She is shorn of feminine traits, particularly since her son is absent throughout, removing any maternal dimension. All three spend much of the play drinking, and the dispute in the club is over their entitlement to free drink as a token of the debt owed to them. They fit the stereotypes of the barbarian wild Irish just as easily as depictions of their republican counterparts do: extreme, working-class, unemployed and unemployable, and drunken (Deane 1985). Theirs is a fate which Kenneth McCallister in *A Night in November* escapes because he moved away from the area in which he was brought up and got enough of an education to get a job. His childhood friend, Norman Dawson, a dead paramilitary, had not had McCallister's opportunities and was condemned to be left behind, no more than a memory and a photograph on a club wall.

Whilst Jones does not accommodate any sense of the political dimensions of loyalism in her treatment, Mitchell's representation of the loyalist politician, Alec, has little to say about politics or policy. Instead of commitment to a specific cause, he is presented as pursuing 'serious suits, serious style, serious accommodation and serious transportation' (Mitchell 2001: 76). Just in case the audience should miss the point, the gap between the reality and his rhetoric of peaceful negotiation and dialogue is pointed up by Larry, who says he sounds as if he is on television when he uses it. Even at the point where he delivers a diatribe against the unionist leaders of the past who are 'either very rich or very Christian' (ibid.: 20), the sense is that Alec wants to replace them, not necessarily deliver a different future for the people he claims to represent. This sceptical representation of political leadership is repeated in *Caught Red Handed*. The Leader, before his demise, is caught up in his own rhetoric which is caricatured further by Pat's *reductio ad absurdum* when he extemporises in the television studio. Political self-interest drives each of his henchmen: part of the dynamic of the play is the way in which loyalties switch between them as they vie for control or influence. Even the involvement of Pat and Constance serves each of them primarily: Pat seeks the love of a good woman, which he finds in Constance; Constance likewise needs a man; and each takes the actions they do to preserve their relationship. Of course, the play is to be regarded as the kind of caricature one associates with a political cartoon, in which the outer appearance of characters is distorted by their inner corruption (although one of the problems of the production was that this was not carried through consistently in performance). Only Wayne in the final scenes articulates an altruistic defence of his intervention as a means of ensuring that the voice of the people be heard, a voice which the other contenders for the leadership ignore or disregard. However, at no stage does any character have the opportunity to suggest that there might be a rational political basis to resistance to constitutional change: indeed, when Pat as the Leader tries to present this on the television programme, the Presenter's questioning effectively undercuts any attempt at presenting a political basis for the loyalist position. Again, as in *A Night in November*, Wayne's final speech focuses on identity, rather than politics: it is a rallying cry invoking the tradition of dissent associated with the radical Presbyterianism of the United Irishmen, rather than an articulation of why such a tradition might reject a united Ireland.

The arguments of each of the plays on the nature of identity suggest that there is no sustained or sustainable substance to loyalism. In both *A Night in November* and *Caught Red Handed*, identity can be shucked off and replaced with a change of clothing. While this is a theatrical device in each play marking a more fundamental shift, in each it also follows what Cornell argues is the (re) construction approach which 'seeks to remove the causes of conflict by. . . suggesting that some cultures are less essential than others, and therefore may be modified or erased without ill effect' (1999b: 211).[16] Such an approach in these plays suggests that loyalist identity is plastic: only ill-founded loyalist intransigence therefore seems to be standing between the wider society and a lasting peace. In *As the Beast Sleeps*, the changes within the UDA suggest that the kind of loyalism to which Freddie and Sandra cling can be discarded by their political leaders (and other members of the community) as an awkward memento of the past, rather than a valued communal history. This is clearly distinct from the treatment of the past within republican communities (see Chapter 3).

The negative reading of the depictions of loyalism in these plays is not, of course, the only reading. A loyalist audience (or audience members) may well have been engaged positively in a process of self-reflection on the fate of the constituency, and the plays may be considered to be part of a necessary dialogue within that constituency. However, the context of production of each of the performances did not lend itself easily to such a dialogue. *A Night in November* opened as part of Féile an Phobail, deep within republican West Belfast. Playing out these representations in front of a republican audience simultaneously invites a triumphalist reaction to the recognition of the republican analysis of the conditions of the conflict; affirms the rightness of the republican-nationalist project; and celebrates Irishness as a fully fledged modern and democratic identity which loyalism cannot emulate. *As the Beast Sleeps* was staged at the Peacock in Dublin. Whilst this is a very different context to that of the Whiterock Road, the audience at the Peacock was just as unlikely to be engaged in a dialogue with or within the loyalist constituency. Indeed, the machinations of the political leaders and the intransigence of the paramilitaries within the play may well confirm the attitudes of Dublin audiences towards Northern Ireland as a foreign country where they do things differently (see Chapter 1). There is a danger for Mitchell that, in the contexts in which his work is staged, audiences are able to engage in a voyeurism inflected with the distance of class and political identity. *Caught Red Handed* was staged initially in a more neutral venue, before touring, but the public profile of the company might well have suggested that its orientation on the constitutional issue would be sympathetic to nationalists.

The argument within this chapter is not that there should be a greater balance in the depiction of loyalists and the politics of unionism within all plays. Rather, in showing how these plays conform to already existing stereotypes for particular audiences, it is argued that they limit the possibility of engaging with loyalism as a political force within the peace processes which they attempt to address. According to these three plays, if loyalists are to be accommodated within the new politics they have only two options. They can exchange their political identification with Britain for an Irish civic (rather than ethnic) nationalism as in *A Night in November* and *Caught Red Handed*. Alternatively, they can maintain a self-defeating violent resistance to the erosion of shared values by forces within and forces outwith the community, as in *As the Beast Sleeps*. In re-presenting such limited depictions, the underlying assumption is that loyalism is an outmoded political project with which other political constituencies cannot or need not engage while they get on with the business of making the peace.

9

The Art and Politics of
Staging the Troubles

From the previous chapters, it is apparent that there has been a great deal of variation in the approaches adopted by the makers of theatre, and that, whilst the clichés of the Troubles play have been reiterated in a number of productions, they have not excluded other forms and functions. There have, however, been other continuities between works which it is helpful to draw out at greater length. In the following, I will identify some of these continuities and the values discernible in the making, performance and reception of plays about the Troubles. These continuities concern principally the approaches to the representation of the conflict on stage. These approaches have been an expression of certain values regarding the relationship between art and politics. These values are most evident in the approach to the representation of violence on the stage. In addition, while these values have been explicitly and voluntarily embraced by the vast majority of theatre makers, they have also been consistent with the interests of the state. The exercise of particular decisions around moments of crisis by public bodies demonstrates the ways in which the Arts Council and other arts funders have policed the representation of the conflict on behalf of the state. The cumulative effect is to create a context in which most work which has staged the Troubles can be regarded at best as political plays, rather than political theatre (Murdock 1980). The radical potential of performance has been blunted.

First, then, what have been the continuities in approaches to representing the Troubles on the stage? The relationship between the audience and the stage representation as a function of familiarity or distance has been a consistent focus of attention. The general issue is captured by Maxwell as the 'problem of finding a dramatic metaphor which will both contain and distance the immediacy and the intransigence of present events' (1990: 2). These approaches work on the basis that the audience's relationship to the conflict prior to the performance needs to be disrupted to provoke alternative conceptions. Historical moments have been reappropriated as a means of achieving the necessary distance. Likewise myths from a variety of sources have been invoked to estrange the audience from the issues with which the play has engaged. Particular formal strategies have been adopted too in order to achieve the same effect. These include the use of metatheatrical devices, such as the play-within-a-play; self-conscious role-playing; and framing devices, such as the use of a narrator. While the emphasis of these approaches has been on providing a distance between the audience and the performance, other approaches have been concerned with establishing the proximity of the audience to the representation. Some of these approaches have shared the assumption that the audience's prior relationship to the conflict needs to be disrupted. This disruption takes the form, however, of exposing areas of the conflict which have been concealed within other modes of representation and dominant discourses. Realism has been a prominent mode of representation in depictions of the Troubles through which the assertion of hidden lives has taken place. Documentary theatre techniques have also been used to achieve this disruption. Proximity has also been the goal of theatre makers who have sought to celebrate the values of their audience as an act or acts of resistance. Here, the use of reminiscence and oral history has emphasised the authority of the constituency being represented. This celebration of subjectivity has also been marked in performances in which the audience has been confronted with the perspective of a single character, or the perspective of a single constituency, which I will discuss in more detail later.

These different approaches can be aligned with one of three dominant strains within representations of the Troubles. The first arose as a reaction to the collapse of civil society in the early 1970s and was based on an attempt to identify or produce a common ground between the different sections of the populace, suggesting that the roots of the conflict lay in extreme elements, rather than in the fundamental structures of the state. Thus, plays such as Boyd's *The Flats* sought to create an identity between their audience and a putative middle-ground position from which the extremists might be rejected as threats to social integration and peace. A reviewer of Patrick Galvin's *Nightfall to Belfast* (1973) noted that 'Watching a play about the present troubles. . . there is the inevitable temptation to ask "Whose side is it on?" ' and is gratified to be able to say that 'it is clear that if the author is taking a side it is for peace and against violence' (Lowry 1973: 12). In Graham Reid's *The Death of Humpty Dumpty* (1979), George Sampson's affair with a fellow teacher is not presented as a threat to his marriage, until he inadvertently stumbles upon paramilitaries when meeting his lover. In shooting Sampson, the paramilitaries set in train the destruction of his physical vitality (he is rendered paraplegic); all Sampson's personal relationships; and his sense of self. Their violence is portrayed as 'intractable to historical analysis or rational explanation' (Pilkington 1990: 20). Likewise, Christina Reid's *The Belle of Belfast City* develops a sinister link between the local loyalists and extreme

British nationalists to demonise both as a threat to the traditional respectable Protestant values of Vi and Dolly. In Gary Mitchell's *Loyal Women*, both Adele and Brenda have to resist the demands of the Women's UDA if they are going to be able to lead normal lives.

A recurrent motif in such work has been the individual or small group which is isolated and resisting the forces of paramilitarism or sectarianism. This could be the owner of a small business, such as Frank Stock in Parker's *Spokesong*, or Vi in Reid's *The Belle of Belfast City*; or a political leader such as Henry Joy McCracken in Parker's *The Northern Star*. In Gary Mitchell's *In a Little World of Our Own* (1997), even though Ray is himself a member of the UDA, the family is exposed to the threat of punishment for an attack on the daughter of a local loyalist leader. Cleary identifies this as a recurrent formulation in domestic tragedy: 'as the action comes to a climax in each play, the "inside" space where everything happens (the place of the stage proper) is completely besieged by a hostile "outside" space (the offstage world)' (1999: 518).

The division between the personal/domestic and the political/public reaches its apogee in plays which draw on what Christopher Murray has called 'The Romeo and Juliet typos' (1997: 192–4), or the 'love-across-the-barricades' scenario familiar from the novels of Joan Lindgard.[1] As Murray explains, the narrative of a love story across sectarian divides has served both to assert the humanity of the individuals caught up in the political struggle; and in some more radical versions to point to how 'difference is manipulated by forces working to prevent a 'working-class' marriage of differences' (ibid.: 192). Cleary suggests that this kind of romance 'seems to be operating as an allegory for some kind of national romance: in the erotic embrace of the lovers, traditionally antagonistic communities come to recognize each other as political allies' (1999: 514). In Graham Reid's *Remembrance* (1984) Bert Andrews is an English-born Protestant widower and Theresa Donaghy an Irish Catholic widow. Each has lost a son in the conflict; each has another child still caught up on opposing sides. Bert and Theresa fall in love and have to confront the objections of their families, eventually achieving a reconciliation with them all. In Christina Reid's *Did You Hear the One about the Irishman?*, Brian is a working-class Catholic, Allison a middle-class Protestant, each of whom is connected to the paramilitary prisoners held in Long Kesh. Their relationship is put under pressure by their families and their histories and aspirations. Brian's father was shot by loyalists. Allison's Uncle Henry is a loyalist politician. Brian sees in the common experience of visiting the prisoners in Long Kesh the possibility of a unifying moment: 'where else in Northern Ireland can a Provie wife and a UDA wife take a long look at each other and realise that they're both on board the same sinking ship. Common ground. Common enemy' (Reid 1997: 77). Both groups of paramilitaries, however, regard the relationship as a threat and the couple are murdered. In *At the Black*

Pig's Dyke, despite their escape across the border to Fermanagh, the union of the Catholic Lizzie Flynn and Protestant Jack Boles leads to the murder of Jack by the local republican leader, Frank Beirne (see Chapter 2).

In 1999, Martin Lynch and Marie Jones collaborated with community groups in East Belfast on the Wedding Community Play Project to produce a site-specific performance focusing on the actual wedding day of a mixed couple. The audience were divided into groups of eight or nine and bussed to various locales across the city to witness the preparations taking place in each household; to attend the ceremony itself; and to sit in on the wedding reception. Whilst the narrative of the play was resolved sentimentally, the process was seen by the participating communities as being as much an opportunity for emphasising the distinctiveness of their particular community as a means of resolving inter-communal tension. A novel spin on the Romeo and Juliet play occurs in Joseph Crilly's *On McQuillan's Hill* where the love affair is between two men, one a former IRA prisoner, the other a member of the UDR. Likewise Owen McCafferty's *Mojo Mickybo* (1998) takes the conceit of a relationship across the divide in exploring the friendship between two boys growing up in Belfast in the 1970s. The Hole in the Wall Gang satirised the use of this narrative in their *Too Late to Talk to Billy and Emer about Love Across the Barricades in the Terror Triangle* which became the basis of their television film *Two Ceasefires and a Wedding* (BBC Northern Ireland, 1996) and eventual sit-com series *Give My Head Peace* (BBC Northern Ireland). There is a certain irony that *Two Ceasefires and a Wedding* received part-funding from the Community Relations Council on the basis that it would aid mutual understanding (Bradbury 1996: 33).

The Romeo and Juliet scenario connects also to a second strain of work. Since the late 1970s, works have emerged which attempt to identify similarities of experience within other constituencies as correctives to the divisions of the conflict. A play such as *Dockers* tries to suggest that the roots of the conflict lie in the failure of the working class to act together, and Lynch has been prominent in producing work which has attempted to address that failure. Paddy Devlin, a life-long socialist activist (and father of playwright Anne Devlin), likewise tried to give a sense of class solidarity in his 1984 *Strike*. Similarly, the work of Charabanc can be seen as part of an attempt to present a common picture of the experience of working-class women in particular. This assertion of commonality across sectarian divisions seeks to reorientate the politics of the Troubles as an attack on the interests of the working class rather than as an effect of ethno-political conflict. Likewise, Anne Devlin's *Ourselves Alone* and Rona Munro's *Bold Girls* draw attention to the effects of the conflict on women as a group marginalised by the concentration on the politics of nationalism.

Emerging since the 1980s, a third strain of dramas has served as an articulation of a particular identity perspective in lieu of common experience. This has produced anomalous examples such as Frank McGuinness's *Observe the Sons of Ulster Marching towards the Somme* through which a Catholic (at least by background) has represented a core myth of Northern Irish Protestant history. More usually, this work has been produced within or on behalf of specific communities of identity, often in specific locales. Thus, Charabanc staged *Weddin's, Wee'ins and Wakes* for the loyalist community of Belfast's Shankill Road. Plays such as *Forced Upon Us* and *Bin Lids* have likewise spoken to and for their specific republican constituency in West Belfast. The rise of community plays and projects has been an important development in this respect (Grant 1993). Other plays have addressed the concerns of a specific constituency, though their performance in locales outwith such constituencies has complicated their reception. Lynch's *The Stone Chair* can be seen as an act of strategic occupation in taking over the Grand Opera House and representing the community of the Short Strand to other communities. However, Charabanc's *Somewhere Over the Balcony* at the Drill Hall in London, Rona Munro's *Bold Girls* in Scotland and London, and the staging of many of Gary Mitchell's plays in London and Dublin have created an uneasy relationship between subject matter, audience and a context of reception within which the figuration of Northern Ireland's conflict is presented for the entertainment of those outside it.

A further dimension of this last strain of work is an emphasis on the subjective experience of the conflict, particularly expressed in story-telling modes of performance.[2] In Reid's *Tea in a China Cup* Beth's narration of her family history is the controlling mechanism of the performance, leading one reviewer to suggest that 'with its storytelling format, [it] is less visually stimulating than " a good listen." ' (Bell 1983: 13). This mechanism becomes the performance mode of her later *My Name, Shall I Tell You My Name?* in which the two characters tell stories which intersect and through which they each have constructed competing versions of their shared history. In McGuinness's *Observe the Sons of Ulster Marching Towards the Somme* the play's action which is set in 1916 is framed by Old Pyper's remembering with which it is juxtaposed. The most notable development within this strain has been the emergence of a mode of performance in which a controlling narrative is erected from the perspective of one figure. In plays such as Parker's *Northern Star*, and Lynch, Grimes and McKee's *The History of the Troubles (According to My Da')*, the act of remembering and retelling the narrative by one character is central to the performance. Of course, in Friel's *Faith Healer*, the divergence between the monologues of Frank, Grace and Teddy is the source of the dramatic tension in the performance.

The development of monodramatic performances represents the essence of this story-telling performance. Thus, in plays like Jones's *A Night in November*, Morrison's *Hard to Believe*, McElhinney's *The Green Shoot* and Vallely's *Peacefire* the performance is constituted primarily by the words and actions of a single character/performer. Whilst far from the kind of shock strategies associated with the brutalist drama of Mark Ravenhill and Sarah Kane, the direct confrontation of the audience by a figure whose perspective challenges their values has been a particular kind of 'in-yer-face theatre' (Sierz 2001). In Caffrey's *Out Come the Bastards*, for example, the audience is confronted with the figure of a former loyalist paramilitary murderer whose retelling of his role in a sectarian murder gang recalls the most heinous acts of the Troubles carried out by the Shankill Butchers. This was a UVF gang who carried out indiscriminate attacks on Catholic targets.[3] McKittrick and McVea describe their most infamous acts as the killing of seven Catholics who were randomly abducted between 1975 and 1977: 'The victims were picked out solely for their religion. They were then killed with implements such as cleavers, axes and the butchers' knives which earned the gang their nickname. Some had their throats cut and others were tortured.' (2001: 115). Listening to the (albeit fictional) testimony of such a killer is a particularly disconcerting and potentially distressing theatrical experience.

Such an experience threatens to dissolve any sense of boundary between art and politics. Nonetheless, much of the drama in Northern Ireland has been constituted according to the dominant understanding of the relationship between the two as necessarily separate. This understanding has been expressed in declarations by theatre makers and reviews by critics which demonstrate a consensus of resistance to any perspective which is deemed to be partial or propagandist. We may perhaps note that: 'the recognition of propaganda can be seen as a function of the ideological distance which separates the observer from the act of communication observed' (Foulkes 1983: 7). Crucially, the force of such values has depended on whether or not the perspective of the play can be aligned with or located within discourses of representation dominant within the society as a whole or within particular blocs. As seen within Chapter 6, this avoidance of partiality extends as far as an unwillingness to be identified with feminism. However, it has been most particular in relation to the taking of stances in relation to the conflict. Whilst Ronan Bennett's charges are problematic in regard to the novelists he criticises, they can be sustained more readily with regard to the drama of the conflict: 'mainstream artistic mediators of the conflict have tended to opt, like the largely middle-class audience they serve, for an apolitical vision. Theirs is the culture of aloofness, of 'being above it all', of distance from the two sets of proletarian tribes fighting out their bloody atavistic war' (1994: 55). Thus, for example, Christina Reid resisted any attempt to label her as a political playwright, stating: 'I would be appalled at any sort of label—I mistrust labels, whether they be social, religious or sexual. I think labels diminish good art. I don't make political statements, I present words and images that are open to interpretation' (Campbell 1983: 24). Moreover, as the reception of Friel's *The Freedom of the City* demonstrates (see Chapter 3), critics are likewise resistant to productions which they deem to be too partial. Time and again, productions have been criticised for being didactic, preaching, or for the partiality of their message.

The boundary between art and politics, between the stage act and political action, is further codified in the conventions of spectatorship governing audience behaviour within theatre institutions. Even in productions where the convention of fourth wall naturalism is disregarded by having actors/characters address the audience or implicate them in the dramatic fiction (such as in *Northern Star* and *Caught Red Handed*), rarely has the audience been empowered to take action within the symbolic sphere of the performance. Two notable acts of transgression against this convention have provoked very similar responses. When a satirical revue by Eugene Watters, John D. Stewart and Tomás MacAnna, entitled *A State of Chassis* was staged at the Peacock in 1970, it excited fierce anger amongst civil rights campaigners in Northern Ireland.[4] At the opening night two civil rights activists mounted the stage to condemn the revue for its staging of a 'caricature of minority politics in Northern Ireland' (Pilkington 2001: 193). The two activists were physically removed from the theatre to the sound of a slow handclap by the audience. The following day, newspaper reports were keen to condemn the upstaging of the legitimate performance by this very public protest. The assumption that theatre should be distanced from the politics of its society had clearly become so institutionalised that there was a consensus between the theatre makers and a majority of the audience. When in 1992, members of Derry Frontline took to the stage to add an unannounced extra scene to the performance of *At the Black Pig's Dyke* in Derry (see Chapter 2), this consensus was made visible again. Actor Frankie McCafferty said that 'the group had the right to protest, but that was not the way. They failed to get their message across, because nobody knew what they were doing or saying. They just succeeded in terrifying people' (cited Murphy 1993: 4). McCafferty's comments highlight inadvertently the ways in which dominant cultural values appear to support democratic protest, while at the same time resisting access to such protest outwith specific institutionalised processes and procedures: an illustration of repressive tolerance. In circumstances in which republican access to the means of cultural production and political representation were restricted within the media and government, McCafferty's suggestion that there might be another way in which to protest ignored the reality of the context. Restrictions on the representation of the conflict have been imposed from the outset (Curtis 1984), with a ban on the broadcasting of direct interviews with members of Sinn Féin imposed by the British Home Secretary, Douglas Hurd, in 1988. In so challenging the frame through which the theatre is made and experienced, these moments have called into question the fundamental tenets of Yeats's vision and of bourgeois values in art. 'The protesters stepped from the auditorium onto hallowed ground. Spectators became

actors; the powerless assumed power, confronting the affront to their history'
(King 2001: 94).

The separation of art and politics which these interventions rejected is
articulated within the composition of performances particularly in regard to
the perspective taken on representation of violence on the stage. The representation of violence more widely can be seen to depend on the emphasis
placed (primarily or exclusively) on the motivations of those perpetrating the
violence; the nature of the actions themselves; or, the consequences of the
violence (see Elliot et al. 1996). An emphasis on motivation seeks to identify
the political context in which the violence has arisen and the political ends to
which it is put. This discourse has largely been championed by republicans
in their defence of a 'just war', although loyalist paramilitaries too have
successfully employed it to win some measure of political influence. A focus
on the actions involved in violence has tended to present them as repugnant
to civilised people, encouraging the view that anyone capable of such actions
must somehow be outside the scope of the law: a criminal, a barbarian or a
madman. This has largely been the discourse of the state and those involved
in 'legitimate politics', particularly in refusing to negotiate (at least publicly)
with terrorists or former terrorists. Finally, accounts which emphasise the
consequences of the violence seek to identify the human cost of it and therefore to assume the broadly humanitarian perspective that no cause is worth
causing suffering of this kind. The effect of this has been to dissolve 'political disputes into a de-contextualised humanism' (Hill 1987: 161). While this
final discourse has been harnessed tactically to the one which emphasises the
actions involved in violence, it is the most apolitical position and one which
has attracted broad support at specific moments in the conflict, often through
mass demonstrations.

As indicated, these emphases have been used selectively by each set of
participants in relation to their own actions and those of other groups within
self-sustaining and mutually contradictory narratives. These narratives have
themselves been altered or revised at various stages of the conflict, in response
to or as part of the political manoeuvrings of the participants, most clearly in
the rehabilitation of paramilitaries as a preparation for direct negotiations with
them (see Edge 1998: 223, for example). The paradigmatic choice of such
selective focus in dramatic representations aligns them with the discourses at
work in the wider society, often producing distortions by omission. Fintan
O'Toole's comments on Graham Reid's *Callers* (1985) capture the dominant
trend in theatrical representation:

> Writing out of a Belfast experience, he has consistently tried to root
> violence in the community from which it springs, exploring the intersec-
> tions between personal family relations, the daily intimate cruelties and
> the problems of endemic pathological aggression. Like almost everyone

else, however, he has held back from exploring the mind and motivations of the killers.

(1985b: 11)

As O'Toole suggests, then, most representations of the Troubles on the stage have preferred to avoid presenting the motivations of the perpetrators of violence. In a number of plays this avoidance is achieved by a focus on the effects of the violence. Boyd's *The Flats* ends with the introduction of the dead body of Monica, a Protestant neighbour who is killed while running for help for her invalid mother. This established a convention by which the introduction of the wounded or dead body on the stage is used to confound any analysis which might justify or explain the use of violence. Reid's *The Death of Humpty Dumpty* explores the effects of the attack on George Sampson, not the context in which the original attack was mounted. Only the Irishman and the racist Comedian speak after the discovery of the corpses of Brian and Allison is announced in *Did You Hear the One About the Irishman. . .?* They do not offer any verdict on the deaths, rather the Irishman's reaction to the Comedian's insistently racist jokes is to tear up the news bulletin in which the deaths are announced and to issue a reminder of the power of the paramilitaries in the form of a 'knock-knock' joke. In *At the Black Pig's Dyke*, the revelation of the bodies of each of the victims of the straw men is part of a dramaturgical strategy which forestalls any exploration of political violence beyond the personal jealousies of Beirne as discussed in Chapter 2.

In Mitchell's *Tearing the Loom*, the culmination of the play's central action is the death of Ruth Moore, who hangs herself rather than betray the whereabouts of a nearby encampment of United Irishmen soldiers to the local Orangemen. The resolution of the plot and the play's argument structure evacuates the stage of the two Orangemen (William Hamill and his son Samuel), leaving the space free for a final tableau around Ruth's body. This dramaturgical manoeuvre reduces the articulation of other perspectives to silence, presenting a definitive conclusion on the debates around different loyalties which are so central in the rest of the play. An exception to this strategy by which the introduction of a corpse silences discussion might appear to be Friel's *The Freedom of the City*. The first act of the play opens on the dead bodies of Michael, Lily and Skinner. This presence of the dead bodies provokes both retrospective and future action in the scenes in the Mayor's Parlour and the Tribunal respectively. Yet while this action explores a range of possible motivations for the killing as presented to the Tribunal, the gap between the explanations offered and the audience's knowledge of the victim's perspective ensures that the motivations of the army for such extra-judicial killings are never actually explored.

Only in a small number of plays is violence represented directly on the stage. This can be explained, in part, by the difficulties in finding appropriate conventions for depicting violence. The ancient Greek convention, used in Thompson's *Over the Bridge*, is to report the violence which occurs offstage. In *Pentecost*, the violence is represented through the sound effects of distant explosions, bottles breaking, a military helicopter. Each time one of the characters enters the house, they bring reports from outside of the violence, its effects marked in their own costume and body. Ruth has disguised her head wound with a bandana when she first appears. Marian's rescue of her car from a barricade results in scratches on her face and her coat is ripped and mud-spattered. Peter's hand is cut in climbing the wall to escape a gang of drunken hooligans. These physical characteristics function as metonymies for the violence, connecting with the first perspective of focusing on the effects of violence. In Mitchell's *Trust*, the stabbing through which Jake, son of a UDA Commander, avenges himself on the boy who has been bullying him at school is recounted in dialogue rather than shown. The same use of report rather than action is achieved through the introduction of radio and television news reports. For example, the community radio which is featured in Boyd's *The Flats* reappears in *Somewhere Over the Balcony*, a play in which all the events are reported.

The direct depiction of violence has been a feature of the realist dramas of Martin Lynch in *Dockers* and *The Interrogation of Ambrose Fogarty* where the beatings of John Graham and Ambrose Fogarty, respectively, are vivid and disturbing. Police violence against suspects is represented too in Mitchell's *The Force of Change* where it erupts momentarily, being quickly displaced by psychological violence as an interrogation method. Much of Mitchell's work is notable, however, for the graphic representation of violence. Sierz notes that, 'stage violence is inherently dramatic, almost always marking a point of no return. Taking place in real time and real space, aggression seems to leap across the footlights, emotionally if not literally. So when the characters onstage start pushing each other around, it is often the audience that gets battered and bruised' (2001: 209). In *As the Beast Sleeps*, Freddie's interrogation in the punishment room is brutal and sustained, his physical deterioration a rebuke to the rhetoric of the new politics of loyalism. In *Loyal Women*, Adele is being held by the Women's UDA as a warning to stop seeing her Catholic boyfriend. She is tarred and feathered on stage, an action which in turn provokes Brenda into stabbing one of the perpetrators, Heather. Here, these acts are core to an understanding of the situation in which the characters are placed and the values which dominate their thinking. The depiction encompasses the enactment of the violence and the resulting abjection of its victims. Furthermore, both Lynch and Mitchell create a context in which the violence is clearly motivated as a consequence of the culture within which the stage figures operate and the understanding they demonstrate of the situation in which they must act. In *The Interrogation of Ambrose Fogarty*, the Special Branch officers provide an elaboration of the principle that the end justifies the means, contrasted with the audience's direct experience of the violence which they perpetrate. In Mitchell's plays such acts are demonstrated as the inevitable consequences of a self-harming culture of violence, in which status, respect and approval are garnered only by the ability to physically dominate others. Moreover, these dramas avoid (or attempt to avoid) what Sierz has called 'politically correct "victim drama", where perpetrators were bad and victims good' (2001: 231). In these plays, this is not as Sierz suggests, an avoidance of ideology: rather, it is a means of making manifest the ideologies of the communities which are the milieu for the action.[5]

The values which see art and politics as separate are not restricted to Northern Ireland, of course: they are an important part of a bourgeois ideology that seeks to render itself invisible and in which 'culture is a noble universal thing, placed outside social choices: culture has no weight. Ideologies on the other hand are partisan interventions' (Barthes 1972: 81). The hegemony of this view is demonstrated in the reactions to the interventions in the performances of *State of Chassis* and *At the Black Pig's Dyke* discussed earlier. It has meant that the role of the state within the conflict in policing overtly its own representation has been much less marked than in television and film (Curtis 1984). In only a few instances have state bodies intervened directly to control representations of the Troubles. Seamus Deane notes, for example, that 'Field Day wanted to do a production of *The Island*, Athol Fugard's adaptation of *Antigone*; but it could not get financing for this, on the ground that it would be politically too sensitive, from the Arts Council of Northern Ireland' (2002: 161). The pressure to which ACNI was sensitive was manifested later around the production of *Binlids* (see Chapter 3). *Private Eye* had ridiculed ACNI for funding the play and the West Belfast Festival (Moroney 1999: online). An article in the *Daily Telegraph* included a quotation from Lord Tebbit condemning the play[6] and selectively reported incidents from the play, including one which 'showed four women befriending a soldier from the Welsh guards. The audience laughed and clapped as one woman stole his gun and two IRA terrorists walked on to the stage and shot him dead' (Harnden 1997: online). The point of this account is made clear in the article's headline: 'Arts Council funds play that jokes at IRA killings'. Philip Hammond from ACNI is quoted as saying that, 'What we are concerned with is purely artistic standards. We are not in the position of censoring anyone' (ibid.). This apparent resistance to political pressure is predicated on a division between art and politics, and the convention of an 'arm's-length' relationship between government and arts councils throughout Britain.[7]

The limits of this independence are marked by the treatment of the company's next controversial production with JustUs, *Forced Upon Us*. ACNI withdrew £20,000 of funding in the week before the production was due to open.[8] ACNI insisted that the withdrawal of funding was based purely on artistic judgements on the script which had been supplied late to it. However, the requirement on DubbelJoint to supply a copy of the script for assessment was in itself unusual, particularly given a track record in producing scripts based on documentary evidence and involving new writers.[9] Moreover, a comment from the anonymous panel of assessors was leaked to the press in which the play is described as 'shockingly distasteful and exploitative' and 'a clumsy propagandist play [that] could only serve to deepen existing prejudices' (Gentleman 1999: online). Although a number of reviews concur that the final production was both partisan and the script weak in conventional dramatic terms, Moroney's detailed article for the *Irish Times* concluded that the production was 'classic, left-wing agit-prop theatre'(1999: online). With a basis in detailed historical research by writer Brenda Murphy, including the use of verbatim accounts and recreated historical incidents, the play's polemic was well grounded and its avoidance of psychological depth a characteristic of its form.

Thus, the focus of the assessors' critique lay in the play's partisan nature and its potential to increase divisions. Exactly the same argument had been used in the justification of J. Richie McKee for the refusal of the Group Theatre Board of Directors to produce Sam Thompson's *Over The Bridge* in 1959:

> We are determined not to mount any play which would offend or affront the religious or political beliefs or sensitivities of the man in the street of any denomination or class in the community and which would give rise to sectarian or political controversy of an extreme nature.
>
> (cited Keyes 1997: 12)[10]

In both circumstances, it would appear that the preservation of a manufactured political consensus was uppermost in the minds of those controlling the funding for the productions. In 1999, ACNI was wedded to the same values as the playwrights who have sought to find middle ground in a tribal conflict, without acknowledging its own role on behalf of the state. DubbelJoint's Pam Brighton argued that 'The reality is that the NIAC [*sic*] is embarrassed to be seen to be funding a piece it believes has a nationalist perspective' (ibid.) Moreover, according to Gentleman's article, a DubbelJoint representative felt that the decision was as much about the embarrassment caused to ACNI by *Binlids* as by criticisms of *Forced Upon Us* itself.

A further controlling value within the operation of ACNI is in its view of culture which locates the production of theatre which it seeks to fund within a rigid frame of cultural commodification. Thus, for example, state funding has been targeted primarily at professional companies playing within recognised theatre venues, rather than at projects designed at engaging with grassroots or working-class community audiences or participants. Where practitioners have tried to engage with other ways of making work or of reaching out to such audiences they have often struggled to have their work recognised or sustained by public funders, such as the case with Charabanc in the 1980s (Martin 1987; Dicenzo 1993), or Martin Lynch's *The Stone Chair* (see Chapter 7 and Grant 1993). The capacity of the state to contain the activities of the theatre makers it funds through financial allocations and administrative processes is a repeated refrain within the industry. It has had a specific effect in Northern Ireland of limiting the sustained development of radical alternatives to the values of mainstream theatre institutions. Thus, even where individual productions have engaged directly with the issues of the situation within an institutionalised theatrical context, they have by and large been no more than political plays, as described in Sandy Craig's definition of British theatre:

> Political plays seek to appeal to, and influence, the middle-class, in partic-
> ular that section of the middle-class which is influential in moulding
> 'public opinion'. The implication of this is that society can be reformed
> and liberalized, where necessary, by the shock troops of the middle-
> class. . . But further, political plays in bourgeois theatre implicitly recog-
> nize that the middle-class remains the progressive class in society.
>
> (1980: 30)

In such a context, however, these plays may well be limited in their impact on even this audience. According to Coppieters, 'the traditional theatre event is safely framed in a programmed life. It is a cultural and/or entertainment packet of commodity, the contours of which are relatively clear and predictable' (1981: 38). This framing of the theatre event, then, reduces the scope for individual productions, Craig's 'political plays', to make radical interventions which will reorientate the audience's view of the world. Dramaturgical manoeuvres on the part of theatre makers, then, have to work against strong audience expectations. As Arnold notes:

> Theatre is increasingly seen now as a marginal art form. It has lost its polit-
> ical power. It no longer provokes much argument or debate. . . Audiences
> do not go to their theatre in order to develop their understanding of nation-
> alism, their grasp on social change, or to listen to debate about issues
> affecting the country's future.
>
> (2000: 60)

From this it would appear, then, that the potential for theatre to intervene in the politics of its society is not determined by the intentions of the theatre makers; the dramaturgical strategies of the performance; the context of the production; or, even the constitution of the audience. The conditions in which theatre can intervene politically only exist where the spectator is receptive to the possibility of applying aesthetically derived experience to the ways in which he or she lives in and understands the world. For specific constituencies at particular moments in Northern Ireland, these conditions have been available, most notably in circumstances where the theatre event is framed within a wider cultural context in which representation is seen as a vital part of a political movement or struggle. This suggests a reason for the importance accorded by working-class communities to finding a space on a cultural battleground from which they have largely been excluded. A slogan adorning an Ardoyne mural in 1996 speaks particularly then to the people who do not see performance as a means of depicting a conflict in which they have no part, but rather as a means of finding a new role beyond the stereotypes: 'Meon an Phobail a Thogáil Tríd an Chultúir' or 'Building the identity of people through culture' (White 1996: online).

Notes

Chapter 1

1. I am conscious also of the ways in which productions originating and set in other contexts, or revivals of existing plays, nonetheless retain the capacity to speak to, or be read by, audiences in ways which resist or reinforce dominant discourses. Thus, much of the work of Tinderbox Theatre Company and Prime Cut Productions might be considered political in a more general sense than can be accommodated here. Moreover, the context in which revivals of canonical texts have dominated the Irish stage for over thirty years is itself something against which the productions discussed here have had to operate but which can be addressed only sporadically in my discussions.
2. Date references in parentheses to the initial citation of a play are to the date of its first production. Page references are given to the edition of the play cited in the bibliography.
3. Under partition, the state of Northern Ireland included only six of the historic nine counties of Ulster. This ensured that approximately two-thirds of the million and a half population were unionist and almost entirely Protestant. The first Stormont administration consolidated Protestant unionist power through the abolition of proportional representation for local elections in 1922 (and the Stormont parliament in 1929) and the redrawing of the electoral boundaries which had existed prior to partition to ensure the return of unionist candidates. Voting in local government elections was restricted to ratepayers and their spouses, so that tenants and lodgers had no vote. The allocation of housing then was distorted by the need to preserve unionist majorities rather than housing need. Nationalists were effectively disenfranchised at every turn.

Chapter 2

1. This is not to suggest that there is not a politics of the personal, but to draw attention to the ways in which the political dimensions of personal conflict may be occluded in a realist representation.
2. This is known colloquially in Northern Ireland as 'whataboutery', a rhetorical strategy of defending political or violent actions by reference to grievances inflicted on one's own side in the past.
3. Gilbert and Tompkins (1996) identify metatheatrical devices through which

attention is drawn to the structures of power at work within the given circumstances of the drama as a recurrent feature of post-colonial theatre:

> By developing multiple self-reflexive discourses through role playing, role doubling/splitting, plays within plays, interventionary frameworks, and other metatheatrical devices, post-colonial works interrogate received models of theatre at the same time as they illustrate, quite self-consciously, that they are acting out their own histories/identities in a complex replay that can never be finished or final.
>
> (Gilbert and Tompkins 1996: 23)

4. These biographical details are taken from an unpublished interview with the author and a range of sources including Cassidy (1981), McAughtry (1981), Triesman and Lynch (1983), Byrne 2001b and the Princess Grace Irish Library database [online].

5. Networks of clubs sprang into existence in nationalist areas as a feature of the Troubles: in some instances they existed as or replaced working men's and ex-servicemen's clubs; others were run as part of multi-functional community centres or GAA clubs; others were illegal shebeens run to fund various political or paramilitary activities. Taking material around these to be performed in the intervals between acts represented an experience akin to many of the left-wing groups in Britain in the 1970s and early 1980s.

6. *A Roof Under Our Heads* was toured around community centres and later mounted as a professional production as *Castles in The Air* at the Lyric Theatre, Belfast in June 1983 under the direction of Leon Rubin. Michael Poynor directed these plays for the Fellowship under an Arts Council of Northern Ireland (ACNI) scheme (Triesman and Lynch 1983: 3).

7. Rubin's two-year stint as artistic director of the Lyric was significant for the number of local writers whose works were premiered there. These included Lynch, Graham Reid and Christina Reid.

8. The character was based on a local man Hughie Dargan, who attended the rehearsals on three occasions to watch Ian McElhinney's playing of him.

9. The Reverend Ian Paisley is the founder of the Democratic Unionist Party and the Free Presbyterian Church, both of which organisations he leads. His history in politics is marked by a resolute resistance to any involvement of the Republic of Ireland in the government of Northern Ireland, a fervent anti-Catholicism and a dogmatic conservatism in social matters.

10. Brian Phelan's play *Article 5* was commissioned by the BBC and filmed in 1975. It was never shown in case it would 'cause offence' to viewers (Curtis 1984: 36).

11. Despite its apparently resolute stance, the British government conceded to a number of the prisoners' demands, including the right to wear their own clothes. McKittrick and McVea comment also that although they were not granted special category status by the British government, the hunger strikers achieved a recognition of their political status in the eyes of the world (2001: 147).

12. These biographical details are taken from Clancy (1994) and Woods and Barry (2001). An Irish language version of the play under the title *Ag Claí na Muice Duibhe* was directed by Maelíosa Stafford at the Taidhearc Theatre as part of the Galway Arts Festival in July 2001.

13. Hill discusses the link between sexuality and republican violence in cinematic representations in particular relation to the films *Shake Hands with the Devil* (1959) and *A Terrible Beauty* (1960). In each of these IRA commandants are 'not simply cold and emotionless but positively pathological. In both cases, this pathology is closely connected to sexual abnormality' (1987: 166). Rolston's discussion of the representation of republicans in novels of the conflict suggests this analysis can be applied more widely within cultural representations (1996: 404–5). This suggests that in Beirne, Woods has drawn on a long-established typification of the militant republican.

14. See Rolston 1998b for a further discussion of the rise of revisionism.

15. By contrast, Canada's Catalyst Theatre Society, for example, explored methods of 'involving the audience directly in the performance' (Filewod 1987: 154), eventually developing work similar to Boal's Forum Theatre.

Chapter 3

1. Anthony Roche identified the rise of story-telling modes of performance in a review of Dublin Festival Theatre in 1988, suggesting that 'storytelling has not so much died as transferred from the family hearth to the public stage' (1989: 21).

2. The following biographical details are drawn from Dantanus (1988) and Lojek (2004).

3. The company's name is taken as an amalgamation of Friel and Rea's surnames. See Richtarik (1995) for a detailed account of the company's early history.

4. Schrank gives a useful summary of the initial events and subsequent inquiry (2000: 124–8). In January 1998 a second inquiry into the deaths on Bloody Sunday was announced by British Prime Minister Tony Blair. Chaired by Lord Saville, this inquiry was in marked contrast to the original Widgery Inquiry in the volume of material gathered and the length of time spent in its investigations.

5. The title of the play appears both as *Binlids* and *Bin Lids* in the script, publicity material and reviews. I have adopted the single-word version in an earlier article (Maguire 2000b) and continue to use that version here.

6. The festival originally began as the Falls Road Festival; becoming known later as the West Belfast Festival or Féile an Phobail. It is now one of the largest community-based festivals in Europe.

7. In 1970 the continued escalation of clashes in Belfast between republicans and loyalists led to the introduction of a curfew on the Falls Road in July in which the area was sealed off by the army for several days while the army conducted house searches in an effort to defeat the IRA. Under pressure from public demonstrations demanding the introduction of internment, this military approach to conflict resolution resulted in a large-scale arrest operation on 9 August 1971. In the first six months of the operation over 2,400 people were arrested on suspicion of IRA membership (McKittrick and McVea 2001: 68). Many were released without charge, although numerous wrongful arrests, the 'casual brutality' of the troops involved (ibid.: 69), and the use of brutal interrogation techniques radicalised the nationalist population in ways which would have severe repercussions for the development of the conflict.

8. Lance Pettit's (1999) account of the context of production of the television docu-

drama *The Treaty* (1991) explains that the boundaries set for the makers of such programmes by the BBC and the Independent Television Commission included codes for producers which lay stress on the necessity of fidelity to established facts about historical events.

9. It is an irony that Friel has never engaged in the documentary processes of capturing the experiences of real people, yet through his skill as a dramatist is able to so deftly represent the recognisable voice of ordinary people.

10. This emphasis on what the community itself had undergone echoes Filewod's observation that 'The Canadian documentary tends to document experience rather than facts and the actor generally has a first-hand relation to the material of the play' (1987: 17).

11. The title of Lynch, Grimes and McKee's *The History of the Troubles (According to My Da')* captures this shift from *histoire* to *discours*, juxtaposing the concept of the public narrative of history with the personal and subjective memories of the father.

12. Schaefer discusses the reception of the play by reviewers from outside of the nationalist constituency, noting that it was 'predominantly unfavourable' in the English press and 'mixed' in New York reviews (2003: 16).

Chapter 4

1. Initial date references within the main text are to the productions under discussion. References to the scripts are to the following published editions: Martin Lynch (2003a) *Dockers* in *Dockers and Welcome to Bladonmore Road*, Belfast: Lagan Press, pp. 9–72; and Stewart Parker (1989) *Northern Star* in *Three Plays for Ireland*, London: Oberon Books, pp. 11–76.

2. From an account of the production provided in an interview with the author.

3. The cast included Oliver Maguire in the role of John Graham, Louis Rolston as Buckets McGuinness, Stella McCusker as Theresa Graham, J.J. Murphy as Legs McNamara, George Shane as Jack Henry, and Leila Webster as Sarah Montague. Other members of the cast included Ian McElhinney, Mel Austin and Mark Shelley.

4. Biographical details are taken from Cassidy (1981) and Triesman and Lynch (1983).

5. A system operated whereby gangers selected men to load and unload ships from those who gathered within pens at the dockside. Union members, designated by the wearing of a badge (the button), were given first preference, although other men could be selected from a casual workforce should the work demand. The trade union limited the numbers who could be selected for work on any given day by maintaining a closed shop and limited lists of union members. Historically, fathers who were union members were entitled to extend or pass on their membership to their eldest son, though this had to be approved by the trade union hierarchy. My own grandfather and father worked as dockers.

6. The Republican Clubs organisation had historical roots in the Official Republican Movement and was banned in 1967. It later sought cross-community support in changing its name to the Workers' Party. Lynch's older brother served as Chairman of the party and Lynch was a full-time organiser in the early 1970s (Coyle 1989b).

7. His radio plays include: *The Iceberg* (1975) for BBC Radio Ulster and *The Kamikazi Ground Staff Reunion Dinner* (1980) for BBC Radio Three which was filmed for BBC Northern Ireland a year later. His television work includes: *I'm a Dreamer, Montreal* (Thames Television, 1979), *Iris in the Traffic, Ruby in the Rain* (BBC Television, 1981), *Joyce in June* (BBC Television, 1981), *Radio Pictures* (BBC Television, 1985), *Blue Money* (London Weekend Television, 1985) and a six-part series *Lost Belongings* (Thames Television, 1987).

8. Andrews (1989b) refers to it as the Age of Knowledge; whereas Satake notes that 'he may have intended to call [it] the Age of Shame (this is the only Age without a clearly defined name)' (2000: 177).

9. This was published as *Dramatis Personae* (1986) which had been delivered at the John Malone Memorial Lecture.

10. Kearney argues that 'As the prison campaign showed, the Republican-nationalist movement operated in terms of two distinguishable, if not always distinct, discourses: on the one hand, the secular discourse of military action and social struggle; on the other, the mythic discourse of sacrificial martyrdom' (1997: 113).

11. This is based on the actual story of Kipper Lynch who was attacked for singing 'The People's Flag' at a dockers' event in a local social club (Triesman and Lynch 1983: 4).

12. From an unpublished interview with the author.

13. Lynch himself was to comment that one of the difficulties of casting a professional actor in the role of Graham was that he had little grasp of the politics of the role, considering Graham as only a trade unionist (Triesman and Lynch 1983: 3).

Chapter 5

1. M. McDonald (2002) notes that there have been more than thirty adaptations of Greek tragedies by Irish writers in the last twenty years, including Paulin's own *Seize the Fire: A Version of Aeschylus's Prometheus Bound* (1989) and Seamus Heaney's version of Sophocles' *Philoctetes* for Field Day, *The Cure at Troy* (1990).

2. These have included Bertolt Brecht, Jean Anouilh, Jean-Paul Sartre and Athol Fugard, all of whom have adapted the Antigone myth.

3. These biographical details are drawn from various sources including M. McDonald (2002) and Murray (1991a). Of particular help were Paulin's own essay on *Antigone* (2002) and an article 'Who's side are you on?' for the *Independent* in September 2003 to mark the revival of *The Riot Act* at the Gate, London.

4. Connor Cruise O'Brien (1972) *States of Ireland*, London: Hutchinson.

5. Given the lack of infrastructure for touring at that time within the island, it was a mark of the commitment of many members of the cast and crew to the project of the company that they would undertake a tour, often being paid only union minimum rates. Rea notes, for example, that Ray McAnally took the part of Hugh in *Translations*, after Patrick Magee had refused to tour Ireland (Rea and Pelletier 2000: 55).

6. The Board was made up by Friel and Rea together with Seamus Deane (poet, novelist and literary critic), Seamus Heaney (poet and later playwright), David Hammond (film-maker) and Tom Paulin (poet and later playwright).

7. Morrison's 2003 adaptation of the play employed a similar linguistic division, where Pauline Hutton's Antigone used a strong Derry accent and Robert O'Mahoney as Creon employs an English dialect. This is despite the production's insistence, through the use of projected images, on the use of the myth as a critique of Israeli policy in Palestine.

8. The other members of the cast were Joe Reilly, Nuala Hayes, Mark Lambert and Hilary Reynolds.

9. An initial idea had been to do the play alongside Frank McGuinness's *Carthaginians*, although this was abandoned when McGuinness withdrew the play (Rea and Pelletier 2000: 58).

10. Rea noted in a later interview a divergence from Parker in his views about politics, particularly as expressed in *Pentecost*. He suggested that 'Maybe that's what has happened in the North now. We had a northern Catholic, Frank [McGuinness] and a northern Protestant, Stewart [Parker] and they were both suggesting that political involvement had to be avoided somehow. Dealing with a political problem by avoiding it, I don't know that that can be done' (Rea and Pelletier 2000: 59).

11. The cast of the play included Stephen Rea as Lenny, Eileen Pollock as Marion and Jonathan Kent as Peter, with Paula Hamilton as Ruth and Barbara Adair as Lily.

12. This is particularly crucial since, as Pilkington (2001b) argues, Yeats was essentially a constructive unionist rather than a separatist Irish nationalist.

13. Kearney argues that 'The recourse by Yeats and Lady Gregory to the legendary images of Celtic mythology may thus be read as an attempt to make peace between the opposing interests of class, creed and language'(1997: 114). Stewart Parker had attempted a similar enterprise in his six-part television drama for Thames Television based on the Deirdre myth, *Lost Belongings* (1986) which critiqued contemporary Ulster society (see Cornell 1999a for a discussion of this series).

14. Paulin (1985b) summarises the politics of Adamson's approach to language in particular in 'A New Look at the Language Question'.

15. Some of these details are taken from Jane Coyle's (1990) profile of the company in *Theatre Ireland* 23.

16. From an unpublished interview with the author.

17. Zoe Seaton has maintained a relationship with Godber's work, having directed a number of productions for Hull Truck Theatre Company.

18. This may be attributable, at least in part, to the company members' need to work free-lance outside to support themselves.

19. Seaton also devised and directed a version of the Finn McCool myth as *Fi Fi Fo Finn* for the Riverside Youth Theatre, Coleraine. The myth is particularly associated with the Giant's Causeway, a short distance from Portstewart and Coleraine.

20. The Irish form is Fionn McCumhaill.

21. See Barthes (1977) for a development of the idea of the 'grain of the voice'. Parker's use of music is a recurrent feature of his work, based on a passion acknowledged in his stint as music columnist for the *Irish Times* in the 1970s (see Chapter 4).

Chapter 6

1. Following Kruger (1996), I am adopting the term masculinist to refer to the operation of this social construction of gender.

2. I am grateful to Royona Mitra for pointing out the similarities in this respect between the Indian and Irish experiences.

3. Relatedly, Cleary (1999) demonstrates that Catholicism and Protestantism have each in turn been gendered in depictions of the Troubles on stage.

4. That only fourteen out of the total 108 members of that first assembly were women undercuts the grandiloquence of that claim.

5. See, for example: McMullan 2000; O'Dwyer 2000; Pelan 1999; Trotter 2000; White 1989; and Wilmer 1991. It has become commonplace to summarise the exclusion of women from theatrical institutions in Ireland as a preliminary to any discussion of the work of any women whose work has actually been staged.

6. See for example Meany's (1993) discussion of six 'women's' theatre groups in *Theatre Ireland.*

7. At the time of writing, a number of venues were led by women. Paula McFettridge was artistic director at the Lyric Theatre in Belfast, Northern Ireland's main producing house, and Andrea Montgomery was artistic director at the Riverside Theatre in Coleraine, in which role she has developed the theatre's in-house producing. In the receiving venues women play a leading role, with Jill Holmes the Theatre Director of the Market Place in Armagh and Anne McReynolds the Director of the Old Museum Arts Centre in Belfast, for example. Amongst the subsidised touring companies Pam Brighton was Creative Director of DubbelJoint, Zoe Seaton was Artistic Director of Big Telly, and Jackie Doyle was Artistic Director of Prime Cut. Stella Hall had just completed her time as Director of the Belfast Festival at Queen's. The repertoire of dramatic works produced and published includes work by: Anne Devlin, Marie Jones, Nicola McCartney and Christina Reid, for example.

8. Roche has suggested somewhat mischievously that whilst male dramatists have often written strong female characters, 'the question must be asked: is this not a move by male Irish playwrights to appropriate and colonise the concerns of women in a feat of expert ventriloquism, a pre-emptive strike against the increasing number of women writing plays and having them staged?' (1994: 286).

9. Reinelt (1996) notes that discounting the importance of the domestic sphere from consideration of wider society (specifically its economic relations) diminishes its importance and ignores the role women play in society through their role at home.

10. It is ironic that the naïve approach embodied within the role of Kathleen would give rise to a number of ill-fated interventions by women, frequently uniting as mothers, to bring an end to the violence. For example, according to Fairweather et al., 'The Peace People failed because they didn't recognize until it was too late that no amount of prayer, based on an understandable desire for peace, was a substitute for eventual political settlement' (1984: 30).

11. This is not merely a literary or dramatic role, of course. Fairweather et al. (1984) present testimonies of the punishments by paramilitaries (including other women) meted out to women regarded as unfaithful to their absent husbands, including beatings, tarring and feathering, and in at least one incident, murder.

12. These typifications of female roles have provided the recurrent subject for parody, such as in the work of Belfast comedian and theatrical impresario James Young,

stage and television comedy team the Hole in the Wall Gang and comedian Nuala McKeever (see McAleer 1996).

13. Ironically, Charabanc was accused later by Pam Brighton of abandoning its radical practices in mounting a production of Neill Spiers' *Cauterised* at the 1989 Belfast Festival: 'Here it was, at the Belfast Festival, simply maintaining its profile, doing a play whose choice seemed to be born from a 'jobs for the girls' attitude as much as anything else' (1990: 42).

14. Like McGrath's work, it drew on a pre-existing popular performance, in this case that associated with James Young (see note 12). Marie Jones had gained her first experiences as a performer with Young when he was in charge of the Group Theatre in Belfast.

15. Author's note to the published playscript.

16. While dialogue is used to establish the world which the women inhabit, it is also the occasion for a number of set-piece comic exchanges which neither reveal the world outside nor advance the plot in each play.

Chapter 7

1. Woodruff describes how in London in the early 1980s the concept of 'communities of interest' was used to include: '(i) ethnic minorities, (ii) the unemployed, (iii) youth, particularly girls, (iv) women's groups and gay men's groups, (v) the elderly, and (vi) the disabled' (1989: 371).

2. One must be wary of the emphases placed on identity as the central issue in the conflict. Rolston notes the rise of the concept of 'ethnicity' as a marker of the communities of identity in Northern Ireland from the 1980s such that 'By the 1990s an internal conflict explanation resting on 'ethnicity' had become fashionable in academic circles' (1998b: 261). He argues that this conception of the origin of the problem led to the development of policies of multiculturalism by the state which did little to address the fundamental causes of the conflict, through its denial of 'colonialism, politics, triumphalism, institutionalised discrimination, state power' (ibid.: 268). Further, the decisions by the paramilitaries to declare cease-fires in 1994 and the political parties to sign the Good Friday Agreement in 1998 have not weakened any sense of community identity based on the ethno-religious divides suggested. The success of *political* initiatives has, however, been marked by the decrease in violence and a relative normalisation of civic society as a result.

3. The connection between O'Neill and the Short Strand is that his fiefdom extended around Belfast Lough and is commemorated in the naming of a number of streets in the area. O'Neill himself is remembered in the Connswater, a river flowing through the Short Strand.

4. Since the late 1990s, territorial disputes have resulted in inter-community violence. The relationship between the Short Strand and the rest of East Belfast was explored by Lynch alongside Marie Jones in the Wedding Community Play Project in 1999, in which the writers worked with seven different community groups.

5. The concept of an 'interface area' has been generated to describe the locations where highly segregated communities adjoin. They may be marked by physical boundaries such as the highly visible peace-line (a high wall which separates the communities), or a road or park; or, they may be conceptual boundaries known

only to people in the area.

6. These details are taken from an interview with the author.

7. John McGrath makes a similar point about actors trained at the Royal Scottish Academy of Music and Drama and their inability to relate to the audiences for 7:84's work (McGrath 1990).

8. The role of the arts in urban regeneration within Belfast was not recognised until much later, but the extent of its attraction is demonstrated by the (albeit failed) campaign mounted to seek designation for the city as European Capital of Culture 2008.

9. These gantries were built at the nearby Scirocco Works.

10. These and the details which follow are taken from an interview given by Dan Baron Cohen (1994) to Lionel Pilkington, entitled 'Resistance to Liberation with Derry Frontline Culture and Education' and the introduction by Dan Baron Cohen (2001) to *Theatre of Self Determination: The Plays of Derry Frontline Culture and Education*.

Chapter 8

1. Parker had envisaged that the artist should provide a 'working model of whole-ness' (1986: 19). Ronan Bennett's television film *Love Lies Bleeding* (BBC Northern Ireland/Telecip, 1993) was one of the few dramatic explorations of how republicans might actually move from a war footing to embracing purely polit-ical means.

2. This is based on the parties' returns at the elections held for the devolved assembly in November 2003, although the assembly was not reconvened.

3. On 21 November 2001, Dr John Reid, the Secretary of State for Northern Ireland, delivered a speech at the Institute of Irish Studies in Liverpool University, in which he used the phrase to warn of what he foresaw as a future possibility. It was nonetheless seized upon by many unionist commentators as a recognition of the immediate effects of the Agreement.

4. The tight grip of the Provisional Sinn Féin and IRA leaderships on their constituency which prevented the exploration of dissenting voices within the public forum of the theatre should not be underestimated. So, for example, it was not until 2004 that the issue of continued punishment beatings of teenagers for 'anti-social behaviour' by republican paramilitaries was addressed in Seamus Keenan's *Flight* (2004) and Macdara Vallely's *Peacefire* (2004).

5. The creative relationship between Jones and Brighton was the subject of legal scrutiny in 2004 when Brighton sued Jones to claim co-authorship of *Stones in his Pockets* which DubbelJoint had originally staged (see McKeon 2004).

6. Following partition, Protestant unionist power was reinforced across all sectors of government, bolstered by the political appointment of judges and magistrates and the operation of the predominantly Protestant Royal Ulster Constabulary and an auxiliary police force, the Ulster Special Constabulary ('B' Specials). According to McKittrick and McVea, 'the political, legal and policing worlds were thus inextricably linked: one community governed, judged and policed the other' (2001: 11). Despite the abrogation of the Stormont parliament in 1972, the direc-tion of security policy even under direct rule was primarily focused on the nation-alist community. Thus, the location of military bases; the introduction of

internment; the torture of prisoners; collusion between security forces and loyalist paramilitaries; and, extra-judicial killings by state agents have all been focused on defeating the IRA, not ensuring the security of all the citizens of the state.

7. This aspect of story-telling performance has a long history. In Fo's account of the classic piece for the medieval *jongleur*, 'The Resurrection of Lazarus', he notes that 'the jongleur has to act out something like 15 characters in succession, and only indicates the character changes with his body. He does not vary his voice at all; everything is done by gesture' (1992: 64).

8. McIlroy applies it, for example, to the documentary *Dragon's Teeth* (1990) by Tom Collins: 'Collins' technique invites the Protestant unionist spectator to masquerade (a false consciousness) as the aggrieved nationalist, or produces a resistant spectator who feels assured in exposing the intended masquerade, and interprets Collins' sins of omission as symptomatic of yet another IRA apologist' (1998: 17).

9. The involvement of Morrison and O'Kane provides counter-evidence to accusations that Mitchell refuses to work with people from a nationalist background.

10. The title of the play comes from James Simmons's poem 'Ulster Says Yes', which was included in the programme for the first production.

11. The company has produced new work by writers such as Daragh Carville, Joseph Crilly, Marie Jones, Ken Bourke and Owen McCafferty.

12. The terms of that agreement are discussed in Chapter 5.

13. This format allowed the audience to be implicated within the action of the play and is used to stage an open vote on the audience's attitude to the union.

14. McIlroy suggests that this is a politics characterised by 'secular individualism and the belief in civil society, incorporating a pluralist and federalist British Isles' (1998: 13).

15. This demonisation is discussed in relation to film by a number of commentators including McIlroy (1998), Cornell (1999b) and Pettit (2000).

16. Lloyd, for example, refers to 'the figment of Protestant identity [which], with all its racial overtones, masked certain internal differences of sect and geographical origin as well as of economic interest' (1993: 19).

Chapter 9

1. Lindgard has written a quintet of books for children based on the central characters of Kevin and Sadie who form a relationship across the sectarian divides in Belfast and eventually leave to find a new life in England

2. Story-telling performance has emerged as a particular feature of dramatic output across the island since the late 1980s (Roche 1989). Monodrama has become a particularly favoured mode in plays such as O'Kelly's *Bat the Father Rabbit the Son* (1988); Conor McPherson's *Rum and Vodka* (1994) and *The Good Thief* (1994); Dermot Bolger's *In High Germany* and Richard Dormer's *Hurricane* (2002). Robert Welch's *Protestants* is a particular variation on the form in which there is a single framing narration within which the performer creates a kaleidoscope of characters as a means of exploring what it might mean to be a Protestant.

3. Two film treatments have also been made: *Nothing Personal* (1995) and *Resurrection Man* (1998), an adaptation of a novel by Eoin MacNamee.

4. This discussion is based on the details in Pilkington (2001b).

5. Although discussed by Sierz (2001) only in passing, Mitchell's work has much in common with the provocative theatre which he categorises as 'in-yer-face theatre' arising in the early 1990s, including the role of the Royal Court in staging *The Force of Change*, *Trust* and *Loyal Women*.

6. Tebbit was a member of the Conservative Cabinet which was the target of a PIRA bomb attack on the party's conference in Brighton in 1984. As a result of her injuries, his wife was confined to a wheelchair and he has remained an implacable critic of republicans and their involvement in the peace process.

7. This convention has been the object of much criticism historically throughout Great Britain (Pick 1980; Shaw 1987; Pattie 1990) and Williams notes that 'All that is gained by arms length is a certain notion of removal of directly traceable responsibility' (1979: 159). Not only is ACNI a quango, but the assessors in this instance were never identified and no appeals process was available to contest their judgements.

8. The figure varies between £18,000 and £20,000 in different newspaper articles.

9. The companies had been awarded a Belfast City Council Award for Best Arts Partnership for the staging of *Just a Prisoner's Wife*.

10. What is perhaps the most curious aspect of ACNI's relationship to DubbelJoint is that subsequent work by the company has been no less partisan, such as Pearse Elliot's *A Mother's Heart* which focused on the murder of a Catholic by a loyalist terror group. Notably, this play did not call into question the role of the state in the conflict. It can only be a matter of surmise the extent to which the increasing political influence of Sinn Féin may also have offered other productions some degree of protection.

Bibliography

Achilles, J. (1995) '"Homesick for Abroad": The Transition from National to Cultural Identity in Contemporary Irish Drama', *Modern Drama* 38 (4), 435–49

Anderson, B. (1991) *Imagined Communities*, London: Verso Books

Andrews, E. (1989a) 'The Power of Play: Stewart Parker's Theatre', *Theatre Ireland* 18 (April–June), 21–8

—— (1989b) 'The Will to Freedom', *Theatre Ireland* 19 (July-September), 19–23

—— (1995) *The Art of Brian Friel: Neither Reality Nor Dreams*, Basingstoke: Macmillan

Aretxaga, B. (1997) *Shattering Silence: Women, Nationalism and Political Subjectivity in Northern Ireland*, Princeton, NJ: Princeton University Press

Arnold, B. (2000) 'The State of Irish Theatre', in E. Jordan (ed.) *Theatre Stuff: Critical Essays on Contemporary Irish Theatre*, Dublin: Carysfort Press, 59–66

Aston, E. (1995) *An Introduction to Feminism and Theatre*, London: Routledge

Aughey, A. (1996) 'Unionism', in A. Aughey and D. Morrow (eds.) *Northern Ireland Politics*, London: Longman, 31–8

Bairner, A. (1996) 'The Arts and Sport', in A. Aughey and D. Morrow (eds.) *Northern Ireland Politics*, London: Longman, 181–9

—— (1999) 'Masculinity, Violence and the Irish Peace Process', *Capital and Class* 69, 125–44

Bakhtin, M.M. (1981) *The Dialogic Imagination*, Austin, TX: University of Texas Press

Baron Cohen, D. (2001) *Theatre of Self-Determination: The Plays of Derry Frontline: Culture and Education*, Derry: Guildhall Press

Baron Cohen, D. and King, J. (1997) 'Dramatherapy: Radical Intervention or Counter-Insurgency', in S. Jennings (ed.) *Dramatherapy: Theory and Practice 3*, London: Routledge, 269–83

Baron Cohen, D. and Pilkington, L. (1994) 'Resistance to Liberation with Derry Frontline Culture and Education', *The Drama Review* 38 (4), 17–46

Barry, S. (1998) 'Introduction', in J. Fairleigh (ed.) *Far from the Land: Contemporary Irish Plays*, London: Methuen, i-xiv

Barthes, R. (1972) *Mythologies*, selected and trans. A. Lavers, London: Cape

—— (1977) *Image-Music-Text*, trans. S. Heath, London: Fontana Press

Bauman, R. (1975) 'Verbal Art as Performance', *American Anthropologist* 77 (2), 290–311

Bell, D. (1998) 'Modernising History: the Real Politik of Heritage and Cultural Tradition in Northern Ireland', in D. Miller (ed.) *Don't Mention the War: Northern Ireland, Propaganda and the Media*, London: Longman, 228–52

—— (2001) 'Of Monsters and Men: Protestant Identity and Film Culture in Ireland', in D. Bell (ed.) *Dissenting Voices/Imagined Communities*, Belfast: Belfast Film Festival, 3–7

Bell, J. (1983) 'A Skilful Blend', *Belfast Telegraph*, 10 November, 13

—— (1984) 'Reflective Star', *Belfast Telegraph*, 8 November, 7

Bell, J.B. (1998) 'Ireland: The Long End Game', *Studies in Conflict and Terrorism* 21, 5–28

Bennett, R. (1994) 'An Irish Answer', *Guardian Weekend*, 16 July, 55

Bennett, S. (1991) *Theatre Audiences: A Theory of Production and Reception*, London: Routledge

Bentley, E. (1968) 'The Theatre of Commitment', in *The Theatre of Commitment and Other Essays on Drama in Our Society*, London: Methuen, 190–231

Billington, M. (1993) 'At the Black Pig's Dyke, Tricycle Theatre', *Guardian 2*, 9 July, 11

—— (1998) 'He Had a Dream', *Guardian*, 18 November, 12

Bleeker, M. (2004) 'Look Who's Looking! Perspective and the Paradox of Postdramatic Subjectivity', *Theatre Research International* 29 (1), 29–41

Boal, F.W. (1987) 'Segregation', in M. Pacione (ed.) *Social Geography: Progress and Prospect*, London: Croom Helm, 90–128

Boltwood, S. (1998) ' "Swapping Stories about Apollo and Cuchulainn": Brian Friel and the De-gaelicizing of Ireland', *Modern Drama* 41 (4), 573–83

Bort, E. (1993) 'Female Voices in Northern Irish drama: Anne Devlin, Christina Reid, and the Charabanc Theatre Company', in E. Bort (ed.) *'Standing in their shifts itself. . .': Irish Drama from Farquhar to Friel*, Bremen: European Society for Irish Studies, 263–79

Boyce, G. (1991) 'Northern Ireland: a Place Apart?' in E. Hughes (ed.) *Culture and Politics in Northern Ireland, 1960–1990*, Milton Keynes: Open University Press, 13–26

Boyd, J. (1973) *The Flats*, Belfast: Blackstaff Press

Bradbury, J. (1996) 'A Funny Thing Happened on the Way to The Forum', *Causeway* (Autumn), 32–3

Brady, F. (1994) 'The Politics of Community Theatre', *Causeway* (Spring), 9–13

Breen, S. (1994) 'Great Craic and Absent Guests', *Irish Times*, 17 August, 8

Brenton, H. (1980) *The Romans in Britain*, London: Eyre Methuen

Brighton, P. (1990) 'Charabanc', *Theatre Ireland* 23 (Autumn), 41–2

—— (1997) 'Drama's Portrayal of Forgotten Injustices', *Irish News*, 14 August, 8

Brustein, R. (1992) 'The Dreaming of the Bones', *Theatre Ireland* 29 (Autumn), 49–51

Butler Cullingford, E. (1990) ' "Thinking of Her. . . as. . . Ireland": Yeats, Pearse and Heaney', *Textual Practice* 4 (1), 1–21

—— (1996) 'British Romans and Irish Cathaginians: Anticolonial Metaphor in Heaney, Friel and McGuinness', *PMLA* 3 (2), 222–39

Byrne, O. (1997) *The Stage in Ulster from the Eighteenth Century*, Belfast: Linenhall Library

—— (2001a) 'Theatre—Companies and Venues', in M. Carruthers and S. Douds (eds.) *Stepping Stones: The Arts in Ulster 1971–2001*, 1–26

—— (2001b) *State of Play: The Theatre and Cultural Identity in 20th Century Ulster*, Belfast: Linenhall Hall Library

Caffrey, S. (2001) *Out Come the Bastards*, Belfast: Lagan Press

Campbell, K. (1983) 'Cuppas and Corpses: Kerry Campbell talks to Chris Reid', *Belfast Review* (October), 24–5

Carlson, S. (1994) 'Exorcising Bigotry with World Cup Odyssey', *Irish News*, 6 August, 10

Carruthers, M. and Douds, S. (2001) (eds.) *Stepping Stones: The Arts in Ulster 1971–2001*, 1–26

Carty, C. (1985) 'Northern Star Rising on the Tide', *Sunday Tribune*, 29 September, 19

Carville, D. and Patterson, G. (2001) 'Daragh Carville in Conversation with Glenn Patterson', in L. Chambers et al. (eds.) *Theatre Talk: Voices of Irish Theatre Practitioners*, Dublin: Carysfort Press, 64–75

Cassidy, S. (1981) 'Martin Lynch—A Profile', *Gown* (May/June), 11

Castagno, P.C. (1993) 'Varieties of Monologic Strategy: the Dramaturgy of Len Jenkin and Mac Wellman', *New Theatre Quarterly* 9 (34), 134–46

Chambers, L., Fitzgibbon, G. and Jordan, E. (2001) (eds.) *Theatre Talk: Voices of Irish Theatre Practitioners*, Dublin: Carysfort Press

Charabanc Theatre Company (2001) *Somewhere Over the Balcony*, in H. Gilbert (ed.) *Postcolonial Plays: An Anthology*, London: Routledge, 443–69

Clancy, L. (1994) 'Out of the Druid, into the Woods', *Irish Times*, 15 February, 10

Clarke, J. (1993) 'Finding Hope in Horror', *Sunday Tribune*, 18 July, B4

—— (1994) 'Review of A Night in November' *Sunday Tribune*, 14 August, B6

—— (1995) 'Fireworks on and off Stage', *Sunday Tribune: Tribune Magazine*, 12 November

—— (2000) '(Un)critical Conditions', in E. Jordan (ed.) *Theatre Stuff: Critical Essays on Contemporary Irish Theatre*, Dublin: Carysfort Press, 95–106

Cleary, J. (1999) 'Domestic Troubles: Tragedy and the Northern Ireland Conflict', *South Atlantic Quarterly* 98 (3), 501–37

Cleeve, B. and Brady, A. (1985) *A Dictionary of Irish Writers*, Dublin: Lilliput

Clutterbuck, C. (1999) 'Lughnasa After Easter: Treatments of Narrative Imperialism in Friel and Devlin', *Irish University Review* (Spring/Summer), 101–18

Cohen, A. (1985) *The Symbolic Construction of Community*, London: Tavistock

Connolly, L. (1999) 'Feminist Politics and the Peace Process', *Capital and Class* 69, 145–59

Coppieters, F. (1981) 'Performance and Perception', *Poetics Today* 2 (3), 35–48

Corcoran, N. (ed.) (1992) *The Chosen Ground: Essays on the Contemporary Poetry of Northern Ireland*, Bridgend: Seren Books

Cornell, J.C. (1997) ' "The Other Community": Northern Ireland in British Television, 1995', *New Hibernia Review* 1 (2), 37–47

—— (1999a) ' "Different Countries, Different Worlds": the Representation of Northern Ireland in Stewart Parker's Lost Belongings', in J. MacKillop (ed.) *Contemporary Irish Cinema: From The Quiet Man to Dancing at Lughnasa*, Syracuse, NY: Syracuse University Press, 71–84

—— (1999b) 'Recontextualising the Conflict: Northern Ireland, Television Drama, and the Politics of Validation', in J. Harrington and E.J. Mitchell (eds.) *Politics and Performance in Contemporary Northern Ireland*, Amherst, MA: University of Massachusetts Press, 197–218

Coulter, C. (1999) 'The Absence of Class Politics in Northern Ireland', *Capital and*

Class 69, 77–100

Coyle, J. (1988) 'Death of Playwright Stewart Parker', *Irish Times*, 8

—— (1989a) 'Charabanc Motors On', *Theatre Ireland* 18 (Apr–Jun), 41–2

—— (1989b) 'The Blitz, the Short Strand and the Flight of the Earls', *Irish Times*, 13 June, 16

—— (1989c) 'Black Belfast One-liners', *Sunday Tribune*, 18 June, 30

—— (1989d) 'Lynch's Epic Tale of Blitz True Grit', *Sunday Life*, 18 June, 40

—— (1990) 'Big Telly', *Theatre Ireland* 23 (Autumn), 42–3

—— (1991) 'Tinderbox', *Theatre Ireland* 25 (Spring), 20–21

—— (1992) 'Moths', *Theatre Ireland* 29 (Autumn), 72

—— (1993) 'Now We are Ten', *Theatre Ireland* 30 (Winter), 16–18

—— (1998) 'Return of the United Irishmen', *Irish Times*: Belfast Festival at Queens Supplement, 7 November, 1

Craig, S. (ed.) (1980) *Dreams and Deconstructions: Alternative Theatre in Britain*, London: Amber Lane Press

Cranston, D. (1991) 'Skimmers, Spaghetti and the Boiler House', *Theatre Ireland* 25 (Spring), 32–3

Crick, B. (1979) 'The Political in Britain's Two National Theatres', in J. Redmond (ed.) *Themes in Drama Volume 1: Drama and Society*, Cambridge: Cambridge University Press, 169–94

Crozier, M. and Frogat, R. (1990) (eds.) *Cultural Traditions in Northern Ireland: Cultural Diversity in Contemporary Europe. Proceedings of the Cultural Traditions Group Conference, 1997*, Belfast: Institute of Irish Studies, Queens University of Belfast

Cummings, S.T. (2000) 'The End of History: the Millennial Urge in the Plays of Sebastian Barry', in S. Watt, E. Morgan and S. Mustafa (eds.) *A Century of Irish Drama: Widening the Stage*, Bloomington, IN: Indiana University Press, 291–302

Curtice, J. and Dowds, L. (1999) 'Has Northern Ireland Really Changed? Working Paper, 74. Oxford: Centre for Research into Elections and Social Trends' [online]. <http://www.crest.ox.ac.uk>. Accessed 1 September 2003

Curtis, L. (1984) *Ireland: The Propaganda War*, London: Pluto

Dantanus, U. (1988) *Brian Friel: A Study*, London: Faber and Faber

—— (1995) 'Brian Friel's Histories', in C.C. Barfoot and Rias van den Doel (eds.) *Ritual Remembering: History, Myth and Politics in Anglo-Irish Drama*, Amsterdam: Rodopi, 113–26

Darby, J. (1997) *Scorpions in a Bottle. Conflicting Cultures in Northern Ireland*, London: Minority Rights Publications

Day, F. (1999) 'How do I Know who or where I Am until I Hear what I Say?' in J. Fox and H. Dauber (eds.) *Gathering Voices: Essays on Playback Theatre*, New Platz, NY: Tusitala Publishing, 79–91

Deane, S. (1983) *Civilians and Barbarians*, Derry: Field Day Theatre Company

—— (1984) 'Introduction' in B. Friel *Selected Plays of Brian Friel*, London: Faber and Faber, 11–22

—— (1987) 'O'Casey and Yeats: Exemplary Dramatists', in *Celtic Revivals: Essays in Modern Irish Literature, 1880–1980*, Winston Salem, NC: 108–22

—— (2002) 'Field Day's Greeks (and Russians)', in M. McDonald and J.M. Walton (eds.) *Amid Our Troubles: Irish Versions of Greek Tragedy*, London: Methuen, 148–64

Deane, S. et al. (1985) *Ireland's Field Day: Field Day Theatre Company*, London: Hutchinson

Deegan, L. (ed.) (2001) *Irish Theatre Handbook*, 2nd edition, Dublin: The Theatre Shop

Delgado, M.M. (1997) 'Introduction', in C. Reid *Christina Reid Plays: 1*, London: Methuen, vii-xxii

De Marinis, M. (1993) *The Semiotics of Performance*, trans. A. O'Healy, Bloomington, IN: Indiana University Press

De Paor, A (1991) 'Druid in Oz', *Theatre Ireland* 24 (Winter), 46–9

Devlin, A. (1999) *Ourselves Alone*, New York: Dramatists Play Service, Inc.

—— (1994) *After Easter*, London: Faber and Faber

—— (1995) 'Naming the Names' in M. Parker (ed.) *The Hurt World: Short Stories of the Troubles*, Belfast: Blackstaff Press, 315–40

—— (1999) 'Anne Devlin', in D. Edgar (ed.) *State of Play: Playwrights on Playwriting*, London: Faber and Faber, 96–99

Devlin, A. and Cerquoni, E. (2001) 'Anne Devlin in interview with Enrica Cerquoni', in L. Chambers et al. (eds.) *Theatre Talk: Voices of Irish Theatre Practitioners*, Dublin: Carysfort Press, 107–23

Dewhurst, K. (1988) 'Stewart Parker: Uniting Irishman', *Guardian*, 5 November, 39

Dicenzo, M. (1993) 'Charabanc Theatre Company: Placing Women Center-State in Northern Ireland', *Theatre Journal* 45 (2), 175–84

Dixon, P. (2001) *Northern Ireland: the Politics of War and Peace*, Basingstoke: Palgrave Macmillan

Dowler, L. (1998) ' "And They Think I'm just a Nice Old Lady" Women and War in Belfast, Northern Ireland', *Gender, Place and Culture* 5 (2), 159–76

Duggan, D. (1997) 'Making a Drama Out of a Crisis', *Causeway* (Summer), 36–38

Dyer, R. (1992) *Only Entertainment*, London: Routledge

Eagleton, T. (2000) 'Unionism and Utopia: Seamus Heaney's *The Cure at Troy*', in E. Jordan (ed.) *Theatre Stuff: Critical Essays on Contemporary Irish Theatre*, Dublin: Carysfort Press, 172–74

Edge, S. (1998) 'Representing Gender and National Identity', in D. Miller (ed.) *Rethinking Northern Ireland: Culture, Ideology and Colonialism*, London: Longman, 211–27

Edgerton, L. (1987) 'Public Protest, Domestic Acquiescence: Women in Northern Ireland', in R. Ridd and H. Callaway (eds.) *Women and Political Conflict, Portraits of Struggle in Times of Crisis*, New York: New York University Press, 61–83

Elam, K. (1988) *The Semiotics of Theatre and Drama*, London: Routledge

Elliot, P., Murdock, G. and Schlesinger, P. (1996) 'The State and "Terrorism" on British Television', in B. Rolston and D. Miller (eds.) *War and Words. The Northern Ireland Media Reader*, Belfast: Beyond the Pale Publications, 340–76

Ellis, J. (2000) *Seeing Things: Television in the Age of Uncertainty*, London: I.B. Tauris

Etchells, T. (1999) *Certain Fragments: Contemporary Performance and Forced Entertainment*, London: Routledge

Etherton, M. (1987) 'The Field Day Theatre Theatre Company and the New Irish Drama', *New Theatre Quarterly* 3 (9), 64–70

—— (1989) *Contemporary Irish Dramatists*, Basingstoke: Macmillan

Fairleigh, J. (1998) (ed.) *Far from the Land: Contemporary Irish Plays*, London: Methuen

Fairweather, E., McDonough, R. and McFadyean, M. (1984) *Only the Rivers Run Free*, London: Pluto

Favorini, A. (1994) 'Representation and Reality: The Case of Documentary Theatre', *Theatre Survey* 32 (2), 31–42

Fearon, K. and McWilliams, M. (2000) 'Swimming against the Mainstream: the Northern Ireland Women's Coalition', in C. Roulston and C. Davies (eds.) *Gender, Democracy and Inclusion in Northern Ireland*, Basingstoke: Palgrave Macmillan, 117–37

Filewod, A. (1987) *Collective Encounters: Documentary Theatre in English Canada*, Toronto: University of Toronto Press

Finlayson, A. (1999) 'Loyalist Political Identity after the Peace', *Capital and Class* 69, 47–75

Fiske, J. (1987) *Television Culture*, London: Methuen

Fitzgerald, C. (1987) 'Play Probes the Protestant Tradition', *Belfast Newsletter*, 28 September, 11

—— (1989) 'True Grit Theatre Triumph', *Belfast Newsletter*, 16 June, 9

Fitzgibbon, G. (1991) 'Historical Obsessions in Recent Irish Drama', in G. Lernout (ed.) *The Crows behind the Plough: History and Violence in Anglo-Irish Poetry and Drama*, Amsterdam: Rodopi, 41–59

Fletcher, J. (2001) 'Realism, Feminism and the Northern Irish Women Playwrights of the '80s' [online]. <http://www.britishtheatreguide.info/otherresources/academic/realism.PDF>. Accessed 23 June 2004

Fo, D. (1985) 'Some Aspects of Popular Theatre', *New Theatre Quarterly* 1 (2), 131–9

—— (1992) *Dario Fo Plays: One*, London: Methuen

Foley, I. (2003) *The Girls in the Big Picture: Gender in Contemporary Ulster Theatre*, Belfast: Blackstaff Press

Forte, J. (1996) 'Realism, Narrative and the Feminist Playwright—A Problem of Reception', in H. Keyssar (ed.) (1996) *Feminist Theatre and Theory*, Basingstoke: Macmillan, 19–34, reprinted from (1989) *Modern Drama* 32 (March), 115–27

Foster, R.F. (2001) *The Irish Story: Telling Tales and Making It Up in Ireland*, London: Penguin Books

Foulkes, A. (1983) *Literature and Propaganda*, London: Methuen

Freshwater, H. (2002) 'Anti-theatrical Prejudice and the Persistence of Performance: The Lord Chamberlain's Plays and the Correspondence Archive', *Performance Research* 7 (4), 50–58

Friel, B. (1984) *Selected Plays of Brian Friel*, London: Faber and Faber

—— (1989) *Making History*, London: Faber and Faber

—— (1990) *Dancing at Lughnasa*, London: Faber and Faber

Gardner, L. (2003) 'The Riot Act', *Guardian*, 22 September [online]. <http://www.guardian.co.uk/arts/critic/review/0,1169,1046991,00.html>. Accessed 6 September 2004

Gargan, S. et al. (1993) 'Theatre Protest', *Derry Journal*, 9 July, 4

Garland, R. (1999) 'Sitting in the Dark Can Shine a Light on Things', *Irish News*, 2 August [online]. <http://www.irishnews.com>. Accessed 7 September 2004

Genet, J. and Cave, R.A. (eds.) (1991) *Perspectives of Irish Drama and Theatre*, Gerrards Cross: Colin Smythe

Gentleman, A. (1999) 'Dubbel trouble', *Guardian*, 5 August [online]. <http://www.guardian.co.uk/Archive/Article/0,4273,3889619,00.html>.

Accessed 2 October 2000

Gibbons, L. (1998) 'The Harp Re-Strung: The United Irishmen and Cultural Politics', programme note for *Northern Star*, Belfast: Field Day and Tinderbox

Gilbert, H. and Tompkins, J. (1996) *Post-colonial Drama: theory, practice, politics*, London: Routledge

Goodlad, J.S.R. (1971) *A Sociology of Popular Drama*, London: Heinemann

Gould, T. (1991) 'The Uses of Violence in Drama', in J. Redmond (ed.) *Themes in Drama 13: Violence in Drama*, Cambridge: Cambridge University Press, 1–14

Goulish, M. (2000) 'Compendium: A Forced Entertainment Glossary', *Performance Research* 5 (3), 140–48

Graham, C. (1999) ' "... maybe that's just Blarney": Irish Culture and the Persistence of Authenticity', in C. Graham and R. Kirkland (eds.) *Ireland and Cultural Theory: The Mechanics of Authenticity*, Basingstoke: Macmillan, 7–28

—— (2003) 'Subalternity and Gender: Problems of Post-Colonial Irishness', in C. Connolly (ed.) *Theorizing Ireland*, Basingstoke: Palgrave Macmillan, 150–59

Grant, D. (1993) *Playing the Wild Card, Community Drama and Smaller-Scale Professional Theatre*, Belfast: Community Relations Council

—— (2001) 'Theatre—Plays and Playwrights', in M. Carruthers and S. Douds (eds.) *Stepping Stones: The Arts in Ulster 1971–2001*, 27–51

Greenhalgh, S. (1990) 'The Bomb in the Baby Carriage: Women and Terrorism in Contemporary Drama', in J. Orr and D. Klaić (eds.) *Terrorism and Modern Drama*, Edinburgh: Edinburgh University Press, 160–83

Greer, R. (1994) 'A Partial View from Windsor's Terraces', *Belfast Newsletter*, 10 August, 13

—— (1995) 'Ancient Warrior Alive at the Lyric', *Belfast Newsletter*, 9 November, 14

Grene, N. (1986) 'Distancing Drama: Sean O'Casey to Brian Friel', in M. Sekine (ed.), *Irish Writers and the Theatre*, Gerrards Cross: Colin Smythe, 47–70

—— (1999) *The Politics of Irish Drama: Plays in Context from Boucicault to Friel*, Cambridge: Cambridge University Press

Griffiths, T.R. and Llewellyn-Jones, M. (1993) *British and Irish Women Dramatists since 1958: A Critical Handbook*, Buckingham: Open University Press

Hale, E. (1982) 'Reflections of Derry's Bloody Sunday in Literature', in H. Kosok (ed.) *Studies in Anglo-Irish Literature*, Bonn: Bouvier, 411–21

Hanafin, P. (1997) 'Defying the Female: The Irish Constitutional Text as Phallocentric Manifesto', *Textual Practice* 11 (2), 249–73

Hannah Bell, S. (1972) *The Theatre in Ulster*, Dublin: Gill and Macmillan

Harnden, T. (1997) 'Arts Council Funds Play that Jokes at IRA Killings', *Daily Telegraph*, 11 August [online]. <http://www.portal.telegraph.co.uk/htmlContent. jhtml?html+/archive/1997/08/11/nuls111.html>. Accessed 2 September 2000

Harrington, J. and Mitchell, E.J. (1999) (eds.) *Politics and Performance in Contemporary Northern Ireland*, Amherst, MA: University of Massachusetts Press

Harris, C.W. (1988) 'The Martyr-Wish in Contemporary Irish Dramatic Literature', in M. Kenneally (ed.) *Cultural Contexts and Critical Idioms in Contemporary Irish literature*, Gerrards Cross: Colin Smythe, 251–68

—— (1991) 'From Pastness to Wholeness: Stewart Parker's Reinventing Theatre', *Colby Quarterly* 27 (4), 233–41

—— (1996) 'Re-inventing Women: Charabanc Theatre Company', in E. Bort (ed.) *The State of Play: Irish Theatre in the Nineties*, Tübingen: Tübingen Anglo-Irish

Theatre Group, 104–23

—— (1997) 'The Engendered Space: Performing Friel's Women from Cass McGuire to Molly Sweeney', in W. Kerwin (ed.) *Brian Friel: A Casebook*, New York: Garland, 43–75

Harris, M.W. (1995) 'An Ersatz Ministry of Culture: The Political Cultural Function of the Field Day Theatre Company', in C.C. Barfoot and Rias van den Doel (eds.) *Ritual Remembering: History, Myth and Politics in Anglo-Irish Drama*, Amsterdam: Rodopi, 159–64

Hawkins, M.S.G. (1999) 'Brenton's *The Romans in Britain* and Rudkin's *The Saxon Shore*: Audience, Purpose, and Dramatic Response to the Conflict in Northern Ireland', in J. Harrington and E.J. Mitchell (eds.) *Politics and Performance in Contemporary Northern Ireland*. Amherst, MA: University of Massachusetts Press, 157–73

Heaney, M. (2000) 'Spotlight Turns to Orange', *Sunday Times*, Section 9: Culture, June, 22–3

Heaney, S. (1985) 'An Open Letter', in S. Deane et al. *Ireland's Field Day*, London: Hutchinson, 23–32

Henderson, L. (1985) 'The Green Shoot: Transcendance and Imagination in Contemporary Ulster Drama', in G. Dawe and E. Longley (eds.) *Across a Roaring Hill: The Protestant Imagination in Modern Ireland, Essays in Honour of John Hewitt*, Belfast: Blackstaff Press, 196–227

—— (1988) 'A Fondness for Lament', *Theatre Ireland* 17, 18–20

Hennessey, T. (1997) *A History of Northern Ireland, 1920–1996*, Dublin: Gill and Macmillan

Hill, I. (1993) 'Staging the Troubles', *Theatre Ireland* 31 (Summer), 42–6

—— (1998) 'Northern Star', *Guardian*, 8 November, 9

Hill, J. (1986) *Sex, Class and Realism: British Cinema 1956–1963*, London: BFI

—— (1987) 'Images of Violence', in K. Rockett, L. Gibbons and J. Hill *Cinema and Ireland*, London: Croom Helm, 147–93

Hinds, A. (2001) *The Starving and October Song: Two Contemporary Irish Plays*, Dublin: Carysfort Press

Hohenleitner, K. (2000) 'The Book at the Center of the Stage: Friel's *Making History* and *The Field Day Anthology of Irish Writing*', in S. Watt, E. Morgan and S. Mustafa (eds.) *A Century of Irish Drama: Widening the Stage*, Bloomington, IN: Indiana University Press, 239–55

Holderness, G. (1992) *The Politics of Drama and Theatre*, London: Macmillan

Hughes, E. (1990) 'To Define Your Dissent: The Plays and Polemics of the Field Day Theatre Company', *Theatre Research International* 15 (1), 67–77

—— (1991) (ed.) *Culture and Politics in Northern Ireland, 1960–1990*, Milton Keynes: Open University Press

Hunter, C. (1987) 'Something To Be Desired?' *Irish Times*, 16 November, 12

Hurley, J. (1998) 'Ordinary People, Extraordinary Times', *Irish Echo*, 71 (42) [online]. <http://www.irishecho.com/files/article.cfm?id=1781>. Accessed 4 September 2000

Hurt, J. (2000) 'Frank McGuinness and the Ruins of Irish history', in S. Watt, E. Morgan and S. Mustafa (eds.) *A Century of Irish Drama: Widening the Stage*, Bloomington, IN: Indiana University Press, 275–90

Hutchinson, R. (1984) *The Rat in the Skull*, London: Methuen

Hyndman, M. (1996) *Further Afield: Journeys from a Protestant Past*, Belfast: Beyond the Pale Publications

Jellicoe, A. (1987) *Community Plays: How to Put Them On*, London: Methuen

Jones, M. (1990) *The Hamster Wheel*, in D. Grant (ed.) *The Crack in The Emerald*, London: Nick Hern Books, 189–258

—— (1995) *A Night in November*, Dublin: New Island Books

Jones, M. and Moylan, P. (2001) 'Marie Jones in Conversation with Pat Moylan', in L. Chambers et al. (eds.) *Theatre Talk: Voices of Irish Theatre Practitioners*, Dublin: Carysfort Press, 213–19

Jordan, E. (1997) *The Feast of Famine: The Plays of Frank McGuinness*, Bern, Switzerland: Peter Lang

—— (ed.) (2000a) *Theatre Stuff: Critical Essays on Contemporary Irish Theatre*, Dublin: Carysfort Press

—— (2000b) 'From Playground to Battleground: Metatheatricality in the Plays of Frank McGuinness', in E. Jordan (ed.) *Theatre Stuff: Critical Essays on Contemporary Irish Theatre*, Dublin: Carysfort Press, 194–208

Judge, T. (1997) 'The Lid of Me Granny's Bin', *Irish Times Weekend*, 2 August [online]. <http://www.ireland.com/newspaper/weekend/1997/0802/archive.97080200171.html>. Accessed 7 September 2004

JustUs Community Theatre Company (2000) *Strategic Development Plan: Striking Out On Our Own*, Belfast: JustUs Community Theatre Company

Kearney, R. (1977) 'Editorial', *The Crane Bag Journal*, 1 (1), 1

—— (1985) 'Myth and Motherland', in S. Deane et al. *Ireland's Field Day: Field Day Theatre Company*, London: Hutchinson

—— (1997) *Postnationalist Ireland: Politics, Culture, Philosophy*, London: Routledge

Kelly, J., Baird, B. and West, D. (1991) 'The Cure at Troy', *Theatre Ireland* 24 (Winter), 12–16

Kelly, O. (1984) *Community, Art and The State: Storming the Citadels*, London: Commedia

Kerr, A. (1987) 'Well Deserved Pat on the Back', *Irish News*, 29 September, 7

—— (1992) 'Review', *Irish News*, 3 November, 11

Kershaw, B. (1992) *The Politics of Performance: Radical Theatre as Cultural Intervention*, London: Routledge

—— (1996) 'The Politics of Performance in a Postmodern Age', in P. Campbell (ed.) *Analysing Performance: A Critical Reader*, Manchester: Manchester University Press, 133–52

Keyes, J. (1997) 'Introduction' in S. Thompson *Over the Bridge and Other Plays*, Belfast: Lagan Press, 9–18

Keyssar, H. (1996) 'Drama and the dialogic imagination: *The Heidi Chronicles* and *Fefu and her Friends*', in H. Keyssar (ed.) *Feminist Theatre and Theory*, Basingstoke: Macmillan, 109–36, reprinted from (1991) *Modern Drama* 34 (1), 88–106

Kiberd, D. (2002) 'Introduction', in M. McDonald and J.M. Walton (eds.) *Amid Our Troubles: Irish Versions of Greek Tragedy*, London: Methuen, vii-xiii

King, J. (2001) 'A Theatre of the Oppressed', in D. Layiwola (ed.) *Understanding Post-Colonial Identities: Ireland, Africa and the Pacific*, Ibadan, Nigeria: Sefer, 90–99

Klein, M. (1984) 'Life and Theatre in Northern Ireland', *Red Letters* 16 (Spring/Summer), 6–32

Kruger, L. (1992) *The National Stage: Theatre and Cultural Legitimation in England,*

France and America, Chicago, IL: University of Chicago Press

—— (1996) 'The Dis-play's the Thing: Gender and Public Sphere in Contemporary British Theatre', in H. Keyssar (ed.) *Feminist Theatre and Theory*, Basingstoke: Macmillan, 49–77, reprinted from (1990) *Theatre Journal* 42 (1), 27–47

Kurdi, M. (1996) 'Female Self Cure Through Revisioning and Refashioning Male/master Narratives in Anne Devlin's *After Easter*', *Hungarian Journal of English and American Studies* 2 (2), 97–110

Lacey, S. (1995) *British Realist Theatre: The New Wave in its Context, 1956–1965*, London: Routledge

Lee, J. (1995) 'Linguistic Imperialism, the early Abbey Theatre, and the translations of Brian Friel', in J.E. Gainor (ed.) *Imperialism and Theatre. Essays on World Theatre, Drama and Performance*, London: Routledge, 164–81

Leerssen, J. (1996) *Remembrance and Imagination: Patterns in the Historical and Literary Representation of Ireland in the Nineteenth Century*, Cork: Cork University Press in association with Field Day

Lehman, E. (1982) 'England's Ireland: An Analysis of Some Contemporary Plays', in H. Kosok (ed.) *Studies in Anglo-Irish Literature*, Bonn: Bouvier, 431–8

Lernout, G. (1991) (ed.) *The Crows Behind The Plough: History and Violence in Anglo-Irish Poetry and Drama*, Amsterdam: Rodopi

Llewellyn-Jones, M. (2002) *Contemporary Irish Drama and Cultural Identity*, Bristol: Intellect Books

Lloyd, D. (1993) *Anomalous States: Irish Writing and the Post-colonial Moment*, Dublin: The Lilliput Press

Loane, T. (2002) *Caught Red Handed, or How to Prune a Whin Bush*, Belfast: Tinderbox Theatre Company

Loane, T. and D. Grant (2001) 'Tim Loane in Conversation with David Grant', in L. Chambers et al. (eds.) *Theatre Talk: Voices of Irish Theatre Practitioners*, Dublin: Carysfort Press, 264–76

Lojek, H. (1990) 'Difference Without Indifference: The Drama of Frank McGuinness and Anne Devlin', *Eire-Ireland: A Journal of Irish Studies* 25 (2), 56–68

—— (1995) 'Watching over Frank McGuinness' Stereotypes', *Modern Drama* 38 (3), 348–61

—— (1999) 'Playing Politics with Belfast's Charabanc Theatre Company', in J. Harrington and E.J. Mitchell (eds.) *Politics and Performance in Contemporary Northern Ireland*, Amherst, MA: University of Massachusetts Press, 82–102

—— (2002) (ed.) *The Theatre of Frank McGuinness: Stages of Mutability*, Dublin: Carysfort Press

—— (2004) 'Brian Friel's sense of place', in S. Richards (ed.) *The Cambridge Companion to Twentieth Century Irish Drama*, Cambridge: Cambridge University Press, 177–90

Lojek, H. et al. (1994a) 'Seeding New Writing, Seeking More Analysis: Belfast's Charabanc Theatre Company', *Irish Studies Review* 8 (Autumn), 30–34

—— (1994b) 'Challenging Cultural Certainties: Charabanc in its Second Decade', *Causeway* (Autumn), 48–51

Longley, E. (1984) 'More Martyrs to Abstraction', *Fortnight* (July/August), 20

Longley, M. (1971) *Causeway: The Arts in Ulster*, Belfast: Arts Council of Northern Ireland

Lovell, T. (1981) 'Ideology and Coronation Street', in R. Dyer et al. *Coronation Street*, London: British Film Institute, 40–52

Lowry, B. (1973) 'Theatre Review: Nightfall to Belfast', *Belfast Telegraph*, 5 July, 12

Lundy, J. and MacPoilin, A. (1992) (eds.) *Styles of Belonging: The Cultural Identities of Ulster*, Belfast: Lagan Press

Lynch, M. (2003a) *Dockers and Welcome to Bladonmore Road*, Belfast; Lagan Press

—— (2003b) *The Interrogation of Ambrose Fogarty and Castles in the Air*, Belfast: Lagan Press

Lyons, L.E. (2000) 'Of Orangemen and Green Theatres: The Ulster Literary Theatre's Regional Nationalism', in S. Watt, E. Morgan and S. Mustafa (eds.) *A Century of Irish Drama: Widening the Stage*, Bloomington, IN: Indiana University Press, 34–56

MacLaughlin, J. (1999) ' "Pestilence on their Backs, Famine in their Stomachs': The Racial Construction of Irishness and the Irish in Victorian Britain', in C. Graham and R. Kirkland (eds.) *Ireland and Cultural Theory: The Mechanics of Authenticity*, Basingstoke: Macmillan, 50–76

Madden, A. (1992) 'Andy Hinds on Song', *Theatre Ireland* 29 (Autumn), 58–60

Magee, P. (2001) *Gangsters or Guerrillas? Representations of Irish Republicans in 'Troubles' Fiction*, Belfast: Beyond the Pale Publications

Maguire T. (2000a) 'Kicking with Another Foot: Contesting Memories in Marie Jones's *A Night in November* and Dermot Bolger's *In High Germany*', *Performance Research* 5 (3), 76–81

—— (2000b) '*Binlids* at the Boundaries of Being: A West Belfast Community Stages an Authentic Self', *Kunapipi* 22 (2), 106–17

—— (2001) 'Marie Jones', in J. Bull (ed.) *Dictionary of Literary Biography, Vol. 233: British and Irish Dramatists since World War II*, Detroit, MI: Bruccoli Clark Layman, 182–7

Marks, P. (1998) 'People Determined to Have their Say', *New York Times*, 14 October [online]. <http://archives.nytimes.com/archives/>. Accessed 4 September 2000

Marlow, S. (1997) 'Binlids', *Fortnight* (September), 41

Martin, C. (1987) 'Charabanc Theatre Company: 'Quare' Women 'Sleggin' and 'Geggin' the Standards of Northern Ireland by 'Tappin' the People', *The Drama Review* 31 (2), 88–99

Martin, M. (1992) 'The Impact of Electra', *Theatre Ireland* 26 (Spring), 8–12

Maxwell, D.E.S. (1990) 'Northern Ireland's Political Drama', *Modern Drama* 33 (1), 1–14

McAleer, P. (1996) 'Run Away Fun With Comedy Gangsters', *Irish News*, 7 August, 7

McAughtry, S. (1981) 'Workers' Writer', *Irish Times*, 5 March, 8

McAuley, J.W. (1991) 'Cúchulainn and an RPG-7: The Ideology and Politics of the Ulster Defence Association', in E. Hughes (ed.) *Culture and Politics in Northern Ireland*, Milton Keynes: Open University Press, 45–68

—— (1999) 'Still "No Surrender"? New Loyalism and the Peace Process in Ireland', in J.P. Harrington and E.J. Mitchell (eds.) *Politics and Contemporary Performance in Northern Ireland*, Amherst, MA: University of Massachusetts Press, 57–81

McAuley, G. (1999) *Space in Performance: Making Meaning in Theatre*, Ann Arbor, MI: University of Michigan Press

McCafferty, N. (1987) 'A Night Meeting the Family', *Sunday News*, 4 October, 8

McCafferty, O. (1998) *Plays and Monologues*, Belfast: Lagan Press

McCartney, N. (2001) *Heritage*, London: Faber and Faber

McConachie, B. (2001) 'Doing Things with Image Schemas: The Cognitive Turn in Theatre Studies and the Problem of Experience for Historians', *Theatre Journal* 53 (4), 569–94

McCoy, G. (2000) 'Women, Community and Politics in Northern Ireland', in C. Roulston and C. Davies (eds.) *Gender, Democracy and Inclusion in Northern Ireland*, Basingstoke: Palgrave Macmillan, 3–23

McDonald, M. (1997) 'When Despair and History Rhyme: Colonialism and Greek Tragedy', *New Hibernia Review* 1 (2), 57–70

—— (2000) 'Classics as Celtic Firebrand: Greek Tragedy, Irish Playwrights and Colonialism', in E. Jordan (ed.) *Theatre Stuff: Critical Essays on Contemporary Irish Theatre*, Dublin: Carysfort Press, 16–26

—— (2002) 'The Irish and Greek Tragedy', in M. McDonald and J.M. Walton *Amid Our Troubles: Irish Versions of Greek Tragedy*, London: Methuen, 37–86

McDonald, R. (2002) 'Between Hope and History: The Drama of the Troubles' in D. Bolger (ed.) *Druids, Dudes and Beauty Queens: The Changing Face of Irish Theatre*, Dublin: New Island Books, 231–49

McDonough, C.J. (2000) ' "I've Never Been Just Me": Rethinking Women's Positions in the Plays of Christina Reid', in S. Watt, E. Morgan and S. Mustafa (eds.) *A Century of Irish Drama: Widening the Stage*, Bloomington, IN: Indiana University Press, 179–92

McFadden, G. (1989) 'Cast Struggle with Trite Reid Drama', *Belfast Telegraph*, 4 May, 15

—— (1992) 'A Production to Enthral', *Belfast Telegraph*, 4 November, 19

—— (1995) 'Ancient Ireland Lives', *Belfast Telegraph*, 9 November, 21

—— (1997) 'Bin Lids Opens with Passionate Clash of Trouble', *Belfast Telegraph*, 7 August, 11

McGrath, J. (1981) *A Good Night Out. Popular Theatre: Audience, Class and Form*, London: Methuen

—— (1990) *The Bone Won't Break: On Theatre and Hope in Hard Times*, London: Methuen

McGuinness, F. (1986) *Observe the Sons of Ulster Marching Towards the Somme*, London: Faber and Faber

—— (1988), *Carthaginians and Baglady*, London: Faber and Faber

McGuinness, F. and Long, J. (2001) 'Frank McGuinness in conversation with Joseph Long', in L. Chambers et al. (eds.) *Theatre Talk: Voices of Irish Theatre Practitioners*, Dublin: Carysfort Press, 298–307

McIlroy, B. (1996) 'When the Ulster Protestant and Unionist Looks—Spectatorship in (Northern) Irish Cinema', *Irish University Review* 26 (1), 143–54

—— (1998) *Shooting to Kill: Filmmaking and the 'Troubles' in Northern Ireland*, Trowbridge, Wiltshire: Flick Books

McKay, S. (2000) *Northern Protestants: An Unsettled People*, Belfast: Blackstaff Press

McKenna, B. (2003) *Rupture, Representation, and the Refashioning of Identity in Drama from the North of Ireland, 1969–1994*, Westport, CT: Praeger Publishers

McKeon, B. (2004) 'Copyright Considerations', *Irish Theatre Magazine* 4 (20), 12–19

McKittrick, D. and McVea, D. (2001) *Making Sense of the Troubles*, revised edition, London: Penguin

McLoone, M. (2001) 'Psychos and Sickos: Cinematic Representations of Loyalists', in D. Bell (ed.) *Dissenting Voices/Imagined Communities*, Belfast: Belfast Film Festival, 8–9

McMillen, R. (1997) 'Standing Room Only for Binlids', *Andersonstown News*, 2 August, 24

McMullan, A. (2000) 'Gender, Authorship and Performance in Selected Plays by Contemporary Irish Women playwrights: Mary-Elizabeth Burke Kennedy, Marie Jones, Marina Carr, Emma Donoghue', in E. Jordan (ed.) *Theatre Stuff: Critical Essays on Contemporary Irish Theatre*, Dublin: Carysfort Press, 34–46

McQuaid, C. (1981) 'Belfast's Dockland Comes to Life at the Lyric Theatre', *Sunday News*, 18 January, 10

Meany, H. (1993) 'The State of Play' *Theatre Ireland*, 30 (Winter), 32–4

Mengel, H. (1986) *Sam Thompson and the Modern Drama in Ulster*, New York: Peter Lang

Methven, E., Moore, C. and Lojek, H. (2001) 'Eleanor Methven and Carol Moore (Scanlan) in Conversation with Helen Lojek', in L. Chambers et al. (eds.) *Theatre Talk: Voices of Irish Theatre Practitioners*, Dublin: Carysfort Press, 342–54

Mikami, H. (2002) *Frank McGuinness and His Theatre of Paradox*, Gerards Cross: Colin Smythe

Miller, D. (1994) *Don't Mention the War: Northern Ireland, Propaganda and the Media*, London: Pluto

Mitchell, G. (1998) *Tearing the Loom and In a Little World of Our Own*, London: Nick Hern Books

——— (1999) *Trust*, London: Nick Hern Books

——— (2000) *The Force of Change*, London: Nick Hern Books

——— (2001) *As the Beast Sleeps*, London: Nick Hern Books

——— (2003a) 'Balancing Act', *Guardian*, 5 April [online]. <http://www.guardian.co.uk/arts/features/story/0,11710,929911,00.htm>. Accessed 3 September 2003

——— (2003b) *Loyal Women*, London: Nick Hern Books

Moloney, E. 'Parker Gives a Ray of Hope', *Irish News*, 24 September, 3

Morash, C. (2002) *A History of Irish Theatre, 1601–2000*, Cambridge: Cambridge University Press

Morgan, V. and Fraser, V. (1995) 'Women and the Northern Ireland Conflict: Experiences and Responses', in S. Dunn (ed.) *Facets of the Conflict in Northern Ireland*, New York: St Martin's Press, 81–96

Moroney, M. (1999) 'Just a Play', *Irish Times*, 29 July [online]. <http://www.ireland.com/newspaper/features/1999/0729/archive.99072900088.html>. Accessed 7 September 2004

Morrison, Bill (1994) *A Love Song for Ulster*, London: Nick Hern Books

Morrison, Blake (2003) 'Femme Fatale', *Guardian*, 4 October [online]. <http://www.guardian.co.uk/arts/features/story/0,11710,1055507,00.html>. Accessed 6 September 2004

Morrison, C. (1998) *Hard to Believe*, in J. Fairleigh (ed.) *Far from the Land: Contemporary Irish Plays*, London: Methuen, 310–41

Muinzer, L. (2003) 'Between the World and the Stage: A Tribute to John Boyd', *Fortnight* (April)

Muinzer, P. (1987) 'Evacuating the Museum: The Crisis of Playwriting in Ulster', *New Theatre Quarterly*, 3 (9), 44–63

Müller-Schöll, N. (2004) 'Theatre of Potentiality. Communicability and the Political in Contemporary Performance Practice', *Theatre Research International* 29 (1), 42–56

Munro, R. (1993) *Bold Girls*, London: Hodder and Stoughton

Murdock, G. (1980) 'Radical Drama, Radical Theatre', *Media, Culture and Society* 2, 151–68

Murphy, J. (1992) 'Theatre Review: Deeply Moving', *Fortnight* (November), 46

Murphy, J. (1993) 'Druid Carry On Despite Disruption', *Galway Advertiser* 8 July, 4

Murphy, S. (1997) 'Friel and Heaney: Setting the Island Story Straight', *New Hibernia Review* 1 (2), 21–36

Murray, C. (1988) 'The History Play Today', in M. Kenneally (ed.) *Cultural Contexts and Critical Idioms in Contemporary Irish Literature*, Gerrards Cross: Colin Smythe, 269–89

—— (1991a) 'Three Irish Antigones', in G. Genet and R.A. Cave (eds.) *Perspectives of Irish Drama and Theatre*, Gerrards Cross: Colin Smythe, 115–29

—— (1991b) 'Brian Friel's *Making History* and the Problem of Historical Accuracy', in G. Lernout (ed.) *The Crows behind the Plough: History and Violence in Anglo-Irish Poetry and Drama*, Amsterdam: Rodopi, 61–77

—— (1997) *Twentieth Century Irish Drama: Mirror up to Nation*, Manchester: Manchester University Press

Murray, D. (1994) 'Community Drama Gets Priority in West Belfast Féile', *Irish News*, 2 August, 8

Murray, D. (ed.) (2000) *Protestant Perceptions of the Peace Process in Northern Ireland*, Limerick: Centre for Peace and Development Studies, University of Limerick

Murtagh, B. (1995) 'Image Making Versus Reality: Ethnic Division and the Planning Challenge of Belfast's Peace Lines', in W.J.V. Neill, D.S. Fitzsimons and B. Murtagh *Reimaging the Pariah City: Urban Development in Belfast and Detroit*, Aldershot: Avebury, 209–30

—— (1998) 'Community, Conflict and Rural Planning in Northern Ireland', *Journal of Rural Studies* 14 (2), 221–31

Mustafa, S. (2000) 'Saying "No" to Politics: Sean O'Casey's Dublin Trilogy', in S. Watt, E. Morgan and S. Mustafa (eds.) *A Century of Irish Drama: Widening the Stage*, Bloomington, IN: Indiana University Press, 95–113

Neill, W.J.V. (1995) 'Lipstick on the Gorilla? Conflict Management, Urban Development and Image Making in Belfast', in W.J.V. Neill, D.S. Fitzsimons and B. Murtagh *Reimaging the Pariah City: Urban Development in Belfast and Detroit*, Aldershot: Avebury, 50–76

Neumann, R. (2003) 'The Myth of Ulsterization in British Security Policy in Northern Ireland', *Studies in Conflict and Terrorism* 26, 365–77

Nowlan, D. (1984a) 'Field Day Double Bill at Derry Guild Hall', *Irish Times*, 20 September, 12

—— (1984b) 'Politics in the Theatre', *Irish Times*, 27 September, 10

—— (1984c) 'Northern Star' at Belfast Lyric', *Irish Times*, 8 November, 12

—— (1987) 'Pentecost at the Guildhall, Derry', *Irish Times*, 24 September, 10

—— (1992) 'A Remarkable Mix of Passion, Despair', *Irish Times*, 1 October, 8

—— (1994) 'A Play of Power, Terror and Despair', *Irish Times*, 15 February, 10

—— (1999) 'Forced Upon Us', *Irish Times*, 7 September [online]. <http://www.ireland.com/newspaper/features/2000/0907/archive.00090700079.html>.

Accessed 7 September 2004

O'Brien, M. (1981) ' "Dockers" an Action Packed Portrayal', *Belfast Telegraph,* 14 January, 13

—— (1982) 'Lynch's Brilliant, Brutal "Fogarty" ', *Belfast Telegraph,* 28 January, 9

Ó Broin, E. (1997) 'A Community's Starring Role', *An Phoblacht/Republican News,* 7 August, 15

O'Doherty, M. (1987) 'On the Eve of Pentecost', *Hype* (November), 28–9

O'Dowd, L. (1991) 'Intellectuals and Political Culture: A Unionist-Nationalist Comparison', in E. Hughes (ed.) *Culture and Politics in Northern Ireland, 1960–1990,* Milton Keynes: Open University Press, 151–73

O'Dwyer, R. (1991) 'Dancing in the Borderlands: The Plays of Frank McGuinness', in G. Lernout (ed.) *The Crows behind the Plough: History and Violence in Anglo-Irish Poetry and Drama,* Amsterdam: Rodopi, 99–115

—— (2000) 'The Imagination of Women's Reality: Christina Reid and Marina Carr', in E. Jordan (ed.) *Theatre Stuff: Critical Essays on Contemporary Irish Theatre,* Dublin: Carysfort Press, 236–48

O'Kane, W. (1993) 'Shadows Along the Border', *The Linnet* 23, 12–13

Ó Liatháin, C. (1997) 'Banging Binlids', *Andersonstown News,* 16 August, 31

Ó Muiri, P. (1997) 'Binlids', *Irish Times,* 12 August [online]. <http://www.ireland.com/newspaper/features/1997/0812/archive.97081200040.html>. Accessed 7 September 2004

—— (1999) 'Funds for Play on the RUC Refused', *Irish Times,* 23 July 1999 [online]. <http://www.ireland.com/newspaper/ireland/1999/0723/archive.99072300028.html>. Accessed 7 September 2004

O'Neill, T. (1969) *Ulster at the Crossroads,* London: Faber & Faber

O'Rawe, D. (1999) '(Mis)Translating Tragedy: Irish Poets and Greek Plays' [online]. <http://www2.open.ac.uk/ClassicalStudies/GreekPlays/Conf99/Orawe.htm>. Accessed 6 September 2004

Orr, J. and Klaić, D. (1990) *Terrorism and Modern Drama,* Edinburgh: Edinburgh University Press

O'Toole, F. (1982) 'The Man from God Knows Where: An Interview with Brian Friel', *In Dublin* 28 (October), 20–23

—— (1984a) 'Field Day: On the Double', *Sunday Tribune,* 23 September, 16

—— (1984b) 'Stephen Rea: The Great Leap from the Abbey', *Sunday Tribune,* 23 September, 16

—— (1984c) 'Tensions in Past and Present Tense', *Sunday Tribune,* 2 December, 18

—— (1985a) 'A Time for Decisions', *Sunday Tribune,* 22 September, 18

—— (1985b) 'Theatrical Murders Reflect the Real World', *Sunday Tribune,* 6 October, 11

—— (1987) 'Death and the Insurrection', *Sunday Tribune,* 27 September, 34–5

—— (1991) 'In a State', in N. Wallace (ed.) *Thoughts and Fragments about Theatres and Nations,* Manchester: Guardian, 18–23

—— (1994) 'A Space Into Which Theatre May Come', *Irish Times,* 23 February, 12

—— (1997) *The Lie of the Land: Irish Identities,* London: Verso

—— (2000) 'Irish Theatre: The State of the Art', in E. Jordan (ed.) *Theatre Stuff: Critical Essays on Contemporary Irish Theatre,* Dublin: Carysfort Press, 47–58

Parker, M. (ed.) (1995) *The Hurt World: Short Stories of the Troubles,* Belfast: Blackstaff Press

Parker, S. (1986) *Dramatis Personae*, Belfast: John Malone Memorial Committee

—— (1989) *Three Plays for Ireland: Northern Star, Heavenly Bodies, Pentecost*, Birmingham: Oberon Books

Parkin, A. (1986) 'Metaphor as Dramatic Structure in Some Plays of Stewart Parker', in M. Sekine (ed.) *Irish Writers and the Theatre*, Gerrards Cross: Colin Smythe, 135–50

Patrick, M. (1989) 'Trouble with the Troubles', *Theatre Ireland* 20 (September–December), 19–21

Patterson, H. (1996) 'Nationalism', in A. Aughey and D. Morrow (eds.) *Northern Ireland Politics*, London: Longman, 39–47

Pattie, D. (1990) 'Alternative Theatre and the State', unpublished PhD thesis, University of Kent at Canterbury

Paulin, T. (1985a) *The Riot Act: A Version of Sophocles' Antigone*, London: Faber and Faber

—— (1985b) 'A New Look at the Language Question', in S. Deane et al. *Ireland's Field Day. Field Day Theatre Company*, London: Hutchinson, 3–22

—— (1987) *The Hillsborough Script: A Dramatic Satire*, London: Faber and Faber

—— (1990) *Seize the Fire*, London: Faber and Faber

—— (2002) 'Antigone', in M. McDonald and J.M. Walton *Amid Our Troubles: Irish Versions of Greek Tragedy*, London: Methuen, 165–70

—— (2003) 'Whose Side Are You On?', *Independent*, 28 September [online]. <http://enjoyment.independent.co.uk/theatre/features/story.jsp?story=448173>. Accessed 3 June 2004

Pavis, P. (1983) 'Socio-Criticism', *Theater* 15 (1), 8–11

Peacock, D.K. (1991) *Radical Stages: Alternative History in Modern British Drama*, Westport, CT: Greenwood Press

Pelan, R.(1999) 'In a Class of Their Own: Women in Theatre in Contemporary Ireland', in H. Gilbert (ed.) *(Post)colonial Stages: Critical and Creative Views on Drama, Theatre and Performance*, Hebden Bridge: Dangaroo Press, 243–52

Pettit, L. (1992) 'Situation Tragedy? The Troubles in British Television Drama', *Irish Studies Review* 1 (Spring), 20–22

—— (1999) 'Troubles, Terminus and The Treaty', in C. Graham and R. Kirkland (eds.) *Ireland and Cultural Theory: The Mechanics of Authenticity*, Basingstoke: Macmillan, 119–35

—— (2000) *Screening Ireland: Film and Television Representation*, Manchester: Manchester University Press

Pfister, M. (1988) *The Theory and Analysis of Drama*, trans. J. Halliday, Cambridge: Cambridge University Press

Phelan, P. (1999) 'Performing Questions, Producing Witnesses', in T. Etchells *Certain Fragments: Contemporary Performance and Forced Entertainment*, London: Routledge, 9–14

Pick, J. (1980) (ed) *The State and the Arts*, Eastbourne: Offord

Pilkington, L. (1990) 'Violence and Identity in Northern Ireland: Graham Reid's *The Death of Humpty Dumpty*', *Modern Drama*, 33 (1), 15–29

—— (1994) 'Theatre and Insurgency in Ireland' *Essays in Theatre/ Etudes Théâtrales*, 12 (2), 129–40

—— (1996) 'Theatre and Cultural Politics in Northern Ireland: the *Over the Bridge* controversy, 1959', *Eire/Ireland*, 30 (4), 76–93

—— (2001a) 'Theatre History and the Beginnings of the Irish National Theatre Project', in E. Jordan (ed.) *Theatre Stuff: Critical Essays on Contemporary Irish Theatre*, Dublin: Carysfort Press, 27–33

—— (2001b) *Theatre and the State in Twentieth Century Ireland: Cultivating the People*, London: Routledge

Pine, R. (1990) *Brian Friel and Ireland's Drama*, London: Routledge

Playfair, N. (1998) 'The First Presbyterian Church' programme note for *Northern Star*, Belfast: Field Day and Tinderbox

Poulter, C. (1997) 'Children of the Troubles', in S. Jennings (ed.) *Dramatherapy: Theory and Practice 3*, London: Routledge, 304–14

Purcell, D. (1987) 'The Illusionist', *Sunday Tribune*: People, 27 September, 1

Purdie, B. (1990) *Politics in the Streets. The Origins of the Civil Rights Movement in Northern Ireland*, Belfast: The Blackstaff Press

Quilligan, P. (1984) 'Field Day's New Double Bill', *Irish Times*, 18 September, 10

Quinn, K.A. (1995) 'Revisioning the Goddess: Drama, Women and Empowerment', in C.C. Barfoot and Rias van den Doel (eds.) *Ritual Remembering: History, Myth and Politics in Anglo-Irish Drama*, Amsterdam: Rodopi, 181–90

Quinn, M.L. (1990) 'Celebrity and the Semiotics of Acting', *New Theatre Quarterly* 22, 154–61

Rabey, D. I. (1986) *British and Irish Political Dramatists in the Twentieth Century*, London: Macmillan

Rafferty, G. (1971) 'Four Words with a Message for All', *Belfast Telegraph*, 16 March, 6

Rafrodi, P. (1991) 'The Worlds of Brian Friel', in J. Genet and R.A. Cave (eds.) *Perspectives of Irish Drama and Theatre*, Gerrards Cross: Colin Smythe, 107–14

Rafrodi, P. et al. (1972) (eds.) *Aspects of the Irish Theatre*, Lille: L'Université de Lille III

Rea, A. (2000) 'Reproducing the Nation: Nationalism, Reproduction, and Paternalism in Anne Devlin's *Ourselves Alone*', in K. Kirkpatrick (ed.) *Border Crossings: Irish Women Writers and National Identities*, Tuscaloosa, AL: University of Alabama Press, 204–26

Rea, S. and Pelletier, M. (2000) ' "Creating Ideas to Live By": An Interview with Stephen Rea', *Sources* (Autumn), 48–65

Reid, C. (1997) *Christina Reid Plays: 1*, London: Methuen

Reid, G.J. (1980) *The Death of Humpty Dumpty*, Dublin: Co-op Books

—— (1986) *Ties of Blood*, London: Faber and Faber

Reinelt, J. (1996) 'Beyond Brecht: Britain's New Feminist Drama', in H. Keyssar (ed.) *Feminist Theatre and Theory*, Basingstoke: Macmillan, 35–48

—— (1999) *After Brecht: British Epic Theatre*, Ann Arbor, MI: University of Michigan Press

Renton, A. (1987) 'Crossing the Troubled Borders of Irish Drama', *Independent*, 27 November

Richards, S. (1991) 'Field Day's Fifth Province: Avenue or Impasse?', in E. Hughes (ed.) *Culture and Politics in Northern Ireland, 1960–1990*, Milton Keynes: Open University Press, 139–150

—— (1995) '*In the Border Country*: Greek Tragedy and Contemporary Irish Drama', in C.C. Barfoot and Rias van den Doel (eds.) *Ritual Remembering: History, Myth and Politics in Anglo-Irish Drama*, Amsterdam: Rodopi, 191–200

—— (2003) 'To Bind the Northern to the Southern Stars: Field Day in Derry and Dublin', in C. Connolly (ed.) *Theorizing Ireland*, Basingstoke: Palgrave Macmillan, 61–8

—— (2004) *The Cambridge Companion to Twentieth Century Irish Drama*, Cambridge: Cambridge University Press

Richie, R. (1985) 'Out of the North', Introduction to R. Hutchinson, *Rat In The Skull*, London: Methuen

Richtarik, M. (1995) *Acting between the Lines: The Field Day Theatre Company, 1980–1984*, Oxford: Clarendon Press

—— (1998) 'Stewart Parker and Northern Star', programme note for *Northern Star*, Belfast: Field Day and Tinderbox

—— (1999) 'Living in Interesting Times: Stewart Parker's *Northern Star*', in J. Harrington and E.J. Mitchell (eds.) *Politics and Performance in Contemporary Northern Ireland*, Amherst, MA: University of Massachusetts Press, 7–28

—— (2000) ' "Ireland, the Continuous Past": Stewart Parker's Belfast History Plays', in S. Watt, E. Morgan and S. Mustafa (eds.) *A Century of Irish Drama: Widening the Stage*, Bloomington, IN: Indiana University Press, 256–74

—— (2004) 'The Field Day Theatre Company', in S. Richards (ed.) *The Cambridge Companion to Twentieth Century Irish Drama*, Cambridge: Cambridge University Press, 191–203

Roche, A. (1988) 'Ireland's Antigones: Tragedy North and South', in M. Kenneally (ed.) *Cultural Contexts and Critical Idioms in Contemporary Irish literature*, Gerrards Cross: Colin Smythe, 221–50

—— (1989) 'The Return of the Story-tellers', *Theatre Ireland* 17 (December 1988–March 1989), 21–3

—— (1994) *Contemporary Irish Drama: From Beckett to McGuinness*, Dublin: Gill and Macmillan

Roll-Hansen, D. (1987) 'Dramatic Strategy in Christina Reid's *Tea in a China Cup*' *Modern Drama* 30 (3), 389–95

Rolston, B. (1991) *Politics and Painting: Murals and Conflict in Northern Ireland*, London and Toronto: Associated University Press

—— (1996) 'Mothers, Whores and Villains: Images of Women in Novels of the Northern Ireland Conflict', in B. Rolston and D. Miller (eds.) *War and Words. The Northern Ireland Media Reader*, Belfast: Beyond the Pale Publications, 403–18 reprinted from *Race and Class* 31 (1), 41–57

—— (1998a) 'Culture as a Battlefield: Political Identity and the State in the North of Ireland', *Race and Class* 39 (4), 23–35

—— (1998b) 'What's Wrong with Multiculturalism? Liberalism and the Irish Conflict', in D. Miller (ed.) *Re-Thinking Northern Ireland*, 253–74

—— (1999) 'Music and Politics in Ireland: The Case of Loyalism', in J. Harrington and E.J. Mitchell (eds.) *Politics and Performance in Contemporary Northern Ireland*, Amherst, MA: University of Massachusetts Press, 29–56

Rolston, B. and Miller, D. (1996) (eds.) *War and Words. The Northern Ireland Media Reader*. Belfast: Beyond the Pale Publications

Rooney, E. (1997) 'Women in Party Politics and Local Groups: Findings from Belfast', in A. Byrne and M. Leonard (eds.) *Women in Irish Society: A Sociological Reader*, Belfast Beyond the Pale Publications, 535–63

Rosenfield, J. (1981) 'Dockers Delighted', *Belfast Newsletter*, 16 January, 4

Rosenfield, R. (1981) ' "Dockers" at the Lyric, Belfast', *Irish Times*, 19 January, 8

—— (1982) 'The Interrogation of Ambrose Fogarty at the Belfast Lyric', *Irish Times*, 3 February, 10

Roulston, C. (1996) 'Equal Opportunities for Women', in A. Aughey and D. Morrow (eds.) *Northern Ireland Politics*, London: Longman, 139–46

Roulston, C. and Davies, C. (eds.) 2000 *Gender, Democracy and Inclusion in Northern Ireland*, Basingstoke: Palgrave Macmillan

Ruane, C. (1999) Falls Community Festival / Féile an Phobail [online]. <http://www.cinni.org/divis/feile.html>. Accessed 2 Oct 2000

Ruane, J. and Todd, J. (1991) ' "Why Can't You Get along with Each Other?": Culture, Structure and the Northern Ireland Conflict', in E. Hughes (ed.) *Culture and Politics in Northern Ireland, 1960–1990*, Milton Keynes: Open University Press, 26–43

—— (1996) *The Dynamics of Conflict in Northern Ireland*, Cambridge: Cambridge University Press

Salaris, L.A. (1991) 'The Mask of Language in *Translations*', in J. Genet and R.A. Cave (eds.) *Perspectives of Irish Drama and Theatre*, Gerrards Cross: Colin Smythe, 101–06

Sales, R. (1997) *Women Divided: Gender, Religion and Politics in Northern Ireland*, London: Routledge

Satake, A. (2000) 'The Seven Ages of Henry Joy McCracken: Stewart Parker's *Northern Star* as a History Play of the United Irishmen in 1798', in E. Jordan (ed.) *Theatre Stuff: Critical Essays on Contemporary Irish Theatre*, Dublin: Carysfort Press, 176–86

Scally, D. (1998) 'Shake, Rattle and Roll—Belfast Play Prepares for U.S. Debut', *The Craic* 22–28 July, 1 and 18

Schaefer, K. (2003) 'The Spectator as Witness? *Binlids* as Case Study', *Studies in Theatre and Performance* 23 (1), 5–20

Schneider, U. (1991) 'Staging History in Contemporary Anglo-Irish Drama: Brian Friel and Frank McGuinness', in J. Genet and R.A. Cave (eds.) *Perspectives of Irish Drama and Theatre*, Gerrards Cross: Colin Smythe, 79–98

Schoenmakers, H. (1982) 'The Tacit Majority in the Theatre', in E.W.B. Hess-Lüttich (ed.) *Multimedial Communication, Vol. II: Theatre Semiotics*, Tübingen: Narr, 108–55

Schrank, B. (2000) 'Politics, Language, Metatheatre: Friel's *The Freedom of the City* and the Formation of an Engaged Audience', in E. Jordan (ed.) *Theatre Stuff: Critical Essays on Contemporary Irish Theatre*, Dublin: Carysfort Press, 122–44

Schroeder, P.R. (1996) 'Locked behind the Proscenium: Feminist Strategies in *Getting Out* and *My Sister in this House*', in H. Keyssar (ed.) *Feminist Theatre and Theory*, Basingstoke: Macmillan, 155–67

Sekine, M. (1986) *Irish Writers and The Theatre*, Gerrards Cross: Colin Smythe

Seymour, A. (1999) 'Welcoming the New Millennium: The Possibilities of Brecht's *The Days of the Commune* for Northern Ireland', *Modern Drama* 42 (2), 176–84

Shaw, R. (1987) *The Arts and the People*, London: Jonathan Cape

Sheridan, P. and Mulrooney, D. (2001) 'Peter Sheridan in Conversation with Deirdre Mulrooney', in L. Chambers et al. (eds.) *Theatre Talk: Voices of Irish Theatre Practitioners*, Dublin: Carysfort Press, 443–58

Shirlow, P. and McGovern, M. (eds.) (1997) *Who are 'The People'? Unionism,*

Protestantism and Loyalism in Northern Ireland, London: Pluto

Shirlow, P. and Shuttleworth, I. (1999) ' "Who is Going to Toss the Burgers?" Social Class and the Reconstruction of the Northern Irish Economy', *Capital and Class* 69 (Autumn), 27–46

Shuttleworth, I. (2004) 'Belfast Blues and Protestants (review)', *Irish Theatre Magazine* 4 (20), 57–60

Sierz, A. (1999) 'Trust', *Tribune* 26 March, in *Theatre Record* 12–25 March, 338

—— (2001) *In-Yer-Face Theatre: British Drama Today*, London: Faber and Faber

Silverstein, M. (1992) ' "It's Only a Name": Schemes of Identification and the National Community in *Translations*', *Essays in Theatre/ Etudes Théâtrales* 10 (2), 133–42

Simpson, D. (1984) 'New Blend Highly Palatable', *Belfast Telegraph*, 5 April, 12

Sloan, B. (1993) 'Sectarianism and the Protestant Mind: Some Approaches to a Current Theme in Irish Drama', *Etudes Irlandaises*, 18 (2), 33–43

—— (1994) ' "The Overall Thing": Brian Friel's *Making History*', *Irish Studies Review* 8 (Autumn), 12–16

—— (2000) *Writers and Protestantism in the North of Ireland: Heirs to Adamnation?* Dublin: Irish Academic Press

Smith, G. (1984) 'Theatre: Field Day', *Sunday Independent*, 30 September, 15

—— (1985) 'Parker's Compassion and Nobility', *Sunday Independent*, 29 September, 17

Smyth, J. (1999) 'Policing Ireland', *Capital and Class* 69 (Autumn), 101–23

Spurr, C. (1992) 'Joyriders USA', *Theatre Ireland*, 26–27 (Winter), 62–5

Stewart, A.T.Q. (1989) *The Narrow Ground: The Roots of Conflict in Ulster*, revised edition, London: Faber & Faber

Stourac, R. and McCreery, K. (1986) *Theatre as a Weapon. Workers' Theatre in the Soviet Union, Germany and Britain, 1917–1934*, London: Routledge and Kegan Paul

Styan, J.L. (1993) *Modern Drama in Theory and Practice. Volume One: Realism and Naturalism*, repr., Cambridge: Cambridge University Press

Szanto, G.H. (1978) *Theater and Propaganda*, Austin, TX: University of Texas Press

Taggart, A. (2000) 'Theatre of War? Contemporary Drama in Northern Ireland', in E. Jordan (ed.) *Theatre Stuff: Critical Essays on Contemporary Irish Theatre*, Dublin: Carysfort Press, 67–83

Tan, E. and Schoenmakers, H. (1984) 'Good Guy; Bad Guy Effects in Political Theatre', in H. Schmid, and A. Van Kesteren (eds.) *Semiotics of Drama and Theatre*, Amsterdam and Philadelphia, PA: John Benjamin, 467–510

Taylor, D. (2001) 'Staging Social Memory: Yuyachkani', in P. Campbell and A. Kear (eds.) *Psychoanalysis and Performance*, London: Routledge, 218–35

Thomas Crane, M. (2001) 'What was Performance?' *Criticism* 43 (2), 169–87

Thompson, P. (1984) 'Playwright Crossing the Sectarian Divide', *Irish Press*, 27 April, 4

Thompson S. (1997) *Over the Bridge and Other Plays*, edited by John Keyes, Belfast: Lagan Press

Timm, E.F. (1982) 'Modern Mind, Myth and History: Brian Friel's *Translations*', in H. Kosok (ed.) *Studies in Anglo-Irish Literature*, Bonn: Bouvier, 447–54

Todd, J. (1987) 'Two Traditions in Unionist Political Culture', *Irish Political Studies* 2, 1–26

Triesman, S. and Lynch, M. (1983) 'Caught by the Goolies', *Platform* 5, 2–6

Trotter, M. (1997) ' "Double Crossing" Irish Borders: The Field Day Production of Tom Kilroy's *Double Cross*', *New Hibernia Review* 1 (1), 31– 43

—— (1999) '*The Beauty Queen of Leenane*, and *A Night in November* (review)', *Theatre Journal* 51 (3), 336

—— (2000) 'Translating Women into Irish Theatre History', in S. Watt, E. Morgan and S. Mustafa (eds.) *A Century of Irish Drama: Widening the Stage*, Bloomington, IN: Indiana University Press, 163–78

—— (2001) *Ireland's National Theaters. Political Performance and the Origins of the Irish Dramatic Movement*, Syracuse, NY: Syracuse University Press

Walter, B. (2000) 'Gendered Irishness in Britain: Changing Constructions', in C. Graham and R. Kirkland (eds.) *Ireland and Cultural Theory: The Mechanics of Authenticity*, Basingstoke: Macmillan, 77–98

Walton, J.M. (2002) 'Hit or Myth: The Greeks and Irish Drama', in M. McDonald and J.M. Walton *Amid Our Troubles: Irish Versions of Greek Tragedy*, London: Methuen, 3–36

Waterman, R. (1985) 'Agit-prop or Naturalism—Which? (1934)', in E. MacColl, S. Cosgrove and R. Samuel (eds.) *Theatres of the Left, 1880–1935*, London: Routledge Kegan Paul, 178–81

Watt, S., Morgan, E. and Mustafa, S. (2000) (eds.) *A Century of Irish Drama: Widening the Stage*, Bloomington, IN: Indiana University Press

Webster, B. (1997) 'Rattling out the Historical Myths of Republican Belfast', *Irish News*, 7 August, 5

Weiss, P. (1971) 'The Material and the Models', *Theatre Quarterly* 1 (1), 41–3

White, V. (1989) 'Towards Post-feminism', *Theatre Ireland* 18 (April–June), 33–5

—— (1993) 'Cathleen Ni Houlihan is not a Playwright', *Theatre Ireland* 30 (Winter), 26–9

—— (1996) 'No Ceasefire in a Cultural Battleground', *Irish Times*, 8 August [online]. <http://www.ireland.com/newspaper/features/1996/0808/archive.96080800036.html>. Accessed 7 September 2004

White McAuley, J. (1999) 'Still "No Surrender"?: New Loyalism and the Peace Process in Ireland', in J. Harrington and E.J. Mitchell (eds.) *Politics and Performance in Contemporary Northern Ireland*, Amherst, MA: University of Massachusetts Press, 57–81

Williams, C. (1993) 'This is One for the Sisters', *Theatre Ireland* 30 (Winter), 6–8

Williams, R. (1977a) 'A Lecture on Realism', *Screen* 18 (1), 61–74

—— (1977b) *Marxism and Literature*, Oxford: Oxford University Press

—— (1979) 'The Arts Council', *Political Quarterly* 50 (2), 157–71

—— (1988) *Keywords. A Vocabulary of Culture and Society*, (2nd edition), London: Fontana

Wilmer, S. (1991) 'Women's Theatre in Ireland', *New Theatre Quarterly* 7 (28), 353–60

Wilson Foster, J. (2001) 'Making Representation: The Literary Imagery of Ulster Protestants: Some Historical Precedents', in D. Bell (ed.) *Dissenting Voices/Imagined Communities*, Belfast: Belfast Film Festival, 12–14

Woodruff, G. (1989) 'Community, Class and Control: a View of Community Plays', *New Theatre Quarterly* 5 (20), 370–73

Woods, V. (1998) *At the Black Pig's Dyke* in J. Fairleigh (ed.) *Far from the Land:*

Contemporary Irish Plays, London: Methuen, 1–61

Woods, V. and Barry, K. (2001) 'Vincent Woods in Conversation with Kevin Barry', in L. Chambers et al. (eds.) *Theatre Talk: Voices of Irish Theatre Practitioners*, Dublin: Carysfort Press, 481–95

Worth, K. (1993) 'Translations of History: Story-telling in Brian Friel's Theatre', in J. Acheson (ed.) *British and Irish Drama since 1960*, Basingstoke: Macmillan, 73–87

Worthern, W. B. (1995) 'Homeless Words': Field Day and the Politics of Translation' *Modern Drama* 38 (1), 22–41

Wren, M. (1982) 'Gruelling Theatre for Audiences at the Lyric', *Irish Times* 3 Februrary, 5

Wright, S. (1989) 'The Stone Chair', *Theatre Ireland*, 19 (July-September), 27

Zach, W. (1992) 'Criticism, Theatre, and Politics: Brian Friel's *The Freedom of the City* and Its Early Reception', in M. Kenneally (ed.) *Irish Literature and Culture*, Gerrards Cross: Colin Smythe, 112–26

Playography

This playography contains details of productions of new work. Entries are listed by year, playwright, title, production company and venue. Entries have been chosen either because they deal with some aspect of life in Northern Ireland, or because they illustrate the oeuvre of a dramatist or company largely associated with Northern Ireland. Adaptations and translations have largely been ommitted, with the exception of productions mentioned earlier in the main body of the text.

1970
Eugene Watters, John D. Stewart and Tomás MacAnna, *A State of Chassis*. Abbey Theatre, Peacock, Dublin

1971
John Boyd, *The Flats*. Lyric Theatre, Belfast

1972
Wilson John Haire, *Within Two Shadows*. Lyric Theatre, Belfast
John Boyd, *The Farm*. Lyric Theatre, Belfast

1973
Tom Murphy, *Famine*. Lyric Theatre, Belfast
Brian Friel, *The Freedom of the City*. Abbey Theatre, Dublin
Patrick Galvin, *Nightfall to Belfast*. Lyric Theatre, Belfast

1974
Patrick Galvin, *The Last Burning*. Lyric Theatre, Belfast
John Boyd, *Guests*. Lyric Theatre, Belfast
Stewart Parker, *Draw Poker*. Group Theatre, Belfast

1975
Brian Friel, *Volunteers*. Abbey Theatre, Dublin
Patrick Galvin, *We Do It For Love*. Lyric Theatre, Belfast
Martin Lynch, *Is There Life Before Death?* Turf Lodge Socialist Fellowship, Turf Lodge Community Centre, Belfast
Stewart Parker, *Spokesong*. World Theatre Productions/Dublin Theatre Festival, John Player Theatre, Dublin

John Arden and Margaretta D'Arcy, *The Non-Stop Connolly Show*. Liberty Hall, Dublin

1976

James Plunket, *The Risen People*. Lyric Theatre, Belfast

Martin Lynch, *We Want Work, We Want Bread*. Turf Lodge Socialist Fellowship, Turf Lodge Community Centre, Belfast

Stewart Parker, *The Actress and the Bishop*. Kings Head Theatre Club, London

Martin Lynch, *They're Taking the Barricades Down*, Turf Lodge Socialist Fellowship, Group Theatre, Belfast

Martin Lynch, *A Roof Under Our Heads,* Turf Lodge Socialist Fellowship, Group Theatre, Belfast

Patrick Galvin, *The Devil's Own People*. Dublin Theatre Festival in association with Gemini Productions, Gaiety Theatre, Dublin

Paddy Scully/David Rudkin *Cries from Casement As His Bones Are Brought To Dublin*. Project Arts Centre, Dublin

1977

John Boyd, *The Street*. Lyric Theatre, Belfast

Brian Friel, *Living Quarters*. Abbey Theatre, Dublin

Frank Dunne, *The Rise and Fall of Barney Kerrigan*. Lyric Theatre, Belfast

Charles Dyer, *Rattle of a Simple Man*. Arts Theatre, Belfast

Stewart Parker, *Catchpenny Twist*. Abbey Theatre, Peacock Stage

1978

Dominic Behan, *Európé*. Lyric Theatre, Belfast

1979

John Boyd, *Facing North*. Lyric Theatre, Belfast

Brian Friel, *Aristocats*. Abbey Theatre, Dublin

Brian Friel, *Faith Healer*. Longacre Theatre, New York

Graham Reid, *The Death of Humpty Dumpty*. Abbey Theatre, Peacock Stage, Dublin

1980

Stewart Parker, *Tall Girls Have Everything*. Actors Theatre of Louisville, Kentucky as part of the America Project

Graham Reid, *The Closed Door*. Abbey Theatre, Peacock Stage, Dublin

Brian Friel, *Translations*. Field Day, Guildhall, Derry

Stewart Parker, *Nightshade*. Abbey Theatre, Peacock Stage, Dublin

Graham Reid, *Dorothy*. Dublin Theatre Festival, Oscar Theatre, Dublin

David Rudkin, *Ashes*, Stage 80, Belfast

1981

Martin Lynch, *Dockers*. Lyric Theatre, Belfast

Frank Dunne, *Old Days*. Lyric Theatre, Belfast

Patrick Galvin, *My Silver Bird*. Lyric Theatre, Belfast

Robin Glendinning, *Jennifer's Vacation*. Edwards-MacLiammoir Gate Theatre Productions, Gate Theatre, Dublin

Jennifer Johnston, *Andante Un Poco Mosso*. New Writers Theatre, Arts Theatre, Belfast

1982

Martin Lynch, *The Interrogation of Ambrose Fogarty*. Lyric Theatre, Belfast

Frank McGuinness, *The Factory Girls*. Abbey Theatre, Dublin

Martin Lynch, *What About Your Ma, Is Your Da Still Working ?* Queen's Fellowship Community Theatre

Graham Reid, *The Hidden Curriculum*. Abbey Theatre, Peacock Stage, Dublin

John Boyd, *Speranza's Boy*. Lyric Theatre, Belfast

Stewart Love, *Football Crazy*. Arts Theatre, Belfast

Brian Friel, *The Communication Cord*. Field Day, Guildhall, Derry

Frank McGuinness, *The Glass God*. Platform Theatre Group, Lourdes Hall, Dublin

Peter Sheridan, *Diary of a Hunger Striker*. Hull Truck Theatre Company, The Round House, London

Stewart Parker, *Kingdom Come*. Lyric Theatre, Belfast

1983

Stewart Parker, *Pratt's Fall*. Tron Theatre, Glasgow

Martin Lynch and The Company, *Lay Up Your Ends*. Charabanc Theatre Company, Belfast Tour

Martin Lynch, *Castles in the Air*. Lyric Theatre, Belfast

Jennifer Johnston, *Indian Summer*. Lyric Theatre, Belfast

Daniel Magee, *Horseman Pass By*. Platform Theatre Group, Lyric Theatre, Belfast

Robert Ellison, *The Unexpected Death of Jummy Blizzard*. Abbey Theatre, Peacock Stage, Dublin

Christina Reid, *Tea in a China Cup*. Lyric Theatre, Belfast

Martin Lynch, *Crack-Up*. Stage 80, Group Theatre, Belfast

1984

Marie Jones and the company in association with Martin Lynch and Pam Brighton, *Oul' Delf and False Teeth*. Charabanc Theatre Company, Arts Theatre, Belfast

Frank McGuinness, *Borderlands*. Team Educational Theatre Company, schools tour

Ron Hutchinson, *Rat in the Skull*. Royal Court Theatre, London

Paddy Devlin, *Strike*. Ulster Actors' Company, Arts Theatre, Belfast

Ron Hutchinson, *Rat in the Skull*. Royal Court, London

Derek Mahon, *High Time*. Field Day Theatre Company, Guildhall, Derry

Tom Paulin, *The Riot Act*. Field Day, Guildhall, Derry

Graham Reid, *Remembrance*. Lyric Theatre, Belfast

Stewart Parker, *Northern Star*. Lyric Theatre, Belfast

1985

Frank McGuinness, *Observe the Sons of Ulster Marching Towards the Somme*. Abbey Theatre, Peacock Stage, Dublin

Marie Jones in association with the company, *Now You're Talkin'*. Charabanc Theatre Company, Arts Theatre, Belfast

Frank McGuinness, *Baglady*. Abbey Theatre, Peacock Stage, Dublin

Thomas Kilroy, *Double Cross*. Field Day Theatre Company, Guildhall, Derry and Irish tour

Frank McGuinness, *Ladybag*. Dublin Theatre Festival in association with the Abbey Theatre, Damer Hall, Dublin

Frank McGuinness, *Gatherers*. Team Educational Theatre Company, Lombard Street Studios, Dublin

Graham Reid, *Callers*. Abbey Theatre, Peacock Stage, Dublin

Anne Devlin, *Ourselves Alone*, Liverpool Playhouse in association with the Royal Court Theatre, Liverpool Playhouse Studio, Liverpool

Martin Lynch, *Minstrel Boys*. Lyric Theatre, Belfast

Christina Reid, *Did You Hear the One About the Irishman. . . ?* Royal Shakespeare Company, American Tour

1986

Charabanc, *Gold in the Streets*. Charabanc Theatre Company, Arts Theatre, Belfast

Christina Reid, *Joyriders*. Paines Plough, Tricycle Theatre, London

Thomas Kilroy, *Double Cross*. Field Day Theatre Company, Guildhall, Derry

Stewart Parker, *Heavenly Bodies*. Birmingham Repertory Theatre, Birmingham

Robin Glendinning, *Mumbo Jumbo*. Royal Exchange, Manchester

Charabanc, *The Girls in the Big Picture*. Charabanc Theatre Company, Ardhowen Theatre, Enniskillen

Frank McGuinness, *Innocence*. The Gate Theatre, Dublin

John Boyd, *Summer Class*. Lyric Theatre, Belfast

1987

Marie Jones, *Somewhere Over the Balcony*. Charabanc Theatre Company, Drill Hall, London

Stewart Parker, *Pentecost*, Field Day, Guildhall, Derry

1988

Brian Friel *The Loves of Cass McGuire*, Lyric Theatre, Belfast

Frank McGuinness *Times In It* (included *Flesh and Blood*, *Brides of Ladybag* and *Feed the Money and Keep Them Coming*) Abbey Theatre, Peacock Stage, Dublin

Kate Batts, Jill Holmes, Zoe Seaton, *Onions Make You Cry*. Big Telly Theatre Company, Flowerfield Arts Centre, Portstewart

Dan Baron Cohen, *Inside Out*. Derry Frontline/Bogside Sculptors, Corn Beef Tin and Pilot's Row, Derry

Brian Friel, *Making History*. Field Day, Guildhall, Derry

Frank McGuinness, *Carthaginians*. Abbey Theatre, Peacock Stage, Dublin

Robin Glendinning, *Culture Vultures*. Lyric Theatre, Belfast

Marie Jones, *Under Napoleon's Nose*. Replay Productions, schools and community tour

Jennifer Johnston, *O Ananias, Azarias and Miseal* and *Twinkletoes*. Abbey Theatre, Peacock Stage, Dublin

Marie Jones, *The Terrible Twins Crazy Christmas*. Charabanc Theatre Company, Riverside Theatre, Coleraine

1989

Dan Baron Cohen, *Time Will Tell*. Derry Frontline. Greater Manchester, Salford, Sheffield and Liverpool

Big Telly Theatre Company, *Crumbs*. Big Telly Theatre Company, Riverside Theatre, Coleraine

Martin Lynch, *Welcome To Bladonmore Road*. Arts Theatre, Belfast

Christina Reid, *The Belle of Belfast City*. Lyric Theatre, Belfast

Martin Lynch, *The Stone Chair*. The Stone Chair Project, Grand Opera House, Belfast

Marie Jones, *Weddin's, Wee'ins and Wakes*. Charabanc Theatre Company, Shankill Festival, Belfast

Neill Speers, *Cauterised*. Charabanc Theatre Company, Lyric Theatre, Belfast

Terry Eagleton, *Saint Oscar*. Field Day, Guildhall, Derry

Christina Reid, *My Name, Shall I Tell You My Name*. Yew Theatre Company, Andrews Lane Theatre, Dublin

Frank McGuinness, *Mary and Lizzie*. Royal Shakespeare Company, The Pit at the Barbican, London

Marie Jones, *It's a Waste of Time, Tracey*. Replay Productions, schools and community tour

Trouble and Strife, *Now and at the Hour of Our Death*. Trouble and Strife, venue unknown

Various, *Stations*, Stranmillis College Theatre, Belfast

1990

Marie Jones, *The Hamster Wheel*. Charabanc Theatre Company, Arts Theatre, Belfast

Brian Friel, *Dancing at Lughnasa*. Abbey Theatre, Dublin

Damian Gorman, *All Being Well*. Replay Productions, school and community tour

Martin Lynch, *Rinty*. Point Fields, Group Theatre, Belfast

Marie Jones, *The Blind Fiddler of Glenadauch*. Charabanc Theatre Company, Amharclann na Carraige, Belfast

Graham Reid, *Too Late To Talk To Billy*. Lyric Theatre, Belfast

Rona Munro, *Bold Girls*. 7:84 (Scotland) Cumbernauld Theatre, Strathclyde

Seamus Heaney, *The Cure at Troy*. Field Day, Guildhall, Derry

Frank McGuinness, *The Bread Man*. The Gate, Dublin

Robin Glendinning, *Donny Boy*. Royal Exchange, Manchester

1991

Marie Jones, *The Cow, The Ship and the Indian*. Replay Productions, schools and community tour

Robert Ellison, *Rough Beginnings*. Lyric Theatre, Belfast

Thomas Carnduff, *The Writing of Thomas Carnduff*, Tinderbox, Old Museum Arts Centre

Marie Jones and Shane Connaughton, *Hang All the Harpers*. DubbelJoint Theatre Company, Ardhowen Theatre, Enniskillen

Gillian Plowman, *Me and My Friend*. Charabanc Theatre Company, Lyric Theatre, Belfast

Thomas Kilroy, *The Madam MacAdam Travelling Theatre*. Field Day Theatre Company, Guildhall, Derry

Marie Jones, *Christmas Eve Can Kill You*. DubbelJoint Theatre Company

Marie Jones, *Don't Look Down*. Replay, St Gerard's Educational Resource Centre

Ron Hutchinson, *Pygmies in the Ruin*. Lyric Theatre, Belfast

Sue Glover, *Bondagers*. Charabanc Theatre Company, St Kevin's Hall, Belfast

Dock Ward, *The Dock Ward Story*. Venue unknown

1992

Marie Jones, *Hiring Days*. Replay Productions, schools and community tour, Belfast

Dan Baron Cohen, *Threshold*. Derry Frontline, The Playhouse, Derry

Hugh Murphy, *Justice*, Point Fields, Old Museum Arts Centre, Belfast

Andrew Hinds, *October Song*. Charabanc Theatre Company, The Playhouse, Derry

Des Wilson, *You're Not Going to Like This, Part 2*, Conway Mill, Belfast

Damian Gorman, *Ground Control to Davy Mental*. Replay Productions, schools and community tour

Frank McGuinness, *Someone Who'll Watch Over Me*. Hampstead Theatre, London

Vincent Woods, *At the Black Pig's Dyke*. Druid Theatre Company, Druid Lane Theatre, Galway

Gerry Stembridge, *Goodnight Strabane*. Ulster Youth Theatre, The Playhouse, Derry

Jill Holmes and Zoe Seaton, *I Can See the Sea*. Big Telly Theatre Company, Riverside Theatre, Coleraine

John Boyd, *Round the Big Clock*. Lyric Theatre, Belfast

Rosemary Magill, *An Immaculate Deception*, Stone Chair Theatre Company, Group Theatre, Belfast

Donal O'Kelly, *The Dogs*. Rough Magic, Dublin

Owen McCafferty, *Winners, Losers and Non-Runners*. Point Fields, Belfast

1993

Theresa Donnelly, *Put that Light Out*. Lyric Theatre, Belfast

Gary Mitchell, *Independent Voice*. Tinderbox Theatre Company, Old Museum Arts Centre, Belfast

Michael Harding, *Hubert Murray's Widow*. Abbey Theatre, Peacock Stage, Dublin

Jennifer Johnston, *How Many Miles to Babylon*. Lyric Theatre, Belfast

Bill Morrison, *A Love Song for Ulster*. Tricycle Theatre, London

Terry Eagleton, *The White, The Gold and The Gangrene*. DubbelJoint, An Culturalann, Belfast

Sue Ashby, *A Wife, A Dog and a Maple Tree*. Charabanc Theatre Company, The Playhouse, Derry

Marie Jones, *The Government Inspector*. Amharclann na Carraige, Belfast

Marie Jones, *Yours Truly*. Replay Productions, Old Museum Arts Centre, Belfast

Brian Friel, *Wonderful Tennessee*. Abbey Theatre, Dublin

Owen McCaffrey, *I Won't Dance, Don't Ask Me*. Who the Hell Theatre Company

1994

Frank McGuinness, *The Bird Sanctuary*. Abbey Theatre, Dublin

Anne Devlin, *After Easter*. Royal Shakespeare Company, the Other Place, Stratford-upon-Avon

Robin Glendinning, *Summer House*. Druid Theatre Company, Druid Lane Theatre, Galway

Brian Friel, *Molly Sweeney*. Gate Theatre, Dublin

Marie Jones, *A Night in November*. DubbelJoint Theatre Company, West Belfast Festival

Owen McCafferty, *The Waiting List*. Point Fields Theatre Company, Old Museum Arts Centre, Belfast as part of Angels with Split Voices

Ken Bourke, *Galloping Buck Jones*. Tinderbox, Lyric Theatre, Belfast

Martin Lynch, *Pictures of Tomorrow*. Point Fields, Lyric Theatre, Belfast

Damian Gorman, *Stones*. Replay Productions, school and community tour

Owen McCafferty, *The Private Picture Show*. Lyric Theatre, Belfast

1995

Conal Morrison, *Hard To Believe*, Bickerstaffe Theatre Company, Cleere's Theatre, Kilkenny

Gina Moxley, *Danti-Dan*. Project Arts Centre, Rough Magic Theatre Company

Gary Mitchell, *Alternative Future*. Point Fields Theatre Company, Old Museum Arts Centre, Belfast as part of 'Angels with Split Voices'

Damian Gorman, *Loved Ones*. Old Museum Arts Centre, Belfast

Marie Jones, *Women on the Verge of HRT*. DubbelJoint Theatre Company, Amharclann na Carraige, Belfast

Graham Reid, *Lengthening Shadows*. Point Fields-Lyric Theatre, Belfast

Zoe Seaton with John Leslie, *Cuchulainn*. Big Telly Theatre Company, Riverside Theatre, Coleraine

Gary Mitchell, *That Driving Ambition*, Replay Productions, schools and community tour

Andy Hinds. *The Starving*. Point Fields, Old Museum Arts Centre, Belfast

1996

Owen McCafferty, *Freefalling*. Kabosh in association with Virtual Reality, Ardhowen Theatre, Enniskillen

Bill Morrrison, *Drive On*. Lyric Theatre, Belfast

Jennifer Johnston, *Desert Lullaby*, Lyric Theatre, Belfast

Christina Reid, *Clowns*. Orange Tree Studio, London

Marie Jones, *Eddie Bottom's Dream*. DubbelJoint Theatre Company, Grand Opera House, Belfast

Daragh Carville, *Language Roulette*. Tinderbox Theatre Company, Old Museum Arts Centre

Marie Jones, *Stones in His Pockets*, DubbelJoint Theatre Company, Amharclann na Carraige, Belfast

1997

Owen McCafferty, *Shoot the Cow*. Druid Theatre Company, Druid Lane Theatre, Galway

Gary Mitchell, *In a Little World of Our Own*. Abbey Theatre, Peacock Stage, Dublin

Brian Friel, *Give Me Your Answer, Do!* Abbey Theatre, Dublin

Christine Poland, Brenda Murphy, Danny Morrison and Jake MacSiacáis, *Binlids*. DubbelJoint and JustUs Community Theatre, Amharclann na Carraige, Belfast

Gary Mitchell, *Sinking*. Replay Productions, schools and community tour

Daragh Carville, *Dumped*. Tinderbox Theatre Company, Royal School Armagh

Frank McGuiness, *Mutabilitie*. Royal National Theatre, London

Dock Ward. *Rebellion*. Venue unknown

David Brett, *Hunger*. Production Company, Waterfront Hall, Belfast

1998

John McClelland, *Into the Heartland*. Tinderbox Theatre Company, Old Museum Arts Centre, Belfast

Pearse Elliot, *A Mother's Heart*. DubbelJoint, Amharclann na Carraige, Belfast

Owen McCafferty, *Mojo-Mickeybo*, Kabosh Productions, Andrews Lane Theatre, Dublin

Gary Mitchell, *Tearing the Loom*. Lyric Theatre, Belfast

Gary Mitchell, *As the Beast Sleeps*. Abbey Theatre, Peacock Stage, Dublin

Joe Crilly, *Second Hand Thunder*. Tinderbox, The Playhouse, Derry

Dave Duggan, *The Shopper and the Boy* and *Without the Walls*, Sole Purpose Productions, Golden Thread Theatre, Belfast

Damian Gorman, *Sometimes*. Replay Productions, schools and community tour

Andrew Hinds, *The Starving*. Open House Theatre/Íomhá Ioldánach Theatre Company, Crypt Arts Centre, Dublin

David Pownall, *Getting the Picture*. Lyric Theatre, Belfast

Nicola McCartney, *Heritage*. Traverse Theatre, Edinburgh

1999

Marie Jones, *The Hamster Wheel*. Charabanc Theatre Company, Arts Theatre, Belfast

Gary Mitchell, *Trust*, Royal Court Theatre, London

Daragh Carville, *Observatory*. Abbey Theatre, Peacock Stage, Dublin

Brenda Murphy and Christine Poland, *Forced Upon Us*, DubbelJoint-JustUs Community Theatre, Amharclann na Carraige, Belfast

Zoe Seaton and Briona Corrigan, *The Pursuit of Diarmuid and Grainne*, Big Telly Theatre Company, Riverside Theatre, Coleraine

Gary Mitchell, *Energy*. The Playhouse, Derry

Colin Teevan, *Iph. . .*, Lyric Theatre, Belfast

Martin Lynch, Marie Jones and the Company, *The Wedding Community Play*. The Wedding Community Play Project, various locations, Belfast

Frank McGuinness, *Dolly West's Kitchen*. Abbey Theatre, Dublin

Sean Caffrey, *Out Come the Bastards*, Crescent Arts Centre

Brian Campbell, *Des*. DubbelJoint, Amharclann na Carraige, Belfast

2000

Joseph Crilly, *On McQuillan's Hill*. Tinderbox, Lyric Theatre, Belfast

Dave Duggan, *Waiting. . .* Sole Purpose Productions, Derry

Brian Campbell, *Des*. DubbelJoint, Amharclann na Carraige, Belfast

Marie Jones, *Ruby*, Tinderbox Theatre Company, Group Theatre, Belfast

Gary Mitchell, *The Force of Change*, Royal Court Theatre, London

Gary Mitchell, *Marching On*. Lyric Theatre, Belfast

Brian Foster, *The Butterfly of Killybegs*, Lyric Theatre, Belfast

Zoe Seaton, *Fish*. Big Telly Theatre Company, Riverside Theatre, Coleraine

2001

Martin McDonagh, The *Lieutenant of Inishmore*, Royal Shakespeare Company, the Other Place, Stratford-upon-Avon

Brian Campbell and Laurence McKeown, *The Laughter of Our Children*. DubbelJoint, Amharclann na Carraige, Belfast

Morna Regan, *Midden*, Rough Magic, Traverse Theatre, Edinburgh

Owen McCafferty, *No Place Like Home* (devised with text by McCafferty). Tinderbox Theatre Company, Northern Bank Building, Belfast

Convictions, Tinderbox Theatre Company, Crumlin Road Courthouse, Belfast: Included

Daragh Carville, *Male Toilets*

Damien Gorman, *Judges' Room*
Marie Jones, *Court Room No. 2*
Martin Lynch, *Main Hall*
Owen McCafferty, *Court Room No. 1*
Nicola McCartney, *Jury Room*
Gary Mitchell, *Holding Room*

2002
Tim Loane, *Caught Red-Handed.* Tinderbox, Northern Bank Building, Belfast
Damian Smyth, *Soldiers of the Queen,* Centre Stage Theatre Company, Belfast
    Institute of Further and Higher Education and tour
Paul Boyd, *McCool XXL,* Big Telly Theatre Company in association with the Lyric
    Theatre, Lyric Theatre, Belfast
Frank McGuinness, *Gates of Gold.* The Gate Theatre, Dublin
Brian Friel, *Afterplay.* The Gate Theatre, Dublin
Brian Moore, *Paddy on the Road.* DubbelJoint, Amharclann na Carraige, Belfast
Brenda Murphy, *Working Class Heroes.* DubbelJoint, Amharclann na Carraige, Belfast
Owen McCafferty, *Closing Time.* Royal National Theatre, London
Maria Connolly, *Massive,* Tinderbox Theatre Company, The Errigal Inn, Belfast
Martin Lynch and Mark Dougherty, *The Belfast Carmen,* Green Shoot Productions,
    Grand Opera House, Belfast

2003
Conall Morrison, *Antigone by Sophocles,* Storytellers Theatre Company in association
    with Cork Opera House, Town Hall Theatre
Nicola McCartney, *The Millies.* Replay Productions, schools and community tour
Owen McCafferty, *Scenes from the Big Picture.* Royal National Theatre, London
Brian Campbell and Laurence McKeown, *A Cold House.* Amharclann na Carraige,
    Belfast
Martin Lynch, Conor Grimes and Alan McKee, *The History of The Troubles Accordin'*
    to My Da, Cathedral Quarter Arts Festival
Brian Moore, *Black Taxis.* DubbelJoint, Amharclann na Carraige, Belfast
Brian Friel, *Performances.* Gate Theatre, Dublin
Gary Mitchell, *Loyal Women.* Royal Court Downstairs, London

2004
Stuart Carolan, *Defender of the Faith,* Abbey Theatre, Peacock Stage, Dublin
Michael Duke, *Revenge,* Tinderbox Theatre Company, Northern Bank Building,
    Belfast
Robert Welch, *Protestants.* Ransom Productions, Old Museum Arts Centre, Belfast
Seamus Heaney, *The Burial at Thebes: Sophocles' Antigone as translated by Seamus*
    Heaney, Abbey Theatre, Dublin
Brian Campbell, *Voyage of No Return.* DubbelJoint, Amharclann na Carraige, Belfast
MacDara Vallely, *Peacefire,* Edinburgh Festival and Irish Tour
Seamas Keenan, *Flight,* The Playhouse, Derry
Padraig Coyle, Conor Grimes, Alan McKee, *Paradise.* Lyric Theatre, Belfast

Index

- page numbers in bold italic denote illustrations
- 'n' indicates an end note.

Abbey Theatre, Dublin 11, 49, 79, 82, 146. *See also* Irish Literary Theatre
abjection 76, 167. *See also* violence
accent 35, 96, 178 n7
Aherne, Bertie 11
Anglo-Irish Agreement 65, 85
Anne Devlin, 79
Antigone 79–84, 168, 177 n3, 178 n7. *See also The Riot Act*
Arden, John and Margaretta D'Arcy, *The Non-Stop Connolly Show* 24, 25
Article 5 174 n10
Arts Council of Northern Ireland (ACNI) 81, 88, 168–70, 174 n6, 183 n7
Arts Theatre, Belfast 110
authenticating conventions 52, 92
authenticity 18, 34, 38, 44–7, 53–9, 63, 86, 94, 110

balance in representation 42, 54–7, 157
barbarism 4, 29; republicans as barbarian criminals 29–30, 34, 165; loyalists as barbarians 154–5
Battle of the Somme 74
Belfast Festival at Queen's 65, 110, 111, 150, 179 n7, 180 n13
Belfast Institute of Further and Higher Education 50, 140
Bennett, Ronan 153, 163; *Love Lies Bleeding* 181 n1
Big Telly 88–9, 179 n7; *Crumbs* 88; *Cu chulainn* 89; *Little Lucy's Magic Box* 88; *Onions Make You Cry* 88; *The Pursuit of Diarmuid and Gráinne* 79, 86, *87*, 89–91, 92–4, 96
Blair, Tony 51, 175 n4

blanket protests 29
Bloody Sunday 33, 48–9, 54–5, 175 n4; 'Bloody Sunday' play 47. *See also The Freedom of the City*; Saville Inquiry, Widgery Tribunal
Boal, Augusto 127, 128; forum theatre 128, 175 n 15, Theatre of the Oppressed 128. *See also* Derry Frontline
Bolger, Dermot *In High Germany* 182 n2
Boyd, John 26; *The Flats*, 14, *15*, 22, 34, 103–4, 159, 166, 167
Brecht, Bertholt 24, 177 n2; Brechtian techniques 55; historicization 61
Brighton, Pam 50, 56–7, 103, 139, 140, 169, 179 n7, 180 n13, 181 n5; with Charabanc 109–10
British Broadcasting Corporation (BBC) 25, 65, 67, 80, 123, 133, 146, 147, 161, 174 n10, 175 n8, 177 n7, 181 n1
British state 4, 8, 13, 14; and loyalism 153; representations of 2, 32, 42
broadcasting ban, 164

Caffrey, Sean, *Out Come the Bastards*, 163
Carville, Daragh 150, 182 n11
Cathedral Quarter Arts Festival, Belfast 26
Catholic Church 128–31; and the Free State 142; and gender 99; representations of Catholics 142; Catholicism 45, 142, 179 n3; anti-Catholicism 174 n9. *See also* sectarianism
censorship 25, 28. *See also Article 5*; broadcasting ban
Charabanc 31, 102, 109–10; 115, 125, 139, 161, 162, 170, 180 n 13; *Gold*

in the Streets 109; *Lay Up Your Ends* 109; *Oul' Delf and False Teeth* 109; *Now You're Talking* 109; *Somewhere Over the Balcony* 99, 105, 109, 110–11, 112–17, 162, 167. See also Jones, Marie

characterisation 27, 68, 91, 96, 126, 155; critique of female characterisations 104, 107; static characterisation 28

Civil Rights Movement 4, 100, 164; and *Antigone* 81; and *The Freedom of the City* 49. See also Bloody Sunday

class 2, 99, 121, 157; and community theatre 122, 131, 169; class consciousness 63; and Charabanc 109, 110; and Derry Frontline 128; and *Dockers* 62–3, 68, 70, 74, 75; and DubbelJoint 103; and ideology 16; and *Interrogation of Ambrose Fogarty* 25, 26, 29, 35; and loyalism 153, 155; and middle-class audiences 170; and *A Night in November* 139–42; and *Northern Star* 66; and the peace process 137; and *Pentecost* 86; and realism 23; and SDLP 72; and *The Stone Chair* 123–7, 133–4; and 7:84 (Scotland) 112; and UWC strike 84; and unionist state 119; class solidarity 161; working class 6, 8, 12, 52

classic narrative 23, 130, 180

colonialism 13, 101; colonial discourses 44, 97, 117

communitas 58

community 3, 58; and *Binlids* 56–9; Community Arts Forum 26; community plays 124–6, 131, 132, 135–6; definitions of 118–19; and loyalism 6; and nationalists 33, 49–51; and Ulster British ideology 6

competitive victimhood 154

Convictions 26, 150. See also Tinderbox

Crilly, Joseph 150, 182 n11; *On McQuillan's Hill* 22, 122, 161

Cruise O'Brien, Connor 81; *States of Ireland* 177 n4

culture 3, 10, 67, 120; and colonialism 44; cultural interpretations of the conflict 2; cultural legitimation 171; and documentary 53; Greek 79, 80; and ideology 16–17; Irish 11, 13, 64, 79, 98, 107, 153; and loyalism 88,

120; middle-class 163, 168; and myth 77; and politics 9, 12, 68, 73, 81, 82, 134, 156; Protestant 151; and resistance 120, 135; Roman 80; and self-sacrifice 132; sub-cultures 121–2; and unionism 119; Ulster 153; and violence 29, 167–8; working class culture 68, 123; workshop culture 127

Cumann na mBan 101

Daly, Edward 54

Deane, Seamus 5, 29, 30, 66, 82, 83, 104, 119, 155, 168, 177 n6

deixis 143

Democratic Unionist Party (DUP) 124, 138,152, 174 n9

Derry City Council 33

Derry Frontline 21, 33, 100, 117, 122, 127–8; *Inside Out* 128–31, 135–6; *Threshold* 17, 21, 128; *Time Will Tell* 128

Devlin, Anne 16, 46, 161, 179 n 7; *My Name, Shall I Tell You My Name?* 47, 162; *Naming the Names* 4, 106; *Ourselves Alone* 102, 105, 106, 117, 161

Devlin, Bernadette 54, 81

Devlin, Paddy 72; *Strike* 161

discours 57, 115, 176 n11

distancing 24–5, 37, 39–41, 49, 61, 79, 91–3, 96, 157–9, 163–4. See also estrangement

documentary theatre 53–4; techniques 55

domesticity 29, 36, 63, 75, 103, 112, 115; domestic settings 62, 86, 99–100, 104, 112–13, 129, 148, 179 n9; domestic tragedy 21, 116, 160; domestic violence 128

Drill Hall, London 110, 162

Druid Theatre Company 31

DubbelJoint 103, 139, 140, 154, 169, 179 n7, 181 n 5, 184 n10; *Binlids* 47, 49–51, 55–9, 176 n12. See also Justus Community Theatre

Dublin and Monaghan bombings 31

Dublin Theatre Festival 12, 65, 67, 85

Duke, Michael *Revenge* 91

efficacy 9, 17–19, 92

Elliot, Pearse, *A Mother's Heart* 184

empathy 23, 35, 57

entertainment 145, 162, 170; and utopia 95
Equal Opportunities Commission 100
Ervine, St John, *Mixed Marriage* 84
estrangement 78, 92. *See also* distancing
European Capital of Culture 8
European Commission of Human Rights 28
European Court of Justice 4
European Economic Community 7
European Parliament 4
European Union 7, 118
expansive acts 134, 136. *See also* community

familiarity 21, 79, 91–4, 158
Féile an Phobail 49, 51, 139–40, 157, 175 n6, 176 n9, 177 n6. *See also* West Belfast Festival
femininity 97, 98, 99, 105, 107 155; feminine forms 116; taxonomy of female figures 103–4, 116, 151. *See also* O'Casey
feminism 98, 163; and nationalism 97–9; and republicanism 102, 116–17; *écriture féminine* 16. *See also* gender
Field Day Theatre Company 5, 10, 48, 78, 80–2. *See also* Friel, Brian; Rea, Stephen
fifth province 82
First Tuesday 31
Fitt, Gerry 72
Flowerfield Arts Centre, Portstewart 88
Fo, Dario 54, 88, 152, 153, 182 n7
Friel, Brian 7, 46, 47, 48, 81, 82, 85, 119, 175 n3; *Dancing at Lughnasa* 47; *Faith Healer* 162; *The Freedom of the City* 11–12, 14, 16, 24, 47–9, 52–9, 81, 162, 166; *Making History* 9–10, 44, 45; *Philadelphia, Here I Come* 47; *Translations* 4, 14, 16, 20, 45, 48, 80, 81, 82, 119, 177 n5; *Volunteers* 14, 60

Gaelic Athlectic Association (GAA) 121, 174 n5
Galvin, Patrick *Nightfall to Belfast* 159; *We Do It For Love* 24, 25
Gate Theatre, London 80, 177 n3
gender 2, 19, 121, 179 n1, n3; and colonialism 97; and Derry Frontline 128; and genre 116; and *Inside Out* 128–31; and nationalism 20, 90, 97–9; and representation 97, 98, 103; and space 104, 116; and unionism 98; and violence 99, 103–7, 110, 116, 129; gender inequality 100; gender politics 7, 72, 99; gender roles 97, 99, 101, 102, 103–7
Godber, John 178 n17; *Teechers* 88
Good Friday Agreement 1, 2, 3, 65, 72, 101, 137, 138, 139, 180
Gordon, Dan 140, 145, 152–3
Government of Ireland Act 7
Grand Opera House, Belfast 26, 123, 126, 133, 162
Group Theatre, Belfast 25, 169, 180 n14
Guildhall, Derry 10, 83, 85, 94; and Field Day 81; in *The Freedom of the City* 49, 52, 54, 55, 81–2

Hall, Peter 96
Hampstead Theatre, London 111
Haughey, Charles 72
H-blocks 76
Heaney, Seamus 8, 66, 79, 177 n6; *The Cure at Troy* 177 n1
Heath, Edward 49
Hinds, Andy, *October Song* 17
histoire 57, 115, 176 n11
history play 77
Hole in the Wall Gang 179 n12; *Give My Head Peace* 161; *Too Late to Talk to Billy and Emer about Love Across the Barricades in the Terror Triangle* 161; *Two Ceasefires and a Wedding* 161
human rights 4, 88, 101. *See also* Civil Rights Movement
Hume, John 31, 81
Hunger Strikes 12, 29, 30, 31
Hurd, Douglas, 164

identity 8, 16, 18, 58, 70, 79, 81, 97–9, 132, 134, 157, 161–2; blocs 5, 7; British 6, 74; and *Caught Red-Handed* 151, 153, 156; communities of 3, 78, 118–21, 133, 171; ethnic 2, 13, 86, 99, 180 n2; gender 98, 101; Irish 8, 41, 157; loyalist 153, 156; and myth 77–8; and *A Night in November* 141–2, 145, 154, 156; Orange 154; Ulster-Protestant 105

182 n16; unionist 5, 138, 155
ideology 16; and Big Telly 89; and
    form 22, 24; loyalist 6, 168; and
    myth 78, 88; nationalist 98; and
    place 66; propaganda 16–18;
    republican 74; Ulster-British 6;
    unionist 74
IMPACT '92 33
implicating the audience 50
institutionalised theatre 43,
internment 28, 30, 50, 56, 59, 101,
    110, 175 n7
in-yer-face theatre 37, 163, 183
Irish Arts Centre, New York 26
Irish Literary Renaissance 86. *See also*
    Yeats, William Butler
Irish Literary Theatre (ILT) 8, 10, 11.
    See also Yeats, William Butler
Irish National Liberation Army (INLA)
    34
Irish Republican Army (IRA) 28, 106,
    175 n7; and GAA 121; and gender
    101, 112–13, 161; ideology 74;
    Continuity 138; Official 124;
    Provisional 2, 31, 59, 72, 181 n4,
    181 n6; Real 138; representation of
    34, 153, 168, 174, 182 n8

Jellicoe, Anne 124–5, 131, 133. *See also*
    community plays
Jones, Marie 16, 109; 139, 179 n7, 180
    n14, 182 n11; *A Night in November*
    47, 103, 104, 139–45, 151, 153,
    154–7, 162; *Somewhere Over the*
    Balcony 99, 105, 109, 110–11,
    112–17, 162, 167; *Stones in His*
    Pockets 181 n5; *The Wedding*
    Community Play 26, 161, 180 n4.
    See also Charabanc; DubbelJoint
Justus Community Theatre 49; *Binlids*
    47, 49–51, 55–9; *Forced Upon Us* 49,
    162, 168, 169; *Just a Prisoner's Wife*
    49, 183 n9. *See also* DubbelJoint

Keenan, Seamus, *Flight* 121, 181 n4

language 'bad language' 37; *The*
    Freedom of the City 52–3; Irish
    language 20, 82, 119; Tom Paulin
    178 n14; power of 67–72, 76, 81,
    94–5; translation 92; vernacular 83,
    96; working-class 62. *See also* accent;
    naming

Loane, Tim 150; *Caught Red-Handed*
    20, 139, 149–53, 156–7. *See also*
    Tinderbox
loyalism 84; loyalists 6, 8, 85, 119, 121,
    139, 175 n7; *Loyal Women* 167;
    representation of loyalists 147–9,
    151–7, 160
Lynch, Martin 24, 25, 63, 109, 122,
    174 n7, 176 n6, 177 n13; *A Roof*
    Under Our Heads, 25, 26, 174 n6;
    The Belfast Carmen 26; *Castles in The*
    Air 174 n6; *Dockers* 26, 61–3, 68–9,
    70–6,161, 167, 176 n1; *The History*
    of The Troubles (accordin' to my Da')
    26, 47, 162, 176 n11; *The*
    Interrogation of Ambrose Fogarty 25,
    26–30, 34–9, 42, 167; *Is There Life*
    before Death? 25; *Minstrel Boys* 75; *A*
    Prayer for the Dying 26; *A Roof Under*
    Our Heads 25, 26, 174 n6; *The Stone*
    Chair 20, 26, 123–7, 131, 133–6,
    162, 170; *They're Taking The*
    Barricades Down 25; *The Wedding*
    Community Play 26, 161,180 n4; *We*
    Want Work, We Want Bread 63;
    What about Your Ma, Is Your Da
    Still Working? 25; *What Did I Know*
    When I Was Nineteen? 26
Lyric Theatre, Belfast 22, 26, 35, 61–3,
    65, 147, 174 n6 and n7, 179 n7;
    Lyric Players Group (later the Lyric
    Players Theatre Trust) 14

Macnas 89
Mahon, Derek, *High Time* 78, 83
Mallon, Seamus 72
martyrdom 73–6, 78, 105, 107, 177
    n10
masculinist discourses 97, 99, 101–3,
    179 n1. *See also* patriarchy; and
    gender
McCafferty, Frankie 31, 164
McCafferty, Owen 182 n11; *Mojo*
    Mickybo 161
McCartney, Nicola 179 n8; *Heritage*
    104–5
McCready, Sam 26, 61
McDonagh, Martin, *The Lieutenant of*
    Inishmore 34
McGrath, John 111–12, 124, 180 n14,
    181 n7
McGuinness, Frank 16; *Carthaginians*
    21, 24, 33, 47, 107, ***108***, 122, 177

n9 and n10; *Observe the Sons of Ulster Marching Towards the Somme* 14, 20, 47, **73**, 74, 82, 122, 162
McLarnon, Gerald, *The Bonefire* 14
McNamara, Gerald, *No Surrender* 154; *Suzanne of the Sovereigns* 154; *Thompson in Tir-na-nOg* 154
McPherson, Conor, *Rum and Vodka* 182 n2; *The Good Thief* 182 n2
memory 44–7, 52; embodied 125
metatheatre 24–5, 39–42, 159, 172–3 n3; play-within-a-play 123
Methven, Eleanor 109, 110
metonymic substitution 3,
Mitchell, Gary 8, 12, 90, 120, 145–7, 162, 168, 182 n9; *As The Beast Sleeps* 105–6, 139, 146, **147**, 147–9, 155–7, 167; *Dividing Force* 146; *The Force of Change* 137–8, 146, 167, 183 n5; *Independent Voice* 146; *In a Little World of Our Own* 146, 147, 160; *Loyal Women* 101, 104, 105, 106–7, 121, 160, 167, 183 n5; *Sinking* 146; *Tearing the Loom* 45, 166; *That Driving Ambition* 146; *Trust* 22, 105, 146, 153, 167, 183 n5; *The World, The Flesh and The Devil* 146
monodrama 142–5, 162–3, 182 n2
monologue 19, 35, 54, 57, 58, 114, 115, 130, 162
Monstrous Regiment 110
Morrison, Conall 79, 147, 178 n7, 182 n9; *Hard to Believe* 162
Mowlam, Mo 51
Munro, Rona 111–12; *Bold Girls* 19, 99, 111, 112–17, 161, 162; *Saturday Night at the Commodore* 111
myth 2, 5, 19, 22, 25, 34, 42, 77, 78–9, 92, 93–6, 134, 159; Celtic 86–8, 89, 90, 178 n13 and n19; Christian 77, 84; Greek 79, 80, 82–3, 84, 93, 103, 177 n1 and n2, 178 n7; ideological myths 78, 134; Protestant 162; utopian myths 78–9, 134. *See also* martyrdom

naming 4, 68–70, 76, 130, 155, 175 n3, 180 n3. *See also* language
National Theatre, London 96, 146
nationalism 2, 5, 6, 11, 12, 83, 120, 153, 170; civic 13, 157; cultural 11; and gender 20, 90, 97–9, 161; and

revisionism 34
Nationalist Party 48
Northern Ireland Assembly 3, 101
Northern Ireland Women's Coalition 101
Northern Ireland Women's Rights Movement 101
Nothing Personal 182 n3

O'Casey, Sean 116; Dublin Trilogy 22, 67, 104; Juno 103; *The Plough and the Stars* 105
Omagh bombing 65
O'Malley, Pearse 26
O'Neill, Terence 1
Oresteia 96

Paisley, Ian 152, 174 n9; Paisleyite 27
paramilitaries 4, 5, 121, 133, 138, 140–1, 160, 165, 166, 174 n5, 180 n2 ; loyalist 4, 28, 84, 90, 120, 128, 137, 139, 146, 147–9, 150, 153, 155, 157, 163, 165, 181–2 n6; republican 139, 181 n4; and women 101–2, 106–7, 179 n11. *See also* Irish Republic Army; loyalists; Republicans; Ulster Defence Association; Ulster Volunteer Force
parity of esteem 3
Parker, Stewart 65, 66–7, 137–8, 178 n21, 181 n1; Stewart Parker Award 146; *Blue Money* 177 n7; *Catchpenny Twist* 67; *Dramatis Personae* 67, 177 n9; *The Iceberg* 177 n7; *I'm a Dreamer, Montreal* 177 n7; *Iris in the Traffic, Ruby in the Rain* 177 n7; *The Kamikazi Ground Staff Reunion Dinner* 177 n7; *Lost Belongings* 177 n7, 178 n13; *Northern Star* 2, 12, 24, 46, 47, 61, 63–6, 69–72, **73**, 76, 160, 162, 178 n10; *Pentecost* 45, 77, 79, 84–6, 94–6; *Radio Pictures* 177 n7; *Spokesong* 67, 160
partition 7, 14, 48, 142, 173 n3, 181 n6
Passionmachine 90
patriarchy 16, 98, 99, 111, 115, 135; and republicans 113, 117. *See also* gender; masculinist discourses
Paulin, Tom 80–1, 177 n6, 178 n14; *All the Way to the Empire Room* 80; *The Hillsborough Script* 80; *The Riot Act* 78, 79, 81, 83–4, 93–6, 177 n3;

Seize the Fire 80, 177
Peace People 100, 179 n10
peace process 2, 65, 72–3; and women
  100–1, 118, 137–9, 157, 183 n6
Peacock Theatre, Dublin 26, 67, 110,
  147, 157, 164. *See also* Abbey
  Theatre
place 2, 99; and accent 35, 44–5;
  communities of location 119; in
  performance 52, 65–6, 86, 104
political drama 13, 41; political plays
  158, 170
post-colonial theory 9, 13; and gender
  98; theatre 173 n3
Prime Cut Productions 173 n1
propaganda 3, 16–18, 25, 29, 47–8, 78,
  163–4; agitational 17; *Binlids* 168–9;
  dialectical 18; integrationist 18;
  propaganda war 3
protective acts 132–4, 136. *See also*
  community
Protestants 5, 6, 26, 29; *Protestants* 182
  n2; 'cold house for' 138; culture and
  identity 151, 182 n16; Protestantism
  45, 142, 151; Protestant Parliament
  and state 2, 173 n3, 181 n6; and
  British identity 74; and Derry 81;
  and gender 99, 179 n3; and
  republicanism 64; and Troubles
  plays 22, 32, 160; representations of
  63, 70, 86, 95, 103, 105, 106, 110,
  141–2, 146, 154, 160–1, 162, 166;
  Ulster Protestants 128, 142, 153;
  unionism 6–7, 80, 119; spectators
  133, 144, 182 n8. *See also*
  Remembrance Day bombing;
  sectarianism; UWC strike
psychological withdrawal 5, 42

Queen's University Belfast 66. *See also*
  Belfast Festival

Rame, Franca 88
Rea, Stephen 48, 64, 65, 66, 81, 82, 83,
  84, 175 n3, 177 n5 and n6, 178 n9,
  n10, n11. *See also* Field Day Theatre
  Company
realism 22–4, 45–6, 47, 64, 110, 129,
  159; classic realism 23; critiques of
  23–4; and *The Interrogation of
  Ambrose Fogarty* 34–9; magical
  realism 45; and *Pentecost* 94–5. *See
  also* classic narrative

reception 9–10, 11–12, 25, 42–3, 158,
  162; *At The Black Pig's Dyke* 32;
  Binlids 176 n12; *Caught Red-Handed*
  149; frames 18–19, 24, 25, 99; *The
  Freedom of the City* 16, 47, 55–6, 59,
  163; and ideology 17–19; image
  schemas 10; *Pentecost* 84, 95; *The
  Pursuit of Diarmuid and Gráinne* 91;
  The Riot Act 83; and women 103;
  and words 94–5
Reid, Christina 12, 16, 163, 174 n7,
  179 n7; *The Belle of Belfast City*
  151–2,159, 160; *Clowns* 24; *Did You
  Hear the One about the Irishman?* 24,
  60, 160, 166; *My Name, Shall I Tell
  You My Name?* 162; *Tea in a China
  Cup* 47, 97, 104, 120
Reid, Graham 12, 174 n7; *Callers* 165;
  The Death of Humpty Dumpty 159;
  Remembrance 160
Reid, John 138, 181 n3
Remembrance Day bombing 31, 110
Replay Theatre Company 102, 146
Republic of Ireland 2, 4, 11, 140, 141,
  142, 174 n9
republicans 4, 6, 26, 49, 128, 137, 139,
  141, 154–5, 156, 157, 162, 165, 175
  n7, 177 n10; collusion with the
  Luftwaffe 133; dissident 65; and
  gender 98, 99, 101, 102, 105, 113,
  116, 117, 129; Official 124, 176 n6;
  prisoners 29, 70, 76; Republican
  Clubs 63, 176 n6; republicanism 11,
  25, 34, 45, 51, 64, 76, 88, 137, 138,
  183 n6; representation of 26, 32–4,
  41, 55, 56, 110, 112, 155, 161, 164,
  175 n13, 181 n1; violence 31, 130,
  181 n4. *See also* martyrdom
Resurrection Man 182 n3
Reynolds, Albert 137, 141
rhetorical conventions 52, 92–3, 94
Rialto Theatre, Derry 32
Roddy, Lalor 150
Royal Court, London 81, 183 n6
Rubin, Leon 26, 174 n7
Rudkin, David, *The Saxon Shore* 82
Royal National Theatre, London: see
  National Theatre
Royal Ulster Constabulary (RUC) 26,
  28, 85, 128; representation of 27–9,
  35–9, 107, 130; and women 101
Russell, Willy, *Educating Rita* 88

Saville Inquiry 175 n4. *See also* Bloody
    Sunday; Widgery Tribunal
Scanlan, Carol 110
Seaton, Zoe 88, 89, 91, 92, 94, 178 n17
    and n19, 179 n7
sectarianism 5, 63, 65, 140, 141, 149,
    154, 160
segregation 13, 119, 134
Shake Hands with the Devil 175 n13
Sheridan, Peter 12, 30, 110; *Diary of a
    Hunger Striker* 12
Sinn Féin 85; Provisional 181 n4
Social Democratic and Labour Party
    (SDLP) 31, 72, 139
A State of Chassis 164, 168
stereotypes 5, 35, 42, 171; Catholics
    154; female 97, 107; loyalists 154,
    155, 157; police 35; terrorists 29, 42,
    116, 155
Stormont 14, 100, 152, 173 n3, 181 n6
Storytellers Theatre Company 79
story-telling 54, 128; performance 47,
    142–5, 162, 175 n1
A Street in Belfast 123
Sunningdale Agreement 72, 84, 85;
    Convention 151

A Terrible Beauty 175 n13
Thatcher, Margaret 72, 85
Thompson, Sam 22, 25, 61, 84; *Over
    The Bridge* 14, 63, 167, 169
Tinderbox 65, 91, 149, 150, 173 n1;
    Convictions 26, 150
The Treaty 175 n8
Tricycle Theatre, London 26, 31, 147
Troubles plays 22, 151
Turf Lodge 25, 122, 123; Housing
    Action Committee 63; Socialist
    Fellowship 25, 123
tragedy 21, 83, 84; domestic 21, 116,
    160; family 116; Greek 79, 80, 96;
    Hegel 81; romantic 182 n1

Ulster 1, 6; Ulster British 6; regionalism
    14. *See also* loyalism; Protestants;
    unionism
Ulster Defence Association (UDA) 88,
    106, 140, 147–9, 155–6, 160, 167
    Women's 101, 106, 107, 160, 167.
    See also Mitchell, Gary

Ulster Defence Regiment (UDR) 101,
    161
Ulster Unionist Party (UUP) 59, 138
Ulster Volunteer Force (UVF) 141, 163
Ulster Workers' Council Strike 84, 151
unionism 5–6; unionists 48, 62, 66,
    85,133, 153; unionist alienation
    138–9, 145, 146–7, 181 n3, 182 n8;
    constructive unionist 178 n12;
    unionist hegemony 14, 54, 81, 119,
    149, 151; ideology 74, 98, 141, 155;
    unionist politicians 11, 30, 155;
    unionist state 4, 119, 173 n3, 181
    n6. *See also* Protestants; loyalism
University of Ulster 26, 98, 124
utopianism 79, 95–6, 138, 145, 149.
    See also myths

Vallely, Macdara, *Peacefire* 121, 162,
    181 n4
violence 11, 16, 29, 30–1, 45, 49, 60,
    72, 73–4, 76, 92,121, 141, 146, 180
    n2; against RUC 84; *At the Black
    Pig's Dyke* 31, 32–3, 39–42; *As The
    Beast Sleeps* 147–9, 155; *Binlids* 56;
    domestic 128; *Caught Red-Handed*
    151, 154; *The Death of Humpty
    Dumpty* 159; inter-community 180
    n4; *The Interrogation of Ambrose
    Fogarty* 28–30, 32, 34–9; and gender
    99, 103–7, 110, 116, 129, 179 n10;
    loyalist 154; *Loyal Women* 106–7;
    police 119; political 2, 4, 23;
    representing 1, 5, 34, 92–3, 96, 158,
    164–8; republican 31, 129, 130. *See
    also* abjection; barbarism; witness
vitality 92–3, 94

West Belfast (Community) Festival 51,
    168, 175 n6
Widgery Tribunal 48, 54, 55, 58, 175
    n4
witness 37–8, 50, 52, 55, 58–9, 145,
    161
Woods, Vincent 31, 174 n12 and n13;
    At the Black Pig's Dyke 24–5, 31–4,
    39–43, 164, 166, 168, 174 n13

Yeats, William Butler 8, 10–11, 68,
    86,116, 164, 178 n12 and n13